Rethinki   'er in Early Chil.... ..u ucation

Rethinking Gender in Early Childhood Education

Glenda MacNaughton

P·C·P

**Paul Chapman
Publishing Ltd**

First published in 2000 by
Allen & Unwin
9 Atchison Street
St Leonards NSW 1590
Australia

This edition published by

Paul Chapman Publishing Ltd
A SAGE Publications Compan
6 Bonhill Street
London EC2A 4PU

SAGE Publications Inc
2455 Teller Road
Thousand Oaks, California 91320

SAGE Publications India Pvt Ltd
32, M-Block Market
Greater Kailash–1
New Delhi 110 048

British Library Cataloguing-in-Publication data

A catalogue record for this book is available from the British Library

ISBN 0-7619-6819-9
ISBN 0-7619-6280-2 (pbk)

Library of Congress catalog card number available

Set in 11/13 pt Palatino by DOCUPRO, Sydney
Printed by SRM Production Services, Sdn, Bhd., Malaysia

10 9 8 7 6 5 4 3 2 1

Contents

Acknowledgments ix
Introduction xiii

1 Seeking gender in early childhood 1
2 There's no point trying to change nature, is there? 11
3 Gender equity's just good practice, isn't it? 36
4 It's not an issue in my centre! 64
5 Too young to know 90
6 We've been doing gender equity for years—what's new? 111
7 What about the boys? 132
8 If it matters that much, just do it yourself 161
9 But what about the parents? 183
10 But it clashes with my multicultural program, doesn't it? 208
11 Reconceptualising early childhood pedagogies 234

References 249
Index 261

Acknowledgments

This book would not have been possible without the energy, generosity and friendship of the women whose work with young children forms its substance. In the book they are represented through pseudonyms to protect their privacy and that of the children, parents and colleagues with whom they worked. My thanks to each of them: Cheryl, Judy, Leanne, Jan, Ruth, Gwen, Helen, Michelle, Trish and Fairlie. The debates and questions that formed in the research group have continued within the Research and Gender Equity Network in Early Childhood (RANGE) that formed from the research project, and more recently with postgraduate students. My thanks to RANGE and to my postgraduate students for continuing to support and challenge my everyday work on gender in early childhood. Patrick Hughes has offered incisive comments on the substance and detail within the book and constant support for its politics and mine.

I have presented earlier versions of the ideas contained within several chapters at a variety of conferences, in journal articles and in chapters in other books. This book builds on this work and in doing so draws on the comments and questions that these earlier papers have provoked. To those who took the time to offer comments and questions, my thanks. My thanks also to Bronwyn Davies, Jennifer Gore and Catherine Patterson for their comments on and encouragement to publish the doctoral research upon which this book is based and to Robin McTaggert for his astute supervision of the research and for his margin notes.

Thank you to the University of Melbourne for providing the institutional base from which to undertake the research on which the book is based and to Elizabeth Weiss at Allen & Unwin for believing in the book's possibilities.

My final thanks go to a group of special women who have in very different ways inspired me and continue to inspire my search for feminist questions and answers in early childhood. They are not insiders to early childhood but feminists outside it. Each has supported me in different ways and at different times to stay as a feminist within early childhood. What they share is a willingness to take the business of early childhood seriously and to take my work within it seriously. I want to acknowledge them now as my thirty-year project as a feminist in early childhood takes flight in this book. In the 1970s I joined my first women's group and in it Brenda, Annette, Liz, Dianne and Perri taught me about the strength to be found in coming together as feminists. They always took my attempts at non-sexist teaching seriously and gave me a thirst for the political and intellectual challenges of feminism which still drives my work.

In the 1980s when I moved to London I joined my second women's group. To Emma Tait, Jane Dempster, Lois Arnold and Sue Lees my thanks for sharing the challenges and joys of living feminism each week as we struggled to do our work as feminists in local government. It was while I was in this group that I learnt to think strategically about how to be a feminist in large institutions. I have much to thank Emma for on this count. While living in London I had the extraordinary experience of working in the Equal Opportunities Unit of Greater London Council, where I found a collegiality that has been unrivalled in my working life. To everyone who was part of the Unit my thanks for taking child care and what happened in it seriously. Judith

Hunt was an inspirational leader who used her political skills and intellect to ensure a strong institutional base for child care work. Judith, thanks for that and for the personal friendship and support between us that flowed from that.

This book is in part my attempt to answer the questions that so often puzzled us about how to make anti-discriminatory practices a reality in the day nurseries. Marion McAlpine has been both friend and colleague whose conversations have always challenged me to stay and seek feminist answers in early childhood. For those conversations that have been so sustaining and supportive, my thanks.

Introduction

In 1991 it took seven months to find twelve early childhood teachers who were interested in gender equity and prepared to join a research project about it. Eighteen months into the project several teachers had been seen by colleagues, parents, friends and family as 'weird', 'odd', 'radical', 'mad feminists', and 'over-the-top' and 'out-of-step' with good early childhood practice.

These reactions themselves seemed out-of-step with the rhetoric of early childhood texts and policies of the time. There had been twenty years of advice to teachers about the need to treat girls and boys in the same way, to work in non-sexist ways with children and to ensure that all children irrespective of gender reached their full potential.

So why did it take so long to find a small group of early childhood teachers willing to explore gender issues in their classrooms? Why did the teachers face the reactions they did? This book tackles these questions through theorising several stories from the action research project on gender equity in early childhood that I initiated in mid-1991 as part of my doctoral studies.

The answers I offer are neither simple nor comfortable for those committed to early childhood traditions and 'truths'. I know this as one who has been committed to them for nearly thirty years. Early childhood traditions and 'truths' incite inclusiveness, acceptance of difference and the right of the individual to reach their full potential. It is uncomfortable to hear that these very traditions and 'truths' can have the opposite effects in practice. Yet this is a key theme throughout this book. How early childhood traditions and 'truths' exclude difference and restrict potential is complex. They do so by relying on understandings of childhood that present simplistic images of how children learn, know and live gender. They do so by insisting that the best way to know and to interact with children is developmentally. They do so by valorising the achievement of the individual's potential above all else. They do so by cloaking the moral, ethical and political nature of teaching.

To show these complexities I use feminist post-structuralist theory. I do this because I think its 'toolbox' of ideas offers powerful tools for seeing the complexities of how children learn, know and live gender and of how teachers learn, know and live teaching. It also offers powerful tools for imagining how to practise early childhood education with feminist intent. These possibilities build from the potentials within feminist poststructuralist theory for new readings of the child, for deep understandings of knowledge-power relations in early childhood education and for generating change with early childhood teachers.

In seeking a publisher for this book I have often been cautioned that early childhood educators do not read theory and that to talk of theory is to doom the book to the remainders list. However, in working with teachers and students in recent years I know that they revel in talking about their teaching, why things happened the way that they did and what they can learn from it. They revel in talking about their 'theories' of teaching. They also seek other people's stories of teaching that excite them to look afresh at their everyday teaching.

The theory in this book arises from teachers talking about their teaching and reflecting on what ideas or principles might help them solve their gender problems. It is grounded in the everyday gender concerns and practices of teachers and the children they taught. It is used to generate questions about what happened in their everyday lives together, how it happened and to provide ways of understanding it. It is also used to provoke debate about what could and should happen about gender in early childhood education. At times these explanations and provocations are unsettling, at times complex and at times intellectually challenging. However, given that teaching young children is unsettling, complex and challenging, would early childhood teachers really accept explanations of it that are not?

1

Seeking gender in early childhood

Myths prevail about the aptness of addressing the gendering of identity through, and in, early childhood education. They range from the view that gender doesn't matter to young children, through a sense that good early childhood practice produces equity for all, to beliefs that pursuing gender equity compromises partnerships with parents and clashes with multicultural perspectives in early childhood.

This book confronts nine common myths about gender equity in early childhood and shows how everyday gender matters in young children's lives. It also shows how everyday teaching practices influence the gendering of young children's identities. It does so by using feminist interpretations of early childhood teachers' research stories, their conversations with each other and with children, and cameos of children's play. The book's aim is to unsettle common myths about gender in early childhood and to revitalise work for gender reform within it.

Why feminist poststructuralist theory?

I have chosen to do this by drawing on feminist poststructuralist theory. Poststructuralist critiques of many modernist discourses, including pedagogical discourses, are circulating widely in the academy, and as many disciplines engage with poststructuralism they are being reformed.

This reformation has barely touched the mainstream literature in early childhood education. Developmentally appropriate practice (DAP) still dominates in contemporary curriculum literature and still has a strong reliance on a research base in developmental psychology, much of which had been gathered in the 1970s and early 1980s (Fleer 1992, 1994; Lambert 1994; Lubeck 1998). However, an increasing number of people touched by postmodernism and poststructuralism are calling for early childhood education to reform its knowledge and its practices and to invent alternatives to DAP (e.g. Silin 1995; Alloway 1995; Canella 1997; Yelland & Grieshaber 1998). The voices of feminist poststructuralists have been strong within these calls; inspired by the work of Valerie Walkerdine (1981, 1989, 1990) and Bronwyn Davies (1988, 1989a), they have high-lighted the gendered nature of early childhood traditions and 'truths' and how these regulate children and their possibilities for being.

Those in early childhood education who see gender as a minor concern in the 'main game' of educating young children may see Davies and Walkerdine as irrelevant. However, their work on gender in early childhood educa-tion has posed several serious challenges to mainstream early childhood traditions and 'truths'. They have variously argued that:

- the innocence and naturalness of childhood is a myth
- child-centred pedagogy regulates rather than frees the child
- gender politics flourish in developmentally appropriate programs
- early childhood practices naturalise gendered violence and aggression between boys and girls and between boys and their teachers. (Walkerdine 1981, 1989; Davies 1989)

It is over ten years since Davies (1988) used these critiques to challenge those in early childhood education to reform

2

its traditions and 'truths'. She suggested that feminist poststructuralism offered a powerful theoretical position from which to understand children's gendering, to re-evaluate gender in early childhood education and hence to build improved feminist pedagogies. Yet the gender equity policies that have flourished in other sectors of education have barely touched, let alone reformed, early childhood education. Martinez (1998) explained: 'Despite the fact that research in the area of early childhood has heavily influenced policy for gender equity in education over the last ten years, for the most part early childhood, more than primary and secondary schooling, seems successfully to evade the focus of gender equity policy' (p. 115).

Moreover, the traditions and 'truths' of early childhood education remain strongly DAP-based and their advocates remain uninterested in the challenges poststructuralism poses (Cannella 1998; Lubeck 1998). This book is an attempt to show how the everyday practices and understandings of early childhood make this so. It is also an attempt to show how feminist poststructuralist ideas might be made practical to teachers who have the will and the desire to seek new possibilities for how they learn and live with young children. It seeks possibilities that recognise the inflections of gender in children's lives and knowings and that produce non-violent ways of living gender. It seeks ways of being gendered that do not regulate but are full of possibilities for girls, for boys and for their teachers. These possibilities will always express a complexity of social relations and social practices. They will not be static or fixed but an expression of constantly negotiated meanings and relationships. The ongoing everyday business of teaching in reformed early childhood education will involve negotiating these meanings and relationships, mindful of the gendered dangers they hold for boys, for girls and for teachers. If teachers can do this then it is they who will reform the traditions and 'truths' of early childhood education. How they can and might do this, helped by the ideas of feminist poststructuralism, forms the substance of this book.

The book's stories and their genesis

Chapters 2 to 9 share a common structure. Each chapter introduces a common myth about working for gender equity using imagined conversations between gender equity protagonists and antagonists. These conversations draw on my countless conversations about gender with early childhood staff and students during the past ten years. They foreshadow the issues that arise for teachers researching gender in their everyday teaching lives. Their research stories illustrate how gender myths influence their teaching decisions and actions. The teachers' words and actions provide a concrete basis for invoking debate about each myth and about what constitutes good early childhood pedagogy. Each chapter presents cameos of children's play to explore the teaching implications of the issues the debate raises.

The teachers' stories and children's cameos that wind through the book come from an eighteen-month action research study. It traced what happened when twelve early childhood teachers and myself (an academic) tried to challenge traditional gender relations between four- and five-year-old children in early childhood centres in Victoria, Australia. During the project individuals initiated several 'gendering projects' which included: gathering gender-inclusive observations, developing processes for challenging sexism, supporting girls' and boys' non-traditional gendering choices and experimenting with gender-inclusive approaches to block play. These projects formed the substance of the action research in individual centres and critical reflection on these projects produced much of the 'data' in this book.

We met as a group fourteen times between May 1991 and February 1993. In these meetings we shared, charted

4

and critically reflected on individuals' work. Our written records of the meetings, individuals' observation notes, research articles and books on gendering in early childhood, articles from the media concerning gender issues, and notes on progress and on issues surfacing within the group that I prepared, helped us critically reflect on our work.

We also had several smaller, formal and informal meetings between individual group members, and we supplemented our observations with a number of videotaped recordings of children's play and of teachers' interactions with children, and with audiotaped discussions with children.

I initiated fifteen 'formal' interviews between individual group members and myself to gain a sense of particular points in the project of individuals' specific concerns and interests. I also used the interviews to check my understandings of how particular individuals were understanding and practising gender equity in their teaching and, on occasion, to critically explore my understandings with them.

Therefore, through the action research project various processes provided information about gendering theories and practices and how teachers and I understood them. In summary these were:

audiotapes of all meetings and interviews
meeting notes
videotapes of children's play and teachers' interactions
with children
audiotaped conversations with children
interviews with teachers and children.

Further information came from individuals' written accounts about themselves (self-profiles), articles and papers written by individuals, my action research project journal and written child observation records collected by individuals.

Each teacher came to the project with different interests, experiences and desires. To capture their work, their discourses, their subjectivities and the subtleties and complexities of who they were, what they did and how they achieved what they did, seemed impossible. To tell of the project's complexity, and their work, and to do it justice, was a practical and theoretical struggle. It has resulted in an account in this book which, by necessity, is partial and highly selective.

I have focused on moments in the project where individuals experienced crisis, or when they disrupted business-as-usual and/or reassembled their pedagogies. I found these moments through a reflexive process of writing and rewriting the original data. Kenway and Willis (1993, p. 5) referred to a process of 'overwriting' case studies of gender and schooling which, in part, captures the process undertaken in this study. Overwriting involved writing a lengthy description of the study from primary data sources, drawing upon this to create a structure and logic for writing up an account of a project and 'layering interpretation' (ibid., p. 5) on this to build case studies and snapshots of a research project. In this book the moments I have chosen to write about expose and confront the everyday gender myths embedded in much mainstream early childhood pedagogy.

The central argument winding through this book is that the power relations weaving between and within everyday pedagogies in early childhood form a regime of truth about the 'developing child' and the teacher's role and responsibility towards the 'developing child'. This regime of truth often hampers feminist interventions in and constructions of gender relations in early childhood settings. For instance, modernist readings of the child, framed within liberal feminist and/or developmental discourses, often restrict teachers' gendering interventions and are associated with facilitative pedagogies to change traditional gendering. The specific nature of the institutionalisation of these discourses in the early childhood field means there is often a lack of gendering reflexivity. By contrast, feminist discourses, principally feminist poststructuralist discourses, provide opportunities for working for gender equity because they often work against this lack of reflexivity.

Local truths and overall strategies

The local truths expressed in the research group's work could be seen as specific to them and, therefore, of little wider consequence. However, as Foucault (1978) cautioned: 'No "local center", no "pattern of transformation" could function if through a series of sequences, it did not eventually enter into an over-all [sic] strategy' (p. 99).

While the research group members' pedagogical understandings and practices were specific to each of us, they were not exceptional. Through a 'series of sequences', our 'local politics of truth' about the developing child did eventually 'enter into' an 'over-all strategy' which regulated teachers' work. For instance, the truths of the developing child competed over in each centre were local to it but not specific to it. These truths about the developing child powerfully regulate the work of early childhood teachers (and academics), and often work against the articulation and practice of feminist pedagogies.

The truths of the developing child winding through the project made gender equity and early childhood education unlikely and uncomfortable allies. As will be seen in the coming chapters, the research group participants' local actions and thoughts went to the heart of this regime of truth, and powerfully illuminated and, at times, disrupted and reformed several aspects of it.

The hope of the book is that illuminating how truths about the developing child restrict work for gender equity might provoke early childhood teachers to challenge their everyday truths and to construct feminist approaches to everyday teaching and learning with young children.

The people within the stories

I refer to all the children, parents and staff involved in the action research project by pseudonyms to protect their privacy. Eleven group members were, like myself, Anglo-Australian. One member was second generation Italian-Australian. All were female. All had formal tertiary early childhood education qualifications, three were studying for their Masters in Education on joining the study. Their pseudonyms are Sally, Nette, Anne, Carlie, Fay, Nellie, Edna, Matti, Sue, Emma, Anna and Tina.

Individuals varied in the time they gave to the action research project overall, and to specific projects in their workplace. The stories in this book derive from five of the six people who remained for the project's duration (Sally, Nette, Anne, Carlie, Fay and Nellie). Their time in the project resulted in a rich and extensive information base from which to explore their changing subjectivities, discourses and practices as they planned work through several action research cycles. Edna didn't stay long but her work is also reported in detail because her contributions to the research group meetings provoked considerable debate early in the project.

The teachers that you will meet most often and in most depth in the coming chapters are:

Sally became a qualified kindergarten teacher in 1961. Sally had been teaching for nearly thirty years when she joined the project. She worked in an outer suburban suburb of Melbourne and the children attending her centre were mainly from Anglo-Australian and Italian-Australian middle class families. Sally described herself as 'definitely feminist'.

Emma qualified as a teacher in 1977 and had been working in kindergarten for thirteen years when she joined the group. Emma worked in a centre where all the children attending were from Jewish middle class families. She

8

described herself as not feminist but committed to equality for women.

Nette held a variety of teaching qualifications and had worked as a primary teacher, a secondary teacher and a kindergarten teacher. Nette had also worked as an industrial chemist. Twelve of Nette's years as a teacher were in kindergartens. She worked in an outer urban area of Melbourne. Children attending her centre were primarily from lower middle class and working class families. The ethnic mix in the group included children from Anglo-Australian and Vietnamese-Australian families. She saw herself as feminist.

Edna qualified as a kindergarten teacher in the 1960s. Edna worked in an outer urban area of Melbourne with families predominantly from middle-class Anglo-Australian and Italian-Australian backgrounds. She saw herself as feminist.

Anne initially qualified as a kindergarten teacher in 1981 and had completed further studies in early childhood in 1985 and in 1990. Anne had been working in kindergartens for ten years when she joined the project. She worked in an ethnically mixed suburb in one of the growth corridor areas of Melbourne. Children attending the centre were mainly from lower middle class and working-class families. Anne did not see herself as feminist.

Carlie completed her initial training as a kindergarten teacher in 1975 and her Bachelor of Education in 1980. Carlie had been teaching for nearly sixteen years when she joined the project. She worked in a leafy outer suburb of Melbourne and the children attending her centre were primarily from upper middle class Anglo-Australian families. A small number of children who attended her centre were from upper middle class Chinese-Australian families. She described herself as a feminist 'but not a fiercely radical one'.

Nellie completed her training as an early childhood teacher in 1989. Nellie had worked briefly in childcare and in kindergarten before joining the project. The children attending her centre were from a mix of class and ethnic backgrounds. She was unsure about whether or not to describe herself as a feminist.

Matti's, Tina's, Anna's and Emma's work will be referred to occasionally. Sue did not initiate any specific projects but because she attended several research group meetings, her contributions will be reported when they are integral to a specific discussion.

The first story of the book, presented in Chapter 2, focuses on Edna's work for gender equity and the disruptions it caused to her everyday ideas and teaching practices.

2

There's no point in trying to change nature, is there?

Patricia: How is your kindergarten group this term?

Maggie: Okay, but I'm getting really frustrated with some of the boys. It doesn't matter where they go or what they play with, they are always noisy. They love fighting with each other. I've been reading them stories about boys who are gentle and they have a non-sexist role model in Sam, my assistant. He's really gentle. They hear and see alternative role models but it's not making any difference yet.

Patricia: I know what you mean, I have boys like that every year. I've decided it's pointless trying to change nature. After all, it's just boys being boys. We might as well accept it's just the way the world is.

Maggie: I really believe that we can make a difference. We just need to provide them with a strong non-sexist environment to make changes.

Patricia: But look at the facts. No matter what you do and say, it just doesn't work!

Maggie and Patricia are discussing how children's gendered identities influence their teaching. Patricia states that gender differences in children are biologically determined rather than socially determined. Her perspective forefronts two questions teachers often pose reflecting on gender issues in their work:

- How can we make a difference to children's behaviours when their genes determine who they are?
- Why should we bother trying to fight nature?

Edna is a teacher from the research group who grappled with these questions in her program. She was committed to gender equity but found it difficult to change boys' and girls' sexist behaviour in the block play area. Like Maggie, she came to wonder if change was possible. Edna began to think that nature must be stronger than nurture, given how hard she had tried to change the children's play. What follows is the story of how she, like so many other teachers, reached this point.

Debating teaching practices: Edna 'fights' nature

Edna was a very experienced kindergarten teacher working in an outer metropolitan suburb of Melbourne, Australia. The children in her centre were predominantly from Anglo-Australian and Italian-Australian families. She vacillated between describing herself as 'probably feminist' and 'definitely feminist'. Edna was concerned with:

> . . . competition for space in different areas, that is, girls in blocks, boys in home corner, broadening my outlook on gender-appropriate play, the demand for attention by loud voices and actions; and providing equal attention for quieter people.

She wanted boys and girls to share similar curriculum experiences, such as play in the home corner, and she wanted to ensure that she gave boys and girls equal attention. Edna's time in the research group coincided with a time when she felt that differences in how boys and girls engaged with her curriculum were intensifying. She was also becoming increasingly alert to how children's relationships with each other were gendered:

> Now, all of a sudden, you get this 'Girls are yuk!' and
> 'The boys are noisy'.

Early meetings of the research group were peppered with debates about what it meant to work for gender equality and gender equity. There was considerable uncertainty about what our aims should be, though there was an initial consensus that children should have access to all curriculum sites. Edna often voiced this view, but also expressed uncertainties about what she felt she wanted to achieve in relation to equality:

> . . . I mean I'm definitely all for equality, but I've got
> mixed feelings about do we have to be the same, given
> the fact that girls do have these lovely qualities. Why
> do we want to make them like boys? I would prefer to
> have the boys a bit more gentle, caring, respecting, like
> the girls seem to be, rather than change the girls . . .

The idea that equality meant everyone being the same was implicit, but she had a sense that this meant everyone being the same as the masculine standard. This clearly concerned her.

Over time, Edna's concern about girls' access to block play intensified and she decided to test strategies to improve their access. Edna actively wrestled with several questions related to this: 'What do I want boys to learn from block play?'; 'What do I want girls to learn from block play?'; 'What do I want all the children to learn from block play?' and, 'How can I work to achieve my equality goals in block play?'

Edna answered this final question using her sense of how children's gender identity was formed. She saw a strong relationship between how women are treated by men in our society and what young girls did in their play. For instance, she believed that women experienced considerable harassment from men when they entered non-traditional areas of work. This meant that they often avoided doing such work. Consequently, girls had no positive role models when they tried to join boys in block play. As Edna saw it, the lack of positive role models for young girls affected their self-esteem in block play and in other areas of the program.

The relationship between gender role models, children's opportunity to observe them and children's own gendered behaviour was a recurring theme in Edna's reflections on how children learn gender. One such reflection concerned how boys in her group struggled against being caring and gentle:

> It is what children see in terms of how men interact
> with children. Even when men take up the role of
> 'mothering', they do it in different ways [to women].

When Edna was planning how to encourage more girls into block play she read the classic early childhood text on working in non-sexist ways with children, *Growing Free* (Cohen & Martin 1976). Published in the mid-1970s by the Association for Childhood Education International (ACEI) and still distributed by them, the booklet details how to 'grow' non-sexist children. The most commonly suggested strategies included adult modelling and encouragement of non-sexist behaviours. Like Edna, Cohen and Martin assumed that gender learning resulted primarily from modelling and social reinforcement. This view is based on sex-role socialisation theory which assumes that people learn gendered behaviour through both indirect and explicit teaching. As agents of socialisation, teachers and parents model, encourage and reinforce in the child those behaviours that they believe to be sex-role appropriate. There is allegedly a simple cause-and-effect relationship between what adults want and do and what children become.

Edna devised her block play strategies by drawing on the advice in *Growing Free* and on her own ideas about how children learn. Initially these involved showing the girls how to play with blocks, encouraging them into the area and reinforcing them as they played.

Edna regarded the results of her work as disappointing:

> . . . I've given them [the girls] space, I've given them
> encouragement, I've given them reinforcement, I've
> given them everything, but they are not perceiving
> those blocks as being relevant to them.

In her assessment the strategies were not changing play patterns, so she tested alternatives. A month later she introduced 'gender rules' in block play. From experience, Edna knew that children obeyed safety rules and she believed children were 'conditioned to obey adult rules' from an early age. However, unthinking adherence to rules was philosophically problematic for her as she believed it contributed to the acceptance of authoritarianism. Her concern was that if children learned to unquestioningly obey rules, they might do so even when it might be morally wrong. She had introduced more and more 'rules' as she worked on gender equity, because if she said, 'This is the rule at kindergarten', children obeyed her.

Drawing on these experiences, Edna developed a strategy she called the 'Badge System' to allow girls in block play. She gave badges to those children she decided to allow in the block area and insisted that only children with badges could enter. As Edna continued with the badge system she found that she could withdraw from the block area more often, as girls were not challenged if they wore badges. However, she was becoming clear that access to play with boys was not, in itself, a positive goal:

> If boys and girls are playing together, what is the
> power structure? They can be playing together and it
> can be quite successful play, but where is the power,
> where is the control?

Naming power as a dynamic of children's relationships increasingly led Edna to understand the relationships between boys and girls in block play as hierarchically organised. By understanding that there were different power experiences for boys and for girls when they played together in block play, Edna began to re-evaluate what was 'correct and proper' behaviour in block play. As part of her rethinking she focused on how to evaluate boys' block play behaviour. When examining the gendering implications in block play, she wavered in how to judge what was 'positive' block play:

> . . . the boys that had been dominating the blocks have actually . . . they now use up the *whole* of the room! The *whole* of the room—the whole of the bathroom. I'm just waiting for them to go outside, and their block play is wonderful. I can't knock it—they are being co-operative with each other, they are being friendly, it's lovely play. But it is very expansive out there. All of this room. (Original emphasis)

Judged within Edna's 'normal' early childhood under-standings the boys were 'playing well' because they were being creative, involved in what they were doing and co-operative with each other. However, the gendering implications of this play were painfully apparent. The boys' successes further reduced the space available to girls. Yet again, boys appeared to benefit from how block play space was organised. Consequently, Edna decided she needed to intervene more in the children's play and to rethink what was 'good' block play.

The intervention strategies Edna tested at this time did not provide comfortable or certain answers to her initial gender concerns. One such moment of uncertainty was evident when her desire as an early childhood teacher to provide a balanced program for all children met her desire as a feminist to encourage girls to play with blocks:

> Well, I was sometimes [actively involved in block play with girls] but I got discouraged, too, as I said. There are other areas of the room that need attention.

Uncertainty also marked Edna's understandings of her power relationships with the children. For Edna, power was the imposition of one's own needs and values on another person. She could impose her view of who should play with blocks and how they should play with them. She could, therefore, control the conditions under which boys and girls gained access to block play. In doing so, she was able to achieve her goal of enabling boys and girls to gain equal access to block play. Exercising power enabled her to challenge gendered power relationships between the children. She found the exercise of power simple and easy, yet problematic. It contradicted her long-held beliefs in child-choice and in the importance of encouraging children to be self-disciplined. She believed that children learnt best when they chose what, when and how they played. She also believed that children learnt self-discipline through exercising these choices and experiencing their consequences.

Edna justified teacher control by highlighting the implications of her perception of its absence in more conventional teaching strategies such as encouragement and modelling. She had tried these for over a month and they had threatened her ability to provide equal time and attention to all children. Introducing the badge system and gender rules had not.

Edna's early experiences in the research group suggested to us that considerable teacher time was required to encourage girls to use blocks. She could never quite shift her sense that if she could just find enough time to model enjoyment in playing with blocks and to encourage girls to play with them, things would change. In the research group, she constantly struggled with the tension between her sense that gendered behaviour could be changed and her sense that it could not. In some instances, the tension was productive, at other times frustrating:

> As I said, I'm feeling quite discouraged . . . Well, it's a priority [girls' involvement in blocks], but there's also another whole big room out there that's requiring attention, and to get them to go there and stay there it [keeping girls involved in block play] takes a lot of energy.

In Edna's moments of greatest disappointment, she felt that biology offered the only sensible explanation for her failure to shift children's behaviours. She felt that perhaps young children might be born with a set of essentially female or male behaviours that 'helped to make the world work' in two ways: they provided a clear basis to differentiate between the strengths and capabilities of females and males so each knew what the other did and could do; and they ensured females and males had separate, distinct and yet complementary ways of being. In a world with two sexes she felt that this might be necessary to ensure that people were certain about who they were, how they should relate to each other and how they should contribute to the world about them. These beliefs translated into explanations for the girls' behaviours in block play. For instance, she speculated that girls might be timid and passive in block play because that's how they were born. It might be that they are genetically predispositioned to want adult support and encouragement. As she put it:

> . . . maybe it is part of being feminine to check back
> with adults about what is appropriate.

Edna wondered if such feminine ways of being might be necessary to complement the more masculine aggressive ways of being. Resorting to biological explanations of gendered behaviour made sense when Edna's alternative theory of how gender is learnt failed her. She could not change the children's behaviour using modelling and social reinforcement. She could change it only when she imposed adult rules that controlled children's behaviour. This felt neither right nor comfortable. It also demanded that she use an alternative theory of why the boys and girls in her centre behaved as they did. The only alternative she had available to her at that time was that biology determined their gendered behaviour, a view known as biological determinism. What other explanation could there be? If gender is socially determined then why couldn't she change it with some gentle persuasion? She provided a non-sexist model for the girls of how to be different. Why didn't this work?

She encouraged and supported them to be non-sexist. Why didn't this work?

We can answer these questions by looking more closely at Edna's theories of how children learn gender.

Why it happened as it did: 'sponge' models of identity formation

Edna believed that children could build a new gender identity through observing and absorbing the social messages she gave them. One image she held of children as learners was of ever-alert 'sponges' who 'soak up' the social environment around them.

Edna shared this image of how children learn gendered behaviours with authors providing advice to staff on how to achieve gender equity with young children (e.g. Cohen & Martin 1976; Hendrick 1990; MacNaughton 1993). These writers tell staff to create a physical and social environment in which children can soak up social justice and equity messages. To achieve this aim, staff are advised to increase non-stereotypical materials, activities and resources and to reduce those that reinforce traditional gender stereotypes. For instance:

> Employ teachers of both sexes who participate equally
> in the majority of activities, that is, the male teachers
> don't always supervise carpentry and female teachers
> don't always present cooking . . . Include pictures of
> boys in caring roles and pictures of boys expressing
> feelings. Include pictures of fathers with children,
> mothers working outside the home, and so forth.
> (Hendrick 1990, p. 230)

I shall refer to this as the sponge model of identity formation.

Such pedagogical advice makes sense. We know there is a simple relationship between what children hear and see and what they do and feel and become. Or do we? The idea that there is a simple relationship between the child's

19

identity and its social environment certainly failed Edna in her initial work. It failed her because the sponge model of identity formation denies the child's need and capacity to *selectively* construct meanings. This flaw reflects a simplistic image of the relationships in identity formation between the individual and the social context. Edna found that this image restricted her role to that of a model, an encourager and a reinforcer. Beyond that it offered her little scope for her action. When she used this simplistic image of children's learning to guide pedagogical practice, it restricted her capacity to construct a meaningful role for herself in children's gender identity formation.

The critique of the sponge model of identity formation is not new (see Davies 1988 and 1989a for a discussion of 'osmosis' socialisation). Its critics have attacked its reliance on a simplistic view of the relationships between the individual's understandings of themselves, who they are and their social and cultural contexts (e.g. Lloyd & Duveen 1992). They have pointed to the fact that the sponge model of identity formation implies that the child is a 'product of social forces' (Hekman 1991, p. 45) with little or no ability to do other than think and feel what he or she is told by society. Put at its most simplistic: individuals become what society wants them to be. Edna's frustration at the girls for not seeing blocks as 'being for them' arose from the fact that they did not do what she told them to. It arose from the fact that the girls did not become what she wanted them to be—keen, active and confident in the block play area.

Hekman (1991, p. 48) used the metaphor of a 'social dupe' to emphasise how this model presents the relationships between the individual and the social. In 'social duping':

- Children acquire identity *from* social institutions such as family, media, etc., via a one-way learning relationship in which children are 'duped' into learning what society wants them to learn.

20

- Children acquire identity from social institutions *through* a process of observation and absorption. Children uncritically absorb what is offered to them. In the case of equity education, children uncritically take up the understandings of gender, race, class, etc. that teachers, peers and/or parents offer them.

This image of identity formation ignores the fact that children do not receive just one message from society about who they should be. They receive many different messages from many different sources. For instance, parents, teachers and grandparents may provide very different messages about how to be normal given their gender, 'race', class and ability.

Consider Edna's story for a moment. The Italian-Australian and Anglo-Australian girls in her centre certainly received different messages about how to be normal four-year-old girls from their parents, their extended families, their teacher and their male peer group. At their simplest these messages ranged from 'normal girls don't play with blocks' to 'normal girls love to play with blocks'. The girls were not merely soaking up images of how to be normal. They were *negotiating* their way through them and taking decisions about how they wanted to be girls.

If children simply form identity through absorbing and observing social messages then how do we explain the girls' negotiation of the different messages they received? Seeing the child as an uncritical and unselective sponge cannot account for the desire to resist teachers such as Edna. The sponge model cannot explain how children such as the girls in Edna's group decide what to do when presented with contradictory expectations about social diversity and equity from family, peers and other institutions such as the early childhood centre or the media.

Social dupe/sponge models of identity formation fail to explain the girls' understandings and actions because they fail to address three inter-related questions:

- How do children construct their social understandings from the competing understandings of gender, race, class, etc. with which various social institutions present them?

- To what extent do they construct their ideas in the ways intended by such institutions?
- How did the girls in Edna's kindergarten decide which messages about girls and blocks they would listen to?

These models of identity formation are based on modernist understandings of the child which assume that children unproblematically acquire a unified and coherent gender identity from their social world. Modernism is characterised by a belief that progress and emancipation for humanity will occur through the use of reason and individual free will. These beliefs derive from Enlightenment's ideals of progress, in which progress was defined through a shift from mythical knowledge to scientific knowledge and a shift from religious faith to reason (Usher & Edwards 1994). Within this context, identity is seen to build from us aspiring ' . . . towards being "free and equal" rational agents who are able to live by the light of reason alone' (Seidler 1997, p. 34). We form ourselves through exercising our free will and through being rational. We become coherent and unified beings through exercising our free will.

Several writers in the early 1990s (e.g. Walkerdine 1990; Davies 1993) heavily critiqued modernist theories of identity formation for their simplistic understandings of how children form and reform their sense of themselves and others. Their work falls under the banner of feminist poststructuralism. Davies (1988, 1989a) has argued in her pathbreaking work on identity construction in early childhood that these modernist accounts offer us inadequate understandings of the relationships between individuals and the social world because they cannot answer questions such as:

- How does the child resist or reject or accent dominant understandings?
- What does the child do when presented with contradictory understandings?

- How does the child make choices between dominant and alternative understandings?
- What influences the child to reject dominant or alternative understandings?

If we think about the girls in Edna's centre, answering these questions becomes important. If we can understand why the girls rejected non-sexist forms of femininity and stuck with traditional ways of being girls, we can plan our gender equity work far more effectively. Without answers to these questions, we don't know what to do for or with such girls and their peer group. We are left with ordering them to act in non-sexist ways or giving up on them.

Social dupe/sponge models of identity formation are of little help pedagogically because they offer the teacher a restricted role. If children learn through observation and absorption, then the teacher's role is to provide an environment in which the child can observe and absorb the messages the adults want them to. The teacher's role is thus restricted to that of creator and curator of the 'right' environment. In gender equity programs, this means having resources with the 'right' messages for children to absorb and having the 'right' role models for them to observe. Can this be all there is to teaching intended to change the world by creating greater equity and justice? Those like Edna who have tried know that it is not! In hindsight, Edna's tensions might have been fewer and her failures avoided if she had had access to an alternative theory of young children's identity formation, such as feminist poststructuralism, with which to inform her work.

Alternative understandings of identity formation

Edna's story shows how her decisions and actions created challenges, frustrations and successes because she relied on modernist understandings of the child to construct her understanding of how children learn gender. Specifically,

23

she often relied on socialisation theory and at times on a simple form of biological determinism.

Socialisation theory and biological determinism worked against gender equity because they skewed Edna's understandings of how children learn and thus her attempts to change what they had learnt about gender. Edna may have altered her approach to her work and thus increased her long-term 'success' in changing sexist behaviours in block play if she had been able to draw on other theories of how identity is formed.

Several recent contributions to identity theory come from poststructuralist perspectives on relationships between the individual and the social world (see Gherardi 1996; Hekman 1991; Davies 1989a & b). They regard the relationships between individuals and social institutions as inseparable. In the process of building identities, the individual and social world do not just interact—instead they are interdependent and mutually constructing. We are born into a social world with pre-existing social structures and meanings. We are, therefore, always and inevitably social. The individual does not and cannot exist outside of the social. Deciding who we are is a complex process that happens within us and without us but is always social. Davies (1993) argued that developing identities involves learning to '. . . read and interpret the landscape of the social world, and to embody, to live, to experience, to know, to desire *as one's own*, to take pleasure in the world, as it is made knowable through the available discourses, social structures and practices' (p. 17, original emphasis).

Identity development is a process in which the child actively constructs meaning through 'reading' and interpreting experiences, but is not free to construct any meanings or any identities she/he wants. The child can construct many and varied meanings but they are limited to the alternatives made available to them. Children do not enter a 'free marketplace' of ideas but form identities in a highly controlled marketplace. Some meanings are more powerful than others because they are more available, more desirable, more pleasurable and more able to be recognised by others (Hughes & MacNaughton 1998).

In constructing identities, children access the particular meanings available to them and then:

read them
interpret them
live them
embody them
express them
desire them
gain pleasure through them
understand them
take them up as their own

All this occurs in a controlled marketplace of ideas and against a background of differential access to ideas. Consequently, models of how we form and reform identities need to be based on more complex images of the relationships between the individual and the social world than those expressed in the osmosis approaches to gender equity. We need metaphors that take us beyond the simplistic view of the child as a sponge. Learning identity is more complex than that imagined in biological determinism (see Rogers 1993) and in the social dupe image of the child.

Poststructuralist theorists are struggling to provide us with alternative images (metaphors) of how we become who we are. In these efforts they try to capture the complexities of the relationships between the individual and the social in identity formation. Their attempts are not fully formed and they disagree about how best to imagine the individual in the social (see, for example, Gherardi 1996). I have chosen two contributions from this work to provoke rethinking about how we tackle gender issues with young children. I have used their metaphors of identity formation to generate questions about pedagogical practice. As you read them you might like to reflect on the extent to which, individually and collectively, they capture some of the complexities missing from our thinking to date. You might also like to reflect on what these metaphors do not capture.

Alternative 1: identity formation as a dialogue

> The central metaphor for identity formation becomes dialogue rather than mirroring: the self is defined by gaining voice and perspective and known in the experience of engagement with others. (Gilligan 1988, p. 17)

Gilligan offered the metaphor of 'dialogue' as an alternative to social duping and osmosis. Dialogue in this context is an active process of talking with others, listening to them and being listened to by them. It also refers to how we respond to others without losing who we are as we do. In dialogue with others we learn about who will attend to us, who will care for us and under what conditions they will do this. We learn who we can and should be as others show us who they are willing to attend to and care for.

Gilligan believed that it is through a dialogue with our social world that we can learn to distinguish ourselves from others (our personal self) and at the same time to find a 'way of being' that shows others that we are recognisably 'normal' (our social self). It is only as we actively engage with others that we learn who we can be, might be and are at a given point in time.

As a metaphor for the process of identity formation, dialogue offers the teacher a strong role in forming the child's identity. From this perspective, learning is seen as a highly interactive process between child and adult. The teachers' role in gender equity programs is to help the child 'gain voice' and perspectives and to engage the child in conversations about different voices in and perspectives on the world. The following questions prompt me to think about what this might mean in practice:

> What might giving voice mean?
> Who should decide what giving voice means?

Whose voices and perspectives are present in the group?
Whose voices and perspectives are silenced, marginalised or trivialised?
How might we give voice to all children in the group?
How do children experience engagement with each other?
How do I engage with the children?
What forms of dialogue are possible within the group?
Who directs the dialogue?
What do we create dialogue about?
Would such questions reinvigorate teaching? Would they add complexity and depth to a gender equity program?

Alternative 2: identity formation as a narrative

> . . . the features of a post-modern concept of identity have been outlined as constituted theatrically through role-playing and image construction . . .
>
> Identities are narrated, they become institutionalized and recognizable by repetitions: actors tell stories, while spectators evaluate them and participate in their construction within a repertoire accessible in situated time and space . . . The telling of one's own story . . . is inherently a creative process by which a situated narrative of identity is constructed. (Gherardi 1996, p. 188)

In Gherardi's view we learn identity through several inter-related theatrical processes: telling stories, playing roles, critiquing our performances and being critiqued by others. We reshape our stories and our roles as we interact with others and with ourselves. Constructing stories of ourselves to others and negotiating these stories as others contribute and react to them can help us distinguish ourselves from others (our personal self) and at the same time find a way of being that shows others that we are recognisably normal (our social self). This allows us to think of our identity as personal to us, but at the same time socially situated and negotiated. Identity is not merely absorbed but has to be worked at with others who are actively engaged with us.

How might such as understanding help us in our gender equity work? As I think of what this might mean in practice, my questions include:

> What stories are narrated in our group?
> What repertoire of stories do individual children have?
> Who is active in narrating stories?
> Who are the spectators in the group?
> What stories do the spectators critique and how do they do this?
> Whose stories are silenced, marginalised or trivialised?
> How do children tell their own stories?
> How do we encourage creative expression of different stories?
> How do children evaluate each others' stories?
> How might story-telling contribute to the formation of anti-bias identities?
> Would such questions reinvigorate teaching? Would they add complexity and depth to a gender equity program?

Themes that emerge from the poststructuralist terrain of identity formation: a summary

- There is not a fixed, coherent immutable gender identity to be learnt.
- The child is an active player in gender identity formation, but not a free agent.
- The child does not receive messages through one single process.
- The child selects her/his messages from a highly controlled marketplace of ideas.
- Interaction with others is central in forming identity.

As children interact with the world about them, their relationships with other people can protect or transform their identities (Gilligan 1988). The challenge in early childhood is to counter those images of identity formation that have underdeveloped and/or simplistic understandings of the relationships between the child and their social world. If this does not happen, gender equity pedagogies will be simplistic and poorly developed. They will be unable to protect or transform the identities of children with gender equity intent.

In hindsight and with the insights of poststructuralism we can see what Edna might have done differently. She might have understood gendering as a social process occurring in and through dialogue and narration and actively engaged children in her attempts to transform their block play decisions. For instance, drawing on Gilligan (1988) and Gherardi (1996), Edna might have created dialogue between herself and the children and between the boys and the girls about what was happening in block play and why. She might have encouraged them to tell each other their stories about it and ensured that all of their stories were told and heard. She might have encouraged them to role-play different ways of being in block play and to comment on each other's role plays. In doing so, she might have expanded the ways through which she and the children made sense of their block play choices.

Some might be tempted to judge her work harshly as simplistic and outdated. However, Edna did what we all do. She used the knowledge of children's learning she had available to her to try to make decisions about how best to do her work. Edna also did what many of us do not. She made her knowledge public, held it up to critical reflection with others and never felt that she had the one true and final answer. Edna's search for a better answer to how children learn gender means that biological determinism will never be her final answer. As she explained:

> . . . it's [understanding gender in children's lives] so complex . . . it is so intangible. As fast as you grasp hold of it, it disappears and pops up elsewhere and as soon as you think 'I've got it' it disappears again, it just moves beyond our reach.

Edna's work shows us just how important it is to continue to reach for the answer. The chapters that follow explore how diverse these answers can be through stories from the work of other teachers in the research group.

Theories into practice

To see what it means to use different theories of how children learn gender to inform our practice let's look at how one child—Tom—understood his gender and how we might read this.

Tom and the after-shave bottle

Tom is a four-year old Anglo-Australian boy who attends an early childhood program in a predominantly Anglo-Australian middle-class suburban area of Melbourne. His mother is actively encouraging him to be non-sexist. His father is less certain about the need for this and about its impact on Tom.

Tom arrives at the centre clutching a small bottle with a gold top. He rushes over to where I am sitting and excitedly shows me his bottle. The conversation about the bottle unfolds like this:

Glenda: That looks interesting. I wonder what it is?

Tom moves closer to me and whispers: It's a perfume bottle. Smell how lovely it is.

Tom offers me the bottle and I smell it.

Tom (whispers to me): Don't tell the other boys it's a perfume bottle. I'll tell them it's an after-shave bottle.

Glenda: Why would you do that?

Tom (smiles at me): You know.

I could certainly guess. Particularly when I combined this moment with a conversation we had had a couple of days previously. Then, Tom had told me that he didn't like being a boy because boys hurt other people and kill people lots. But he didn't want anyone else to know.

Glenda: Who can we tell about the perfume bottle?

Tom: Just us, I think.
Glenda: What about Carlie?
(Carlie was Tom's teacher. She had an active gender equity program and often encouraged Tom in his difference.)
Tom: Not today. Maybe, if . . . (fades). We might tell her later, then.

How did Tom learn to be different to the other boys in his group? How might our preferred explanation influence our teaching decisions about how to work with Tom?

A sex-role socialisation theorist might read it this way: Tom is a non-sexist success. Tom has learnt various non-sexist ways of being male such as disliking violence and enjoying perfume. He has learnt them from the non-sexist messages his mother has modelled and reinforced. His teacher has further reinforced this work.

Tom's teacher might plan in this way: Tom is experiencing some discomfort at being non-sexist in the group. To support him I will:

- continue to provide him with models of gentle, caring non-sexist men through the stories I read to him and by the male visitors I bring into the centre
- positively reinforce his interest in non-traditional pastimes and ways of being.

A biological determinist might read it this way: Tom is behaving in non-traditionally male ways. He seems to lack naturally masculine traits such as aggressiveness and competitiveness and does not seem interested in male bonding. Maybe there has been a genetic 'misprogramming'.

Tom's teacher might plan in this way: Tom is experiencing some difficulty in asserting his natural masculine tendencies. To support him I will talk to his mother about seeking a referral to the pediatrician. This will identify if there is a physical or genetic difficulty.

A poststructuralist feminist might read it this way: Tom had lots of different messages about how to be a normal Anglo-Australian boy. His mother, his father, his teacher and his peer group offered him varied messages about how to be a 'normal' four-year-old boy. Tom was not merely soaking up images of normality; he was negotiating his way through them and learning to 'be' different with different people.

Tom knew that he was a boy and that the other boys in his centre would not share his interest in perfume bottles. He knew at four years of age that there are different ways to be a boy. He knew his particular 'gender-blend' was accepted by some and not by others. Faced with these contradictions he silenced who he was around other boys of his own age but not around an adult. How and why did Tom make this decision? How did he decide this was the most effective strategy for dealing with his desire to play with the perfume bottle? How did he know that different people would read him and his desires differently?

Tom's teacher might plan in this way: Tom is experiencing some difficulty negotiating his own particular 'gender-blend' within the group. To support him I will:

• continue to talk with him about how he is feeling and what he enjoys doing
• show Tom that I recognise that being different to the others in the group is a struggle
• talk with him about what it feels like to be different to the other boys

- discuss with him how I might help him to do the things he enjoys doing most
- discuss with other children in the group the different ways in which we can be male and female
- encourage children to narrate and spectate different stories about being boys and being girls
- encourage Tom to share his gender stories as part of this process within the group.

In summary: feminist poststructuralist possibilities and provocations

Identity is formed and reformed in interaction with others. Reshaping children's gendered identities requires considerable child-child and child-adult interaction. In gender reform programs one aim of this interaction is to expand children's ways of seeing and doing gender. We can do this by inviting dialogue with and between children about gender and provoking their narrations about gender. Specific strategies could include:

- giving a voice to all children about gender irrespective of their gender, race, class or ability
- checking to see whose voices about gender are silenced, marginalised and trivialised in the group
- exploring multiple ways of creating dialogue about who children are and how they see themselves and their genders
- knowing which stories about gender are narrated in the group and which children narrate these
- reflecting on how race, class, gender, disability and sexuality feature in children's narrations, who features them, how do they and how do others react

- encouraging children to evaluate their own and other people's gender stories
- helping all children practise being spectators, commentators and narrators.

Learning more about the debate

The following material should help you in your search for a better understanding of how gender operates in our lives and in the lives of young children.

Further readings

Connell, R.W. 1995, *Masculinities*, Allen & Unwin, Sydney and Polity Press, London. Chapter 2, 'Men's Bodies', is especially useful on current critiques of biological determinism. It is a good introduction for those not familiar with the general literature on gender and biological determinism.

Davies, B. 1989, *Frogs and Snails and Feminist Tales: Preschool Children and Gender*, Allen & Unwin, Sydney. Chapter 1, 'Becoming Male or Female', offers a detailed introduction to different modernist theories of gender and how and why poststructuralist feminists have critiqued them.

Rogers, L. J. 1993, 'Sex differences in cognition: the new rise of biologism', *Australian Educational and Developmental Psychologist*, vol. 10, no. 1, pp. 2–5. Rogers provides a detailed critique of the argument that sex differences in cognition are biologically based. The paper cites research on the brain to show that these differences result from environmental factors and learning. Rogers uses this specific research to provide compelling and detailed arguments against using biological determinism to understand learning in educational contexts.

Weedon, C. 1997, *Feminist Practice and Poststructualist Theory*, 2nd edn, Basil Blackwell, Oxford. Weedon (pp. 122–31) offers a feminist poststructuralist perspective on the debate about the role of biology in sexual difference.

Professional development suggestions

- Talk with two colleagues about how children learn gender. What models of gendering do they adhere to? How do you think their ideas would influence their approach to gender equity work with young children?

- Read Chapter 2: 'Men's Bodies', from R.W Connell's book *Masculinities* and then reread the play cameo in this chapter: 'Tom and the after-shave bottle'. How might Connell read Tom's behaviour?
- Judith Butler (1990) wrote:

  The rules that govern intelligent identity, i.e., that enable and restrict the intelligible assertion of an 'I,' rules that are partially structured along matrices of gender hierarchy and compulsory heterosexuality, operate through *repetition* . . . [As a result] it is only *within* the practices of repetitive signifying that a subversion of identity becomes possible. (p. 145, Original emphasis)

What might Butler's view of identity mean if you worked with Tom?

- Write a story about how gender constructs the life of one young child you know. Then, try to rewrite the story as if you were Butler, Gilligan or Gherardi. Which version of the story offers you the most useful guide to your teaching of the child?

3

Gender equity's just good practice, isn't it?

Lydia: This term I'm trying hard to ensure that each of the girls can use the woodwork equipment effectively.
Nada: Don't worry too much about it. It will just happen.
Lydia: How is that?
Nada: If you make woodwork available to the girls they'll do it when they're ready to. It won't work if you force them to use the equipment.
Lydia: I really disagree. I don't think they'll use the woodwork area unless I take a strong stance against the boys' domination of it.
Nada: I think that you're really over-reacting. Just follow good early childhood practice and it will happen. If you provide the opportunity in an appropriate way the girls will come to it in their own time.
Lydia: Well, they haven't yet!

Lydia felt passionately that gender equity doesn't just happen—she needed to work at it. Nada disagreed. Their discussion revealed a commonly held myth about 'good' early childhood practice and gender equity: if children are 'free' to choose where they play, equal play and equal choice for boys and girls will eventually result.

Nellie and Sally were two teachers in the research group who were prepared to transcend the boundaries of 'good' early childhood practice in their search for gender equity for children. Like Lydia, they were convinced that sexism mattered and that it needed to be challenged. What follows is a story of their attempt to do this in their teaching and their consequent dilemmas about 'good' practice.

Debating teaching practices: 'Free' play? Free for whom?

Nellie had been teaching for two years when she joined the research group. At this time she defined herself as feminist, she was familiar with debates about sexism in children's books and confident in using terms such as 'sexism' and 'counter-sexism'.

In the initial months of the action research, Nellie believed that gender wasn't an issue in her centre. As a feminist, she had worked hard to treat all children equally and to offer them the freedom to choose with what and with whom they played. Nothing from her regular developmental observations of the children suggested that children's friendships or their play choices featured gender inequities.

However, as other research group members shared information about the sexist gender dynamics between children in their centres, Nellie decided to target her observations more specifically on gender issues. Drawing on discussions within the research group, she sought information about gender and power relations between children. She moved rapidly from seeing gender as a non-issue in relationships between children in her centre to recalling their sexist play in detail as a daily occurrence.

Nellie found that many of the boys were involved constantly in a range of strategies to define play spaces as theirs. They physically prevented girls from entering some spaces, they expanded their play to force girls into smaller play spaces and they tried to establish storylines in their dramatic play that were full of aggression and noise. Nellie saw these moves by the boys as highly sexist and she decided to intervene to prevent sexism prevailing. She drew on her understandings of child development to guide her teaching interventions. She understood that young children had limited comprehension of complex sentences, that they were more likely to respond to direct requests than indirect ones and that it was important to be persistent and consistent in her messages to them. These understandings directly parallel advice given to early childhood staff about how best to communicate with young children. For instance, Read et al. (1993, pp. 88–9) state that staff should:

- State suggestions of directions in a positive rather than negative form.
- Make your directives effective by reinforcing them when necessary.
- Define limits clearly and maintain them consistently.

In Nellie's description of her approach we can see how much she drew upon these ideas to structure her gendering interventions:

> . . . just to summarise—I use clear short sentences; I use direct requests—now this is, *some of you may not agree* [my emphasis]—I say things like 'You don't need to', or 'You need to', or in terms of positive reinforcement I encourage—I say, 'I like the way you did that', then, 'You don't need to do that'; persistency and consistency—like all of us, I guess, use similar phrases. I always say, 'All the children can', or 'We're all able to do whatever'. And I've also got to use as much positive type words, use as much positive reinforcement as possible, with either the target child or another child who has previously demonstrated that positive behaviour, or the target behaviour that you're looking for.

What also stood out in Nellie's presentation of her rules for intervention was her certainty that other members of the research group would not approve of them. Later that month I learnt during an informal discussion with Nellie why she had assumed the group would disapprove of her rules for intervention. She felt that others in the group would be uncomfortable with her level of direct intervention in the children's play, that she would be seen as overly interventionist in 'free' play. Free play is a term used widely in early childhood literature to describe child-initiated and child-directed play in which adult intervention is minimal. Children are 'free' to be who they want and to do what they want in their play, as long as it is safe for themselves and for others.

Six months into the action research project, Nellie was consciously challenging the sexism she now observed so clearly between the children. This convinced her that she needed to redefine her understandings of good teaching and to re-evaluate her positions on free play and on intervention in children's play. She decided that good teaching for gender equity must be highly structured and interventionist. Furthermore, she felt that free play in her centre often gave license for sexist play.

The strength and clarity of her rethinking on this issue was apparent in her contribution to a discussion about how to deal with sexist behaviours between children:

> I make no apologies, really, for doing it [intervening], because if we were to make apologies about those sorts of issues, then we should be making apologies about everything. In fact, why can't children come and do what they like: throw things at the wall, hit each other, knock each other out, and why doesn't that continue throughout schooling? I mean, we use those rules throughout their whole entire life. In fact the issues relating to racism and sexism are probably more important than issues relating to safety, like running, in some ways, because it's a lot more valuable and effective and it's very unlikely we are going to kill them letting them run fast, but we still encourage that very consistently.

Nellie believed that her views contravened mainstream early childhood thinking on free play. She felt that the free play school of thought lacked a clear moral agenda. She asked, 'Free to do what?' Nellie contrasted the academic content of her curriculum with children's social and emotional learning. She said, 'Children will learn maths, etc. incidentally, but I want them to have an overt curriculum on gender and human rights.' Nellie had decided that children's incidental gender learning must be deliberately challenged in her curriculum. She saw her role as 'establishing or protecting rights for the girls' and she wanted to provide a 'counter-sexist curriculum'.

Nellie consciously opposed what she believed to be mainstream ideas about good early childhood practice and free play. The eventual firmness of her opposition was a significant change. She knew that her directive style of intervention might not sit comfortably with other research group members, but she found that 'it worked'. She persevered to develop an approach that was consistent with her understandings about children's developmental level in relation to language, concentration and understanding of adult requests. She felt that her approach was tailored appropriately to how young children understood adult rules about social behaviour.

When Nellie had used her approach for nearly six months she reported the outcomes to the research group in the following way:

> **Nellie**: . . . See, I don't really know if it works in practice, because the behaviour stopped and I know that the child thinks about doing it again, and I . . .
> **Sally**: How long does it stop for?
> **Nellie**: Well, it stops completely. Yes. I've never seen the child actually do it again . . . But, I think as long as it develops some sort of awareness, then it has to be positive.

While Nellie had stopped the problematic gendered power relationships she met, she felt uncertain about whether the children's gendering *attitudes* had remained untouched. Despite her uncertainties, Nellie felt that stopping the *behaviour* was an important consciousness-raising activity for the children.

For some children in her group, the outcomes of Nellie's work were clear. There were moments in which some boys' exercise of sexist power was stopped and the girls saw it happening. In addition, her work clearly put the idea of free play as good practice on the group's agenda as contestable on gender equity grounds.

She argued in the research group that intervention was *essential* to gender equity and that we should make no apologies for it. Nellie was certain that she was opening up her teaching practices to criticism. When she first discussed her interventionist approach in the group, she was hesitant and anxious, and she did not share it until quite late in the research group's life, despite the fact that she and I had talked of it much earlier. In her discussions with me, her reasons for hesitancy were clear. She felt 'guilty about being structured in her work' because of the possibility of 'quashing natural creativity'. However, she also felt that 'human rights should never take second place'.

Sally came to a similar conclusion about free play and good practice through her work with a four-year-old Anglo-Australian boy called John. She was concerned with his aggressive sexism. She cited numerous examples of it. They ranged from 'pushing past' the girls shouting 'Bloody girl', through to lifting up their dresses and refusing to allow them to play roles such as firefighters in dramatic play with him.

Sally made a concerted effort to challenge John's sexism by involving him in caring, domestic storylines. She tried in many ways to develop his skills in and understanding of such storylines. For instance, she provided him with specific and detailed information about how to care for babies:

> John was standing next to me and didn't quite know
> what to do next, so I handed him one of the babies
> and said, 'Could you look after my baby for me?',

and when he got it in his arms he really looked
embarrassed. I gave him some techniques of what to
do with a baby, like burping it and so on and he did
that. Then the next day he got into the bed and gave
birth to a baby himself.

It took Sally seven months of this and similar work on
John's storylines to change his sexist behaviours and play
choices. She attributed her eventual 'success' with John to
her active intervention in his play with other children. She
believed it offered her a very powerful position from which
to develop shared storylines between him and the girls. For
example, Sally became involved in some hospital play in
'the imagination area' with the children. She had decided
to be a patient in the play because it would be:

> . . . useful for the storyline . . . well I mean nurses
> really don't know what to do other than give you
> needles, and I was saying well I needed to have
> something to read, I needed to have food, etc. I think
> they learnt a lot in a more meaningful way than sitting
> having a discussion.

Sally's rationale for being more interventionist came from
her understanding of sexism in children's play and from
her experiences of challenging sexism through direct
involvement in children's play. She noted changes in particular children's play when she intervened to make
suggestions and to set rules. She was convinced that this
involvement enabled her to extend children's storylines
and, in doing so, to reduce the sexist behaviours initiated
by John and other boys.

Sally's work on children's storylines changed how John
and several of the boys and girls understood and practised
options in their play:

> . . . the girls were up one end doing home corner stuff,
> and the boys down the other end doing blocks, and
> never the twain would meet, and now at least I've got
> them working together.

42

Videotaping by me at Sally's centre recorded girls and boys involved in a number of non-traditional relationships and roles. Girls were taking lead roles in spaceship play, boys were 'having babies' and girls were 'building ambulances'. Sally reported several other instances of girls and boys crossing traditional gender boundaries in what they played and in how they played.

To achieve and maintain these changes required Sally to develop a heightened alertness to the potential gendered power effects of children's play. One anecdote that indicated this heightened alertness concerned a game of horses which had successfully led to boys and girls playing with each other:

> . . . but I found that I had to be very careful with—say one of the boys who could run really fast was the horse, and we've got the reins, and a girl that was a little bit shy and couldn't run so fast that was the rider . . . Well, I'll leave it to your imagination. So we were having to be pretty careful as to how we teamed them up.

In this and many other anecdotes, Sally demonstrated her alertness to how boys and girls might differentially experience play with each other, and she intervened whenever she felt the girls were disadvantaged by the play.

Increasingly, Sally felt that free play was implicated in the maintenance of sexist relationships and choices for the children. Through her work with John and other boys in her group Sally reshaped her teaching philosophy on free play and increased the diversity of her approaches to teaching. She explained these changes in this way:

> The biggest program change I have made is probably the re-design of my philosophy on free choice in play so that the children's development is enhanced by judicious intervention.
>
> Being part of the research group has encouraged me to try more radical and diverse approaches in my teaching, and to use methods more appropriate to the

age-group than those I had been able to pick up from lectures and reading.

Being 'more radical and diverse' involved being more interventionist by:

- re-organising the room to remove traditional areas such as home corner and block play
- providing detailed alternative storylines and ideas for children's play
- participating in children's play in a specific role
- directing children's play
- directly challenging children when they were sexist
- talking with children about how they understood gender and sexism.

Each of these actions extended Sally's teaching repertoire for challenging children's sexism and in particular for reshaping the boys' sexist understandings and behaviours. Each of them challenged her to rethink how she defined good practice as they each heightened her role in their free play.

Why it happened as it did: DAP pedagogy and good practice

If gender equity results from implementing good early childhood practice, why did Nellie want to reject it and Sally want to redefine it? Why did Nellie stay so silent for so long about her approach to countering sexism in children's play?

Nellie was uncomfortable and coy about her interventionist approach not because she was shy, stupid or ill-informed but because particular theories of children's learning and development have dominated the Western early childhood academy for several years. Many of these theories derive from Jean Piaget's work and its dominance in early childhood education's curriculum philosophies and practices. Nellie had learnt them recently, Sally over 30 years ago.

Dominant pedagogical theory in early childhood has consistently maintained the view that curriculum should be informed by understandings about the developmental levels and interests of each child (Spodek 1988b; Farquhar 1990; Taylor 1992). This produced an approach to curriculum that became known widely as developmentally appropriate (DAP).

DAP results from a long and intimate relationship between developmental psychology and early childhood curriculum theory and practice. The curriculum traditions and expectations of the early childhood profession have been fundamentally preoccupied with the individual child's natural development (Cannella 1997; Jipson 1998; Silin 1995; Walkerdine 1984). To be considered good, early childhood curriculum needs to be developmentally appropriate. Indeed, many argue that it is the emphasis on a developmentally appropriate curriculum for individual children that makes early childhood education distinct from other areas of education and forms its canons of good practice.

Until the late 1980s there was, according to Alloway (1995a), an assumption that all early childhood educators knew what DAP meant—there was, in her terms, a DAP 'onespeak'. This onespeak was certainly evident in much of the 1980s writing of several key early childhood curriculum theorists from the USA. Writers such as Elkind (1986) and Seefeldt (1987) showed remarkable agreement on what constituted DAP. They presented DAP as including:

- providing open-ended materials and experiences
- focusing on learning processes rather than outcomes
- organising materials and the physical environment to encourage child-choice and self-directed learning
- assuming children are self-motivated to learn
- knowledge and use of age and stage appropriate materials

- focusing on individual needs and experiences
- providing concrete experiences relevant to children's interests
- deciding what to teach based on child observations and understandings of the child's developmental needs and potentials
- using play as the central medium for encouraging children's learning and development.
  (Elkind 1986; Moyer, Egerston & Isenberg 1987; Bredekamp 1987; Seefeldt 1987; Hitz & Wright 1988)

DAP was a onespeak that underpinned Nellie's reluctance to come clean about her practices for countering children's sexism! It was a onespeak that made Sally feel that her redefinition of good practice was so radical.

In the late 1980s the term DAP was formalised when the National Association for the Education of Young Children (NAEYC) released the book *Developmentally Appropriate Practice in Early Childhood Programs Serving Children from Birth Through Age 8* (Bredekamp 1987). Like many developments in the USA this booklet and the ideas within it rapidly crossed borders into countries such as Australia, New Zealand and the UK.

The DAP document was based directly on the theories of Jean Piaget (Cannella 1997). Its more recent incarnation (Bredekamp & Copple 1997) acknowledges that a wide variety of theories of child development (e.g. Lev Vygotsky and Howard Gardner) is needed to explain children's learning but is still strongly Piagetian in orientation. The initial document perhaps settled so readily into the early childhood field because during the 1970s and 1980s most early childhood teachers learnt about child development through the theories of Piaget. For this reason, one is likely to recognise much of what is considered good early childhood practice in Piaget's ideas.

Piaget argued that: 'The child can profit from external information—whether it be reinforcement or an adult's explanation or other sources—only when his cognitive structure is sufficiently prepared to assimilate it. In this sense development explains learning and not vice-versa' (Ginsburg & Opper 1969, p. 176).

He saw the 'child as a solitary inquirer, as a "young scientist" engaged in single-handedly building his or her own cognitive structures . . .' (Cleverley & Phillips 1987, p. 89). Thus learning was a self-directed process:

> For Piaget . . . true learning is not something handed down by the teacher, but something that comes from the child. It is a process of active discovery . . . Accordingly, the teacher should not try to impose knowledge on the child, but he or she should find materials that will interest and challenge the child and then permit the child to solve problems on his or her own. (Crain 1980, p. 98, cited in Moncadu 1984, p. 32)

To be compatible with Piaget's view of development and learning, early childhood professionals must support children's exploration and experimentation. Staff may guide the child's learning, but it is the child who actively constructs meaning and learns from what staff provide.

Using Piaget as a guide to good practice led early childhood teachers to:

- emphasise children's self-directed learning and shy away from adult-directed learning
- focus on physical learning materials and be coy about the adult's role in the learning environment
- emphasise learning as a process and become silent about its content.

Direct adult intervention in children's learning became problematic. If children direct their learning and solve their own problems, what were teachers to do? They should allow the natural child to unfold through careful control and supervision of the child's learning environment. Beyond this teachers were almost irrelevant.

Piaget was not the only theorist with these beliefs who has influenced early childhood pedagogies. However, his influence was heightened through the release of the 1987 NAEYC DAP guidelines (see Lubeck 1994).

This emphasis on the child's capacity to self-motivate and self-direct learning was at the heart of Nellie's dilemmas about countering children's sexism and how others might judge her practice. Since her initial pre-service training she had used DAP frameworks to understand her work with children. For instance, she facilitated rather than intervened in children's play, she decoded her child observations using child development norms and she developed teaching goals from these decoded observations. However, in her desire to work for gender equity, she eventually opposed the child-choice/free play features of DAP. In this process she searched for and found a language to explain her role in children's learning but remained unsure if she would be able to convince others of the virtues she saw in being interventionist.

Alternative understandings of good practice

When NAEYC published the DAP guidelines, many argued that they reflected merely a pre-existing consensus within mainstream early childhood literature about good practice (see Jipson 1998), a consensus about how early childhood educators believed children learnt and, therefore, how they believed children should be taught. The publication of the guidelines created consensus concerning good practice in many parts of the early childhood field. However, the guidelines have also created considerable debate and questioning about what is good practice and debate about current and future directions in early childhood education (Lubeck 1994). At the heart of the debate has been a series of questions about the nature of the relationship between early childhood curriculum, teaching and learning and developmental psychology.

Current DAP critics call for a rethink under the banner of 'reconceptualising early childhood education' (e.g. Cannella 1998). These reconceptualists challenge early childhood teachers to realign their relationship with child development and to search for new notions of good practice grounded elsewhere. Their presence and influence has been acknowledged in the revamped NAEYC document (see Bredekamp & Copple 1997, p. xi).

There are three inter-related strands to their critique. Firstly, some reconceptualists argue that DAP has contributed to social inequality and injustice because:

- it offers a necessary but insufficient framework for guiding educational practices for children with disabilities
- the traditional child development theoretical and empirical knowledge base it rests on is ethnocentric
- its values, beliefs, and goals are middle-class
- of its processes and principles and sexist early childhood practices.
(Mallory & New 1994; MacNaughton 1998b)

Secondly, some reconceptualists argue that DAP offers little guidance on the values and goals that should guide our curriculum work with young children. Finally, another group argued that the USA DAP guidelines (as per Bredekamp 1987) were based on outdated understandings of child development which denied the role of social contexts and social relationships in children's learning (Mallory & New 1994; MacNaughton 1998b). In particular, DAP (Bredekamp 1987) was critiqued because it ignored Vygotskian and multi-dimensional perspectives on child development (see Fleer 1995).

In feminist poststructuralist terms the reconceptualists are calling for new discourses of early childhood teaching and learning and within this new understandings of what constitutes good and/or appropriate early childhood practice.

In everyday usage, 'discourse' refers to what is said and/or what is written. Feminist poststructuralism recasts discourse to refer not just to language but to the historically and culturally specific categories through which we give meaning to our lives, practise our lives, invest emotionally in our lives and constitute our social structures. Thus, within poststructuralism, discourse is recast to include the emotional, social and institutional frameworks and practices through which we make meanings in our lives. For example, gender provides many categories through which we give meaning to our lives. Specifically, it offers categories such as masculinity and femininity through which to understand ourselves and others. There are a host of categories within our language that define and delineate people on the basis of gender. For instance, girl, boy, man, woman, husband, wife, bachelor, spinster, mother, father, brother, sister, and so forth.

Within poststructuralism, the description of these categories as a discourse refers to more than language. It refers also to:

- the social practices that constitute masculinity and femininity in our society such as dressing, acting, thinking, feeling, and being
- the emotional investments people make in their gender
- the social practices and structures that are organised on the basis of gender such as family, work, religion, sexuality, education and law.

For example, if poststructuralists refer to Nellie's 'teaching discourses', they are referring to more than the words she has learnt that relate to teaching and learning, such as 'free play', 'child-choice' or 'child development'. They are referring to the social practices in and through which she has learnt the meanings of these words. These practices include how she and other people have produced expectations of her as a teacher, such as when she:

- was judged as a student in practicum on her observational practices and on the developmental appropriateness of her interactions with children
- participated in discussions with other teachers about what they consider good practice

- attended professional development sessions in which good practice was discussed.

Such practices contribute to what it means to be an early childhood teacher. They formed Nellie's understanding of teaching. In other words, they were part of her discourse of teaching and learning.

Furthermore, her understandings will be formed by institutional meanings and practices relating to teaching. Institutions such as the academy (students and lecturers), the government (regulations and guidelines) and the kindergarten (via colleagues and parents) provide frameworks through which she will give meaning to her life as a teacher. Poststructuralists attempt to encapsulate these complex interconnections between language, meaning, the individual and the social in their recast notion of discourse. Thus, if we talk of Nellie's or Sally's discourses of teaching we are talking of how they talk, understand, practice and feel about teaching as they live their lives as teachers.

In addition, poststructuralists believe that each discourse is merely one possible version of events, a possible way of giving meaning to reality, and that each discourse is historically and culturally specific. This implies that no one approach to teaching is 'right'. No one theory or theorist has *the* truth of the matter—we all have different truths. Teachers working within DAP have no special claim on truth. Their particular understanding of best practice is just one of many that are possible. Nellie and Sally weren't wrong to be interventionist; they just produced their understandings about how teachers should understand their role from within non-DAP/feminist/human rights discourses.

In recent years early childhood teachers have become used to different ways of understanding child development. They regularly accommodate the idea that Piaget, Skinner, Freud and Vygotsky understood children's learning differently and they understand that each has different implications for their teaching. However, feminist poststructuralism moves beyond this position in two distinctive but interconnected ways.

Firstly, it recognises that in a given society at a given point of time, only certain discourses are in circulation. How teachers understand children's behaviour will be limited by, or expanded by, the understandings to which they have access. Nellie understood children's behaviour as sexist because she had access to feminist and human rights discourses. Teachers who do not have access to these discourses are less likely to see children's play and relationships as sexist. They are more likely to draw on the dominant discourses to which they have access and in early childhood education these will be DAP discourses. While reconceptualists (e.g. Silin 1995; Jipson 1998; Cannella 1997) are producing new ways of understanding early childhood practices their discourses are yet to circulate widely in early childhood communities. Consequently, they are unlikely to touch the understandings and practices of many early childhood professionals for some time.

Secondly, poststructuralism has a very distinctive view of the relationships between discourses. A multiplicity of discourses about our social world are in circulation, and each one is aligned with, and constitutes, different historically- and culturally-specific power relationships. In other words, particular discourses enable particular groups of people to exercise power in ways that benefit them. They are able to do this because discourses constitute particular ways of being as normal, right and, therefore, desirable (Davies 1993). In this way, discourses (e.g. DAP) institutionalise particular systems of 'morality' (sense of rightness). The power derived from this institutionalisation is hidden because the moral nature of the preferred definition of normal, right and desirable ways of being precludes debate, therefore marginalising and/or silencing alternatives: everyone 'just knows' that they are right and normal.

In early childhood education, many professionals just know that being developmentally appropriate is right and normal. There is no questioning of this and no debate about it. It's so obvious it doesn't require discussion. For instance, the particular meanings given to good practice in early childhood education have within them an implicit moral sense of what is normal and/or right. In early childhood education at this time formal, interventionist and structured teaching form part of the discourse of childhood teaching, but they are rarely seen as desirable, normal or right ways for early childhood teachers to teach.

Teachers' sense of what is right and/or normal in teaching is socially constituted in and through discourse(s). They learn the 'right' way to be an early childhood teacher through their involvement in the social practices which constitute their understandings of teaching and which demonstrate the existence of a moral system. Some reconceptualists argue that DAP institutionalises white, western, middle-class systems of morality (e.g Cannella 1997; Jipson 1998). Cannella provided examples such as:

- The development of Head Start programs in the USA. These were grounded in the idea that working class children were disadvantaged by their home backgrounds and needed to be especially prepared by early education for their years of formal schooling.
- Class-based and differentiated curriculum goals. The goal of early education for the working class child is to remove the disadvantages of their home background and the developmental deficiencies it produces. The goal of early education for the middle class child is to develop the potential they bring from their home background and developmental possibilities it produces.

Early childhood educators often do not debate or question how other ways of understanding the world might help them in their work with young children. For instance, what might a Marxist understanding of class relations and children's needs and interests bring to the early childhood curriculum? For a poststructuralist, moral systems are more than just an individual's expression, or just some accidental and arbitrary occurrence. They exist because 'particular ways of speaking have been institutionalised, have taken on a life of their own, have, in fact, become constitutive of people and their actions' (Davies & Harre 1991/2, p. 3).

From a poststructuralist perspective all ways of being, including teaching, have social and political implications. As Weedon (1997) explained:

> How we live our lives as conscious thinking subjects, and how we give meaning to the material social relations under which we live and with which we structure our everyday lives, depends on the range and social power of existing discourses, our access to them and the political strength of the interests which they represent. (p. 26)

Contradictory discourses about what is normal, right and best circulate and compete with each other in a society at a given point in time. Some discourses dominate, resulting in certain moral systems becoming dominant at specific moments. This is not because such discourses are 'more truthful' or 'right' but because they have more political strength than others, derived from their institutional location.

For feminist poststructuralists, all discourses are implicated in power relationships (and, hence, in the institutionalised moral systems) that constitute gender relations in our society. In early childhood education, developmental psychology's discourses about children's learning are no exception. They have concrete social effects and, therefore, power effects. For instance, they influence how, when and why teachers intervene in children's lives and thus influence children's learning and their gendering.

By way of illustration: Nellie and Sally had the power to articulate and circulate their interventionist, counter-sexist discourses of teaching in their own centres and eventually in the research group. However, they each had little opportunity to circulate their discourses within the academy or the government and thus to establish their moral system on intervention and countersexism as a more powerful one. In contrast, developmental discourses on free play and child-choice do have a well established circulation and location in early childhood training institutions and in government policy (e.g. NCAC 1993). They are, therefore, likely to continue to influence many teachers' decisions about intervention in children's play. Hence, many teachers in Nellie's and Sally's local region and in pre-service training are likely to continue to base their sense of what are normal and/or right ways to be a teacher on these discourses, rather than on those of Nellie and Sally.

Thus, not all teaching discourses have equal social power because particular options about how to understand and practise early childhood teaching are constantly reaffirmed institutionally. For example, dialogue in the early 1990s on DAP in the USA highlighted the dominance within certain sections of the early childhood community of traditional views of good practice and the moral force of these views. Those who critiqued DAP were seen as uninformed about child development. As Kessler (1991) explained:

> What appears to be a debate between those who are well-informed by current research in child development and those who are not is, in reality, a debate between individuals who hold different values about the purposes of schooling, what counts as legitimate knowledge, and presumably the nature of the good life and the just society. (p. 193)

Early childhood teachers' pedagogical discourses will be influenced by the institutional and material power of those discourses. So, for a poststructuralist, each understanding of being a teacher that circulates in our society will be aligned with, and will constitute, specific power relationships. This preordains that some meanings will be marginalised or silenced by being positioned as abnormal, wrong or undesirable. Which meanings these are depend on the social location and institutional power of discourses.

As mentioned previously, feminist poststructuralism suggests that no one discourse on children's learning is

inherently truthful or valid, but all constitute and are constituted by specific institutionalised notions of what is
developmentally normal, right and desirable. Feminist
poststructuralists believe that in order to choose which
discourses should be privileged it is important to have a
clear analysis of how discourses are structured, what power
relations they produce and reproduce and the implications
of different meanings for existing social relations. In other
words, each particular understanding of free play and
child-choice needs to be scrutinised not for its truth, but
for the power relations it produces.

Nellie and Sally had a choice about how they made
sense of children's play and of the gender relations within
it because they had access to a range of different discourses
through which to interpret the children's behaviour (e.g.
child development, feminist, human rights discourses).
Taking the feminist poststructuralist premise that no one
meaning guarantees truth, if we have access to alternative
discourses we all have a choice about which meanings we
use to interpret children's learning and development. To
interpret what was happening we could use a set of meanings similar to those of Nellie and Sally at the beginning
of the research project or those they used toward its end.
We could see good practice as non-interventionist with the
goals of facilitating individual child development. Or we
could see good practice as selectively interventionist to
reduce sexism between children. How do we choose which
meaning to privilege?

Feminist poststructuralists submit that while there
might be different understandings of teaching, it is possible
to judge between them on the basis of their political implications. For feminists, the choice is based upon the political
implications of the discourse for women and girls.

To illustrate, let's revisit ways of looking at the sexism
between the children in Nellie's centre. When Nellie
initially chose to privilege a developmental free play
discourse on the children's play she did nothing about the
sexism between the children. When she chose to use a

feminist interpretation, its focus on the gendered power relationships between the children led her to act in a particular way. For a feminist, like Nellie, concerned with the implications of discourses for the lives and learning of young girls, it is not surprising it became the latter. Nellie's feminism provided her with a strong commitment to ensuring that women and girls could live their lives unrestricted by sexism.

This interpretation of good practice in early childhood teaching shifts our analysis of good teaching practices from the actions of the individual teacher to the discourses through which they understand what it means to be a good teacher. This shift challenges us to think carefully about the gendered power effects of different ways of teaching for boys and for girls: who will be made powerful or powerless through our good practice? Who benefits from our notion of good teaching? Specifically, who benefits from our decisions to intervene or not in children's play? More generally we need to:

- explore the gendered power effects of teaching discourses through which we make sense of ourselves and of children
- challenge teaching discourses that create and re-create sexist power relations between children and between children and teachers
- expand our understandings of what represents good early childhood practice
- reflect on how our early childhood colleagues, our institutions and our daily practices normalise and regulate our teaching.

We have looked briefly at moments in Nellie's and Sally's lives as teachers to depict how discourses work to influence our teaching decisions. Feminist poststructuralism indicates that our positioning within discourses on children's learning will be implicated in how we feel, act and understand our possibilities and challenges within children's learning and their gendering. Nellie's and Sally's work challenges early childhood teachers to decide in whose interests they teach and to be alert to the political and moral implications of their notions of good practice.

Theory into practice

To see what it means to use different discourses of teaching and learning to construct ideas of good practice, let's review a moment in the lives of two children in Nellie's centre using different discourses of teaching and learning. Elizabeth is Anglo-Australian. Tina is Greek-Australian.

How might your preferred explanation influence teaching decisions about how to work with Elizabeth and Tina?

Painting the playhouse

A small group of four-year-old children are playing outside in a large wooden cubby house. The group consists of two girls (Tina and Elizabeth) and four boys (Stephen, Wong, Dave and Thien).

Elizabeth and Tina are sitting at a table inside the cubby house having tea. Elizabeth pours herself some 'tea' (water) from a teapot on the table. Elizabeth is the 'mum' and is taking the lead in this play. She indicates to Tina where to sit and what to eat. Tina seems distracted and she keeps moving to the door and looking outside. She is watching the boys closely.

The boys each have a small bucket of water and a paint brush. They are using them to paint the outside of the playhouse. Stephen and Dave become involved in disputes over where they are painting and begin to jostle each other for painting space.

Inside the cubby house Tina stands up and begins fidgeting. She then leaves the cubby house, saying quietly, 'I don't want to play here any more.' Moments later Elizabeth emerges and follows her to a nearby seat.

The boys have been so busy with their disputes they

have not seen the girls leave. Dave shouts through one of the cracks between the boards on a side-wall, 'You get out you silly girls.' Stephen follows rapidly with, 'I'll blow your house down.'

Stephen jumps from his ladder and bursts into the cubby house. He is astonished to see that the girls have gone. Wong and Thien leave at this point. Stephen attempts to return to his painting but he discovers someone has taken his ladder. More disputes arise between Stephen and Dave. Nellie intervenes.

A teacher steeped in DAP discourses might read it this way: Tina and Elizabeth are role-playing being mums in the outside play area. Elizabeth's fine motor skill development is progressing well as she easily poured her tea into her cup without spills. Her social development for a four-year-old is also progressing normally as she and Tina are co-operating well in their play with each other. However, Tina's cognitive development needs more support as she is having difficulty settling into extended play and is easily distracted by what is happening about her. Her concentration skills are quite limited for a four-year-old and she has few ideas of her own to contribute to the play.

The children's teacher might plan in this way: As Tina seems to enjoy playing with Elizabeth, I will foster this relationship and use it and her interest in the cubby house to facilitate the development of her concentration skills. To do this, I will provide her with lots of opportunities for free play in the cubby house and allow her to follow her own interests while in it. To attract Tina's interest in the cubby house I will place some picnic utensils in it and show them to her and Elizabeth when they first arrive. I will extend this later in the morning with a story and some songs about picnics.

A feminist poststructuralist teacher might read it this way: Tina and Elizabeth are trying to establish some play with each other. They are co-operating well, though Elizabeth is leading the play. However, their play has been disrupted by their concerns about the boys' disputes. Tina seems particularly aware of them and distracted by them. She eventually leaves, thus allowing the boys and their disputes to determine where she will play.

The children's teacher might plan in this way: The boys' use of space around the cubby house was intimidating for Tina and Elizabeth. In the short term, if they are to play in the cubby house it will be important to stop this intimidation and to ensure that Tina and Elizabeth see it as a safe space. I will ensure that I place myself by the cubby house in the morning and let Tina and Elizabeth know that I will be there. I will intervene in any attempts by the boys to disrupt the girls' play, explaining what I am unhappy about and how they might behave differently. In the longer term, it will be important to work with the boys to encourage them to use less aggressive storylines in their play and to develop some shared and safe storylines between the girls and the boys. I will need to reflect carefully on how my interventions create and/or challenge the possibilities of sexism between Tina, Elizabeth and the boys. What am I doing or not doing that has made this instant of play possible?

Feminist poststructuralist possibilities and provocations: a summary

Early childhood teachers can make choices about how they define and practise good teaching. Their choices will be made from within the understandings of good practice to which they have access. These understandings will have encoded within them a specific politics of teaching that makes some choices more likely than others and more right than others. Teachers who want to base their notions of good teaching on feminist(s) politics will be led to choices about how and when to intervene in children's play to counter sexism. To provoke this possibility teachers could:

- reflect on how their notions of good practice might create and re-create sexism in their classroom
- experiment with different ways to intervene to lessen sexism between children
- reflect on what holds them back from experimenting with and in their teaching interventions
- choose how and when to intervene in children's sexism on the basis of its political ramifications (who wins and who loses)
- imagine what good feminist practice might feel like and look like.

Learning more about the debate

The following material examines how different teaching and learning discourses are implicated in our understandings of teaching and, especially, of gender equity in our teaching.

Further readings

Jipson, J. 1998, 'Developmentally appropriate practice: culture, curriculum, connections', in M. Hauser and J. Jipson, (eds), *Intersections: Feminisms/Early Childhoods*, Peter Lang Publishing, New York, pp. 221–40.

In this chapter Jipson drew on research about teachers' perceptions of developmentally appropriate practice to show how it regularly failed them in their attempts to work in the interests of children from diverse backgrounds.

Cannella, G.S. 1997, *Deconstructing Early Childhood Education*, Peter Lang Publishing, New York. In Chapter VI, 'Privileging child-centred play-based instruction', Cannella discussed how discourses of child-centred teaching and learning have influenced early childhood education. She argued that these discourses have privileged the values of the socially and economically advantaged and have produced a monocultural knowledge of young children and how we teach them.

Lubeck, S. 1994, 'The politics of developmentally appropriate practice: exploring issues of culture, class and curriculum', in B. Mallory and R. New (eds), *Diversity and Developmentally Appropriate Practices: Challenges for Early Childhood Education*, Teachers College Press, New York, pp. 17–43. Lubeck provides an excellent overview of the history, politics and substance of the debate surrounding developmentally appropriate practice. She also offers an alternative vision of how early childhood education might be practised.

Weedon, C. 1997, *Feminist Practice and Poststructuralist Theory*, 2nd edn, Basil Blackwell, Oxford. Chapter 5, 'Discourse, power and resistance' offers an extended discussion of how poststructuralists understand discourse and how discourses work to produce power and privilege for particular groups.

Professional development suggestions

- Talk with two colleagues about what they think 'good' early childhood teaching looks like? To what extent do their views parallel DAP discourse on 'good' teaching? How do you think their ideas would influence their approach to gender equity work with young children? How would you describe the political and moral implications of their position on 'good' practice?
- Read Jipson's chapter (see above) and then reread the 'Painting the cubby house' story. How might Jipson and/or one of the teachers in her study read this story?
- One of the teachers in Jipson's study asked these questions about DAP discourses:

How well do they reflect the diversity of perspective, world-view, experience, values, and traditions present in the United States? About the values represented in the underlying assumptions of an 'appropriate practice,' whose are they? . . . And who supports the lonely voices and who might speak to different traditions, values, goals or practices? (Jipson 1998, p. 229).

How would you answer these questions? Whose voices and traditions do you think are represented in DAP? Whose voices about good practice might be lonely in your local area?

- Describe a good early childhood teacher. Try to rewrite your description as if you were Nellie, Jipson or Cannella. Which teaching discourse(s) did you feel most comfortable using to describe a good early childhood teacher? Why do you think this was so?

4

It's not an issue in my centre!

Jennifer: Did you see that article about gender in the early childhood journal this month?
Carla: Yes, I did. I don't know what they were on about. In my centre, gender is just not an issue.
Jennifer: Are you sure?
Carla: Yes, I take regular developmental observations of the children and gender's just not an issue for them. I treat boys and girls the same. I allow them to play with whatever they want. For instance, I've never stopped the boys dressing up or playing with the dolls if they want to.
Jennifer: I think I'd like to look a little more closely at what's happening in my group. I think I know what's happening but I've never looked specifically at the gender dynamics in the group. I wonder if I should?
Carla: Where on earth would you find the time for that? I'm busy enough doing my normal observations!

Many early childhood staff share Carla's scepticism about the relevance of gender to their work. Carla's sense that gender was irrelevant for children in her centre arose from her confidence in the information she gained about them from her regular developmental observations.

Jennifer typifies those early childhood staff who feel unsure that they know what is happening in their group.

Like many staff, she had never specifically targeted gender dynamics when observing the children in her centre. Deciding to do this might seem simple and it might seem obvious. However, as Anne's story will show, it is neither simple nor obvious. It means trading in your developmental observation lens for one with a feminist hue.

An 'observational lens' is the perspective/theory staff 'wear' to produce, analyse and interpret what they observe about the children in their group. For instance, when staff wear a developmental lens they produce, analyse and interpret their observations of children using child development knowledge. In contrast, when staff wear a feminist lens they produce, analyse and interpret their observations of children using feminist theories and politics. Trading a developmental lens for a feminist lens does not come easily to staff steeped in the ideas of developmentally appropriate practice and its focus on the individual child.

Debating teaching practices: Anne's story—putting on the gender lens

Anne worked as a kindergarten teacher in a western suburb of Melbourne. The children were from primarily Anglo-Australian, working-class backgrounds. She said of joining the research group:

> . . . I don't think until I actually got into the group that I knew why I was there. I can't really say that I had to be there for any particular reason. It [gender] wasn't a major issue at that time. Boys were revolting in blocks, you knew that was the way it was, so it wasn't an issue.

In Anne's initial training, 'gender just didn't exist' as an issue. Anne did not define herself as feminist but she strongly believed in 'the ability and rights of women to be and do whatever they want'. Alongside this belief, Anne's experiences suggested to her that gender was subtly involved in children's play. She had noticed that boys were 'revolting' in block play. Their 'revolting' behaviour included being noisy, knocking blocks over and being aggressive with each other.

Anne's curriculum, like that of many early childhood staff, was based on her developmental knowledge of individual children that she gained via observation. She regularly made anecdotal observations of individual children, related to moments and events she believed to be of significance to their development. For instance, she took brief notes of significant incidents in a child's day, which described her/his language, expression and posture, so that she could identify how the child had felt or reacted during the incident. She organised this information into comments about the child's developmental strengths and weaknesses and then used these comments to judge how, when and what to plan for individual children.

Anne explained this when I asked her to recall her approach to observation on joining the research group:

> I used my basic observations to do my planning. I can't plan, I don't think anyone can plan an adequate program, unless you observe where the children *are at* [her emphasis]. So I have always done it and I think it stems from way back in the Diploma of Teaching days.

She explained that deciding where children 'are at' was based on information about their development in relation to their 'cognition, social, emotional, gross motor, fine motor, creativity'. Anne's approach to curriculum planning was consistent with several tenets of developmentally appropriate practice (DAP): she planned for individual children, had a developmental focus in this planning and used observations to learn about children's developmental needs.

Anne entered the research group believing that she should have minimal direct involvement in block play. Block play was a curriculum area that the teacher set up and 'more or less let the children get on with it'. Anne's understanding of block play as an area where 'you let the children get on with it' derived partly from her understanding of the learning that takes place there:

> I think traditionally we have been taught that blocks
> are about problem solving and maths that's generally
> what it is. It is where you come from and that's
> formed the basis of what we have been doing.

During informal discussions with Anne it became apparent that she understood from her teacher training that when children played with blocks, problem solving and learning about maths automatically took place. The teacher's role in block play was to set the blocks up. The blocks would do the rest.

Anne experienced moments in which 'letting the children get on with it' was difficult because of the behaviour of particular groups of boys. At times, their behaviour was sufficiently disruptive for her to actively intervene in block play. She accepted this as unfortunate but inevitable.

Anne decided that her first project in the research group would involve closer observation of gender-based patterns in children's use of materials. Over the next few months, she tracked these patterns and refined her approaches to observing gender.

Anne adapted her well-tested observational methods ('checklists, anecdotal records and notes') to her new gender focus. For two months she observed girls' and boys' play patterns and the gender-based differences in how children worked with each other and with curriculum materials. She used timed observations of who played where and when and took detailed anecdotal observations of boys' and girls' interactions and of their play styles.

Through this work Anne reported a heightened and more detailed awareness of differences in play between boys and girls:

> Glenda: Are you finding focusing on gender is helping
> you pick up the differences?
> Anne: Yes, I think with those sort of [gender] objectives

in mind, you pick up a lot of those little things you
don't pick up usually.

Evidence abounded of gender-based differences in how
children worked with each other and with the curriculum
materials. Anne's block play observations provided telling
evidence of the extent to which gender was implicated in
much of children's play. She could not avoid concluding
that:

> . . . [the boys] dominate strongly in sand play, they
> dominate strongly in blocks, because the boys' block
> building is always expansive and they take over, and
> the girls—if they are allowed into the block corner—can
> have that little bit over there.

Anne focused on block play to detail what she meant and
described one episode in which 'the boys actually barri-
caded [the block play area] off':

> But [the boys] had this great huge wall—the girls were
> not allowed to cross it, they just decided they didn't
> want the girls in there whatsoever, and the girls didn't
> bother about it. As soon as they were told, 'You're not
> allowed in here today, because we're gonna play here
> and you can't come in', they'd go off elsewhere.

Overall, Anne was surprised by what she learnt from her
observations. At the time she did not expect to see negative,
gender-based differences in children's play. She was especially surprised about what she learned from observing
block play. She had previously felt that boys and girls were
playing equally with blocks, although she had known that
particular children had an interest in blocks, and that boys
could be difficult in block play. However, the intensity of
the gendered power dynamics of boys' and girls' relationships in block play surprised her. The gender-focus in her
observations indicated to her that specific ways of being
male in block play had specific negative consequences for
the girls' involvement. Her observations during the early
months of the research group consistently highlighted

issues such as invasion of space, dominance of space and dominance of the sound-scape by boys as critical features of many children's play experiences. She spent some time puzzling over what she had observed and how she could summarise it to others in the research group and found that she needed to use particular language such as, 'boys are expansive, girls are controlled'.

Anne gathered and interpreted her gender observations in ways that expanded her understandings about what constituted an adequate reading of children's behaviour. Her initial observations suggested to her that many girls restrict their use of space in places such as block play because of boys' reactions. Boys used very direct actions to challenge girls' presence in block play, such as knocking over their buildings or barricading the block corner. She presented the following summary of how boys and girls used block play space:

> . . . we got to the stage that in blocks you notice the girls sitting on the edge. Now if I go to the centre of the block area where the boys will go, they will expand [into the space]. The girls know they are going to get pushed aside, so why bother setting up there when the boys come in and take over?

Her observations compelled Anne to rethink the concepts she used to understand children's play. She used concepts that evoked power as a central dynamic of children's relationships to describe how particular groups of boys were involved in. For example:

'intimidation' of girls
'domination' of collective space
'expansiveness' in their use of space and materials
'invasion' of girls' space.

She recalls thinking that children's play could be seen as '. . . a sort of power struggle. Who was going to be the strongest in the group? Who was going to have control?' Power relationships between children were a major shift in her observational foci and using 'power' to summarise what she was talking about was a noticeable shift in her vocabulary. Each concept that evoked power influenced how Anne understood children's learning in block play and she increasingly focused on 'social interaction' rather than 'problem-solving . . . because of the gender thing'.

Simultaneously, Anne struggled to discuss gender relationships in ways that did not assume that all boys were the same and all girls were the same. At times, her descriptions of what was happening faltered as she tried to avoid statements such as 'all girls', or 'all boys' while wanting to be clear that what she was describing had gender relations at its heart. She described the more traditionally gendered boys as the 'boy' boys and the 'macho' boys to distinguish them from the less traditionally gendered boys, whom she described as the 'feminine' boys.

Several of the research group members felt that Anne's descriptions of boys' and girls' differences in use of space ('expansiveness', 'dominance', 'invasiveness') helped them to name the gender relations they had observed in block play. Others felt less certain, but began to grapple with her ideas. The following exchange encapsulates the uncertainty about Anne's findings and their relevance to other centres and the feeling that, just maybe, Anne's descriptions did fit with what was happening elsewhere:

> **Anne**: . . . But even in activities like where [voice fades] . . . the boys are predominant, they're expansive. Even in an activity where the girls are predominant, they are not expansive at all. Would other people feel that?
> **Nellie**: When they play outside, the girls are quite expansive there. I am thinking of a couple of particular items, which is really interesting because when I tried—I found it really difficult to actually compare the boys to the girls. I guess I can't see them in—I don't see them working in those categories. I think after a couple of weeks of observations I possibly could.

Nellie vacillated several times during the meeting between feeling that categorising boys' and girls' play in this way was problematic (maybe she wasn't seeing the differences because she wasn't looking), and feeling that maybe Anne had 'got it right'. Anne's interpretations of her observations broadened the concepts through which others could understand block play. Over the next few weeks, three other teachers (Nellie, Fay and Emma) all tested how well these ideas described gender relations in their own centres.

Anne's novel interpretation of children's play led us to tentatively discuss the exercise of power as an important component of gender relations, and hence the knowledge we might, therefore, need to gather and use in working with children.

Around this time, Emma, Tina and Edna found that they experienced problems trying to observe gender issues in their centres because it interfered with the time they had available to do their 'normal' (DAP) child observations. For Emma, Edna and Nellie, normal observations of children's development got in the way of the gender observations. The two forms of observation were seen as disconnected. This was not because they necessarily were, but because the staff had learnt to read children's behaviour using traditional child development categories: gender appeared to be a novel and, therefore, an additional category to the normal.

Anne's decision to privilege gender in her observations for a period of time disrupted the idea that gender was necessarily additional. Her work implied that vital information about the children may be missed by not investigating gender relations. For example, girls' avoidance of block play was more easily understood once gender was a focus for understanding their actions. As such, her work raised the possibility that gender could be *central* to understanding children's behaviour, rather than *additional* to it.

71

Why it happened as it did: DAP observation and the gender gaze

Despite Anne's long history of monitoring children's development, a focus on children's individual development seemed to be directly associated with a lack of knowledge of gender relations in her centre. Anne was sufficiently concerned about her lack of knowledge to work in a detailed and systematic way to increase it. The desire to increase her knowledge was fundamentally rooted in her approach to planning. She could not imagine having a basis for action without gaining specific information about what was occurring between the children in her group. Such knowledge was essential to her teaching. A way to resolve her lack of knowledge was to use her tried and trusted skills of child study to improve her gender expertise.

So, Anne's long history of monitoring children's development was central in improving her understandings of gender construction in her centre. Her confident practice of, and belief in, child study as the basis of curriculum planning provided the skills and desires that drove the changes she made in her observational practices. Within this context, using gender as a key observational category seemed a simple change to make. However, it required Anne to skew her normal observational practices in two ways.

Firstly, she had to move away, for a time at least, from the principle of taking balanced developmental observations. In choosing to prioritise gender she privileged one aspect of social development. Using gender as the prime category for observing children and, within this, focusing on relationships *between* children, not just on individual development, was a major change in her practices. Anne had never before formally used gender as a basis of her observations and had rarely examined patterns of play between children. The individual, not the group, had been the focus of her curriculum decision-making.

The second way in which she had to change her normal

observation practices was by using power-related concepts to interpret her observations. This required her to move beyond her own normal ways of understanding children's behaviour (which were DAP-derived) and to begin to theorise her observational categories differently. As recommended in many early childhood texts (e.g. Gordon & Browne 1993; Blenkin & Kelly 1996; Faragher & MacNaughton 1998), Anne categorised and decoded these observations using developmental theory. For instance, she classified her observations into those that described incidents concerning a child's cognitive, emotional, social and physical development. This process gave her detailed information about how each child was progressing across these developmental areas. Anne then drew on her knowledge of developmental norms in each of these areas to decode the developmental significance of her observations. She could identify if a child was behaving according to developmental norms or not. On the basis of this information, she individualised her program to assist with each child's developmental strengths and weaknesses.

Anne's work suggests that early childhood staff may often fail to see the significance of gender in children's learning because of the conventions that underpin the DAP ways of looking at children. DAP-based observational practices hide gender. They see children through what I shall refer to as the 'DAP gaze'. In the DAP gaze, gender is hidden by the discursive dominance of developmentalism and individualism within early childhood education and the marginalisation of feminist discourses within it (MacNaughton 1997). Developmentalism refers to the over-reliance on developmental ways of seeing children within DAP. Individualism refers to the over-emphasis within DAP on the individual child's growth and development. (See Chapter 3 for a more in-depth discussion of DAP and its tenets.)

To understand how these discourses interact to hide gender we first need to understand how pervasive and dominant DAP-based observation has become within early childhood education.

In western mainstream early childhood education there is a long and well-documented practice of teachers using developmental information about individual children as their core information base in planning for children's learning (Feeney & Christensen 1979; Cartwright & Ward 1982; Bentzen 1985; Lambert, Clyde & Reeves 1986; Arthur et al. 1996; Faragher & MacNaughton 1998). Teachers are encouraged to use their developmental understandings of each child in the group to plan developmentally appropriate learning experiences for each child (Spodek 1988; Farquhar 1990; Taylor 1992). Anne, like many other early childhood teachers, based her planning for children's learning on these well-tested practices.

Within this approach to planning children's learning, particular conventions structure how a teacher looks (gazes) at children. The teacher's gaze should be on the individual child. The aim is to gather information that allows the teacher to measure each child against developmental norms and from this to plan programs to facilitate their development towards these norms. This convention has the individual child as the object and reads her/him through developmental psychology (MacNaughton 1997; Smith & Campbell 1998).

Developmental psychology regards the child as having essential and naturally emerging human qualities, rather than as socially-constituted and gendered (Pateman 1988). Developmental programs monitor the developing child's *individual* human development against these goals and facilitate their progress towards them. To insert gender relations and gendered power dynamics into the DAP gaze skews it considerably. The focus shifts from the individual towards the *gendered* individual *in relationship with others*.

Developmentalism's dominance in the early childhood field is evidenced in its unchallenged position in government policy. For instance, in Australia it has been institutionalised through the Federal Government's Quality

Assurance and Improvement System (QAIS) for child care centres (National Child Care Accreditation Council [NCAC] 1993). Only those centres that can demonstrate adherence to developmental monitoring and planning for individual children will gain government accreditation and thus financial subsidies via fee relief for parents (NCAC 1993). Similar demands are made on centres in the USA which wish to be quality accredited by the National Association for the Education of Young Children (NAEYC) (see Bredekamp & Copple, 1997).

More recent developments in curriculum policy at the State level of government in Australia extend the areas through which the child is monitored to include those associated with various 'Foundation Areas of Learning' such as technology, language, science and the arts (see Fleer 1996). Discussing this development in Queensland, Greishaber (1998) argued that the preschool child is now seen as:

> . . . one in transition, no longer the subject and object
> of child development, but as a potential first grade
> student and able to be classified accorded to ten areas
> . . . Observations and surveillance, coupled with the
> precise recording and classification of what has been
> observed are the primary techniques through which
> the regulation and training of the child, parent and
> teaching population occurs. (pp. 9–10)

These developments in Queensland have been echoed in other States, including South Australia and Tasmania (Children's Services Office 1991; Department of Education and the Arts 1996). However, in these States developmental psychology still provides the foundation for reading how the developing child might engage with specific areas of learning. For instance, in Tasmania 'The Kindergarten Development Check' has as its focus 'key elements of development that underpin programs in the early years' (back cover) and charts through teacher observation a child's development.

When Anne privileged the developmentalist gaze, as she had when she joined the group, it hid gender

differences in children's play choices and cloaked the construction of gendered power relations between children,
thus enabling them to continue. This was because the
object of Anne's developmental gaze was the individual,
gender-neutral child, not the gendered child constructing
gendering with others. This meant that she did not see and,
thus, could not challenge sexism between the children.
As a result, boys were able to exercise power over girls in
areas such as block play; and patriarchal gender relations
between the children were maintained.

Anne's move to gender-specific observations was an
important staging post in her gender equity work. It
marked a move to feminist readings of the child in that the
object of her gaze was the gendered child. Anne's shift
away from a developmentalist gaze and towards a feminist
gaze meant that she privileged searching for gendered
power dynamics and that she sharpened her search for
sexism in relationships between children. This increased her
knowledge of sexism and of the boys that contributed to
it, and led to action to challenge it. Hence, Anne's refocused
gaze provided a beginning position from which to
challenge patriarchal gender relations between children in
her centre.

For Anne to reinvent what she had learnt in training
about good observational practice was a professional struggle. She achieved it because she was prepared to privilege
her particular gender readings of the child over
developmentalist readings of the child. Her ability to do
this and her desires to do so derived from the specific
context in which her work took place—a research project
in which gender was a key focus of work with young
children.

Alternative understandings of observation

How Anne reinvented her own observational practice offers
just one of many ways of seeing gender in children's lives.

There are many feminisms and thus many feminist pedagogical visions (Kenway & Moudra 1992) that insert gender into our gaze in different ways. Feminism thus offers us many lenses we can wear when observing children.

Not all feminist reconstructions of the pedagogic gaze will be equally productive for challenging sexism. For instance, Chapter 7 explores in greater detail some of the specific difficulties in relying on liberal feminism. This chapter reinforces recent critiques that suggest that liberal feminist reconstructions of the pedagogic gaze in the early years are unlikely to challenge individualistic, humanist notion of the natural child (e.g. Mawson 1993; Alloway 1995b; MacNaughton 1998c). Furthermore, several writers have convincingly argued that liberal feminism cannot lead to major educational reconstruction because liberal feminist theories of gendering ignore girls' *experiences* of gendering (e.g. Alloway 1995b; Weilor 1988). Instead, they focus on describing what happens to demonstrate how inequality is manifested. They ignore why and how girls can begin to challenge traditional gendering. Hence, a liberal feminist gaze in early childhood education is in danger of reinforcing observational practices of describing children's behaviour rather than action and intervention in it.

The challenge in constructing a teaching gaze with feminist intent(s) in early childhood is twofold: to find ways to increasingly articulate, circulate and centre feminist reconstructions within early childhood education; and to continue to critique the pedagogical and political implications of these feminist constructions. As Kenway, Blackmore and Willis (1996) remind us, differing feminist educational discourses 'have different dividends for different groupings of women and girls' (p. 1). If we are to successfully work through the challenges of reconstructing the pedagogic gaze with feminist intent we must be vigilant to the limits and the possibilities of the differing feminist ways we make sense of children.

One feminism that alerts us to the limitations within specific feminist gazes is known as 'multiracial feminism'

(Collins 1989; Zinn & Dill 1996). Multiracial feminism reminds us that not all feminisms are racially inclusive and focuses on the ways in which gender and race intersect in women's lives and on who wins and loses in this process. This approach also focuses on how class and sexuality intersect in women's lives. Zinn and Dill (1996) explain the concerns of multiracial feminism as follows:

> This perspective is an attempt to go beyond a mere recognition of diversity and difference among women to examine structures of domination, specifically the importance of 'race' in understanding the social construction of gender . . . It is the centrality of 'race', of institutionalized racism, and of struggles against racial oppression that link the various feminist perspectives within this framework. (p. 321)

They go on to identify six distinguishing features of multiracial feminism:

- Identity is formed in a complex interaction between a person's gender, race, class and sexuality. For instance, a person's gender works with and through their race, class and sexuality to constitute their identity.
- All aspects of a person's life are formed by how class, race, gender and sexuality are socially structured and by personal experiences of this.
- All women are connected to each other through relations of dominance and subordination.
- Women make lives for themselves and for others around them that work within and sometimes challenge the constraints of race, class, and gender oppression.
- Studying women's lives requires diverse methods that allow us to see the complexity and specificity of *all* women's lives.
- All women's lives are constantly changing and it is important to study the changing nature of their differences and of their commonalities.

Using multiracial feminism as a lens through which to see children, teachers could look at how race, class, gender and sexuality are lived by the children in the group and how the relations between them shift as a result of their differences. Reinterpreting Zinn and Dill (1996), teachers could structure our observations of children through questions such as these:

- How do children within the centre differ in relation to gender, race and class and how does this enable them to shape the experiences of themselves and of others?
- How are those relationships defined and enforced through our early childhood practices?
- How is power negotiated in relationships between different children and between children and adults?
- How are race, class, gender and sexuality implicated in the negotiation of power within the group?
- How does children's diversity contribute to the construction of both individual and group identities?

Teachers need to be vigilant to what will be lost and what will be gained through each of the lenses they wear. Early childhood teachers reflecting on the implications of multiracial feminist gazes for young children should ask, 'What are the limits and the possibilities of this way of making sense of children?' For me, using a multiracial feminist lens is one way to see the complex and often hierarchical ways in which children's race, gender, class and sexuality will construct them, their lives in early childhood centres and their relationships with each other.

A multiracial feminist lens also has the potential to underscore how teachers' own race, gender, class and sexuality constructs them and the lives of children with whom they work. In doing so, this lens could illuminate the productive nature of teaching: how do teachers in part produce who it is possible for the children to be in our classrooms? This relies on early childhood teachers developing a 'critical positioning' (Caraway 1991, p. 114) on themselves (as teachers) in children's lives. They would scrutinise their teaching and the children's ways of being and knowing for the effects of race, gender, class and

79

sexuality. For instance, they would scrutinise the following conversation for information on how race, gender, class and sexuality construct and are constructed within it. In this conversation Rebecca and Connie work hard to construct Barbie as a heterosexual married mother with a father. The girls defined Barbie through her relationships to men. They are talking with me about a videotape of their play with Barbie.

Barbie's baby wants a daddy

Glenda: Can you tell me what you were doing here?
Rebecca: Yes, we were making a Ken for the Barbie.
Glenda: Why were you making a Ken?
Rebecca: Because we didn't have a Ken and we wanted Barbie to get married.
Glenda: Does Barbie need Ken to get married?
Connie: Yes.
Glenda: Why?
Connie: Because then she wouldn't have any father or anything.
Rebecca: No. How can they make the baby?
(There is then some debate between Connie and Rebecca about whether or not Ken is the father or the boyfriend. Connie prevailed with the following statement):
Connie: We were just playing, 'your baby wants a daddy' Barbie.

A multiracial feminist who reads this might ask several questions to see how class, race, gender and sexuality are intersecting in this conversation and in the children's play that provoked it. For instance, she might ask:

- What is the race and class background of Connie and Rebecca?
- How does their background intersect with their efforts to construct Barbie as heterosexual, married, etc.?
- What are the discourses through which these girls understand gender?

Selected feminist poststructuralist perspectives provide some additional conceptual tools to help build this process of analysing the complexity of children's lives in their learning. They do this by taking our gaze away from the developing individual and towards the individual-in-the-social-world. This is achieved through using the teaching gaze to analyse how power and gender operate in discourse in children's lives (Jones 1993). One tool for doing this centres on analysing children's storylines to identify the discourses through which they make sense of their world, how power is exercised through their positioning within these discourses and how they invest within these positionings. Storylines structure young children's dramatic play and offer us one way to see how they are making sense of gender in their lives and the lives of other children (Davies 1989a). Questions to guide gender analysis of children-in-the-social-world through their storylines might be:

- What storylines are the boys and the girls using in this play? What is similar, what is different about their storylines?
- What were the power effects of these storylines for the girls and boys as they used them in their play? For instance:

  Who chose the storyline?
  Who made the rules for how the storyline evolved?
  How was power exercised in the play?
  Who got their own way in and through the storyline and how?
  Who ended the play and how?
  Who benefited, and to what extent, from the exercise of power in the play?

- Who was emotionally invested in the storyline?
- What were the emotional pleasures and desires expressed by boys and girls through the storyline?
- To what extent are the gender politics of the children's storylines patriarchal?

- What discourses of masculinity and femininity are being expressed in these storylines and in the relationships constructed in them?

Another feminist poststructuralist tool for seeing how power and gender are infused in children's lives-in-their-social-world is reading the gender ethics of children's discourses. This tool builds from the work of the French poststructuralist theorist Michel Foucault. Foucault sees ethics in terms of the 'care of the self' (Rabinow 1984, pp. 352–5). He uses the term 'ethics' to describe the discursive construction of our shifting relationships with ourselves. The discursive construction of this relationship can be analysed along four intersecting dimensions: its ethical substance, its mode of subjection, its self-forming activity and its *telos* (our goals for ourselves). If we want to understand how gender discursively regulates children's sense of themselves, we need to 'see' and analyse how each dimension works in their lives.

The ethical substance of our relationship with ourself refers to 'the gestures, postures, and attitudes which are in need of disciplining or styling' (Gore 1993, p. 63). If we apply this notion to observing children and gender we can look for those gestures, postures and attitudes which children try to keep in check (discipline) and to style in particular ways. For instance, teachers could look at how children's ways of standing, looking and gesturing express their gendered beings and how children struggle to get these 'right' as gendered beings.

The mode of subjection refers to the discourses/goals that drive our obligation to self-discipline. It refers to how we explain our efforts to discipline or to style ourselves as particular types of people. In young children it would refer to their explanations for behaving, feeling and being particular types of gendered people. Teachers could seek their explanations for why they do what they do in gendered ways.

The self-forming activities refer to the techniques we use to achieve a particular gender gesture, posture and attitude that forms the gendered self. The techniques produce us as correctly gendered. For children, this could include how they check whether or not they are dressed correctly for their gender, if they have the right toys for their gender, etc.

The *telos* refers to the kind of person we aspire to form and the state of being we desire. Our self-forming activities help us to act on our 'own bodies, souls, thoughts, conduct, way of being, in order to transform themselves and attain a certain state of being' (Gore 1993, p. 91). If teachers adapt this idea to observing children and gendering, then they could look at how children act on their own bodies, thoughts, conduct and way of being, in order to transform themselves and attain a certain state of gendered being.

To illustrate how this might happen I'll draw on a conversation with two Anglo-Australian children, Paul and Amber, about their mud-play in their early childhood centre.

Glenda: Paul was just telling me what you were doing. Can you remember what you were doing that day.
Paul: Yes, you were trying to get some more water—you were axing the water too hard. Remember the day you got too wet?
Amber: Yes. Sat in the mud. (Screwing up her face.)
Glenda: You didn't like getting wet Amber?
Amber: No way.
Glenda: Why?
Amber: Because, I got a dirty top.
Glenda: Does that matter?
Amber: No, I wasn't allowed.
Glenda: Who wouldn't let you?
Amber: Mummy.

Later in this conversation, Amber explained that she did like getting wet but she really didn't want to play in the mud any more because girls don't like getting dirty.

How was Amber involved in the care of her gendered self in this exchange and in the mud-play? If the ethical substance of Amber's relationship with herself is evident in her 'gestures, postures, and attitudes which are in need of disciplining or styling' (Gore 1993, p. 63), then which gestures, postures, and attitudes did she try to keep in check (discipline) and to style in particular ways? In this instance, her attitudes to getting wet and her screwing up her face signalled her attempts to get herself right as a female gendered being. She explained her efforts to style herself as a girl 'who enjoys being clean' by saying that her mother would disapprove of her being dirty and by saying that girls in general don't like getting dirty. Amber acted on her clothes to keep them clean and on her own desires to do so in order to be a normal girl seen through the eyes of her mother and her peers.

Using an 'ethics of the self' lens to read Amber's gestures, postures and attitudes in this conversation begins to tells us how her gender possibilities are constructed through the ethics of her discourses of masculinity and femininity as she lives her life with others. We could learn more about how she constructs her sense of herself in these discourses by putting on a 'storylines lens'. We could look at what storylines filtered through her play, how she exercised power in them and what the gender politics of this might be.

Putting on a storyline lens and an ethics of the self lens are just two examples of how teachers could construct a feminist poststructuralist gaze. There are many diverse ways a feminist poststructuralist gaze might be accomplished. Each chapter in this book touches on different concepts from within poststructuralist thinking that could be used to construct a complex and shifting feminist poststructuralist gaze. However, threading through each of them are some common intentions: to highlight the gendered nature of children's lives, our own part in this and the possibilities for freeing children from the constraints and inequities that gender places on them. To do this, teachers must emphasise how their teaching is implicated in:

- How gender is lived and experienced by children and how this shifts over time and in different spaces
- How gendered power is lived and experienced by children and how this shifts over time and in different spaces
- How all of the above shift and move over time for children and for us but always impact on their educational lives.

Anne's initial failure to see the significance of gender for children in her group is not unusual. Work from the United Kingdom (e.g. Skelton 1989) and Australia (e.g. Kenway et al. 1994) suggests that teachers will often resist acknowledging the influence of gender on children's learning and that feminist teachers may often meet hostility (Robinson 1992). As long as this remains the case, many teachers' abilities and desires to move to gender-specific observations and to analyse the power dynamics within these are likely to be minimal. However, for those staff committed to basing their practice on knowledge of children's needs and interests, ignoring gender is barely defensible. As Anne's work showed, gender is present even if we do not always choose to see it. The challenge is to find ways of seeing it that help us create greater opportunities for equity and justice in *all* children's lives. In doing so, teachers need to acknowledge the challenge posed by the multiracial feminists to see the connections between gender, race, class and sexuality in this work. Who will be the losers and the winners if they cannot meet this challenge?

Theory into practice

To provoke reflection on the limits and possibilities of differing feminist and non-feminist ways of observing children, let's look at some moments in the lives of two groups of children as they play together.

Snack time at Nellie's
It is snack time at Nellie's centre. The children have just washed their hands and can choose where to sit during snack time. Tony, a Turkish-Australian boy, has rushed to an empty table and sat at one end of it. He beckons to three other boys to join him. One of the boys is Turkish-Australian and two are Vietnamese-Australian. A Vietnamese-Australian girl (Stephanie) moves to join them. Tony grabs successfully for the chair she is attempting to pull out from the table. He frowns at her and holds the chair until she moves away. When she has gone he folds his arms in front of his chest and pronounces loudly that, 'This is a boys' table.' The other boys nod. Stephanie sits crying at a nearby table.

A teacher using a developmental observation lens might read it this way: Tony has strong tendencies to take a leadership role in his relationships with other children. He asserts himself both verbally and non-verbally. He appears to not understand the impact of his assertion on Stephanie or to understand that 'we are all friends at kindergarten'.
The teacher might plan this way: Tony needs some help to see the implications of his assertiveness for other children. I will need to remind him that 'we are all friends' in this kindergarten and that each of us can sit where we want to.

A teacher using a multiracial, poststructuralist feminist lens might read it this way: Tony's way of being male is being formed in a complex interaction between his Turkish-Australian background, his heterosexual family background, his gender and his class. These intersections clearly place all girls in a subordinate position to him and allow him to exert dominance over Stephanie physically and non-verbally. It will be important to understand more about Stephanie's family history and background to see how she might find a viable way to be a girl in her relationship with Tony.

The teacher might plan in this way: Tony will require help to understand my position on gender relations at kindergarten. He has very little experience of seeing gender relations non-hierarchically. I will need to learn more about Stephanie's family background and how she understands herself before acting with her to challenge Tony's view that males should dominate females.

Feminist poststructuralist possibilities and provocations: a summary

Traditional DAP-based observational practices in early childhood education risk obscuring the daily gendered politics of children's lives with each other. To see these politics teachers could experiment with changing the lenses through which they read children. They could put on and combine a multiracial feminist lens, a storylines lens or an ethics of the self lens. As a result of doing so, they could:

- Look for the relationships between children's gender, race, class, ability and sexuality and how these influence the children's experiences in and contributions to the group
- Research the children's experiences of power and its effects in their storylines on themselves and on others
- Find out how the children take care of their gendered self: seeking the reasons for their gestures, postures,

attitudes, feelings and behaviours and how they transform these to become correctly gendered

- Reflect on how their own gender, race, class, ability and sexuality influence who it is possible for the children to be.

Learning more about the debate

The following material aims to help you reflect further on how the lenses through which we observe children influence our teaching.

Further readings

MacNaughton, G. 1997, 'Feminist praxis and the gaze in early childhood curriculum', *Gender and Education*, vol. 9, no. 3, pp. 317–26. This paper provides an argument for reconstructing the teaching gaze in early childhood education with feminist intents.

Smith, K. and Campbell, S. 1998, 'Images of the child: constructing the lived meaning of fairness', paper presented at the *Representing the Child Conference*, 2–3 October, Monash University, Melbourne. This paper provides a critical overview of the role of DAP-based observation in early childhood programs. It also explores the possibilities of a feminist poststructuralist reading of the child for understanding how young children live 'fairness' in their lives with each other.

Gore, J. 1995, 'Foucault's poststructuralism and observational education research: a study of power relations', in R. Smith and P. Wexler (eds), *After Postmodernism: Education, Politics and Identity*, Falmer Press, London, pp. 98–111.

Professional development suggestions

- How much does gender influence children's lives in your centre? How do you know this?
- What are the lenses you currently wear to observe children's lives? What are the discourses that produce the lenses through which you observe children?
- Talk with two of your colleagues about how they gain information about children and their learning. To what

extent do they wear a developmental lens in this work? What other lenses do they use?

- Use a Foucauldian ethics of the self lens to observe a group of children at play. What did you learn about the children and about your knowledge of them through this work? How comfortable did you feel putting on this lens?

5

Too young to know

Juan: I'm really looking forward to reading that new non-sexist book to the preschool children. I wonder how they will react to it?

Penelope: Don't you think that the children in your group are a little too young to cope with it?

Juan: I don't think so. I think gender is already affecting their play decisions.

Penelope: I think it's in your head, not theirs. I just don't think that gender matters to young children. You should let them keep their innocence while they can. You'll be planting ideas in their head that they are not ready for.

When do children start to notice gender in their world? When do they start to care about their gender and that of other people? Juan and Penelope had diametrically opposite answers to these questions. Penelope felt that young children were innocent to gender and so did not see the point of introducing them to stories with a 'gender message'. Juan felt that young children were 'gender knowing' and so was keen for them to hear his gender message.

Teachers in the research group found it impossible to ignore the impact of gender in children's lives. However, they differed in their beliefs about how much young children really knew about gender. This chapter looks at how these differences emerged and at the implications for how we talk to children about gender.

Debating teaching practices: what do children know?

Musing on what children know about gender was a regular feature of the early research group meetings. To find out what children knew, we did two things. Firstly, each teacher looked more closely at how gender influenced children's play styles and play choices. Secondly, we read published research about young children and gender. We learnt about the gendered choices children were making but not why they made them. Edna was especially puzzled about why the girls avoided block play:

> **Edna**: I see them [the girls] as very confident, very capable little people, that maybe in a broader scheme that we might perceive them as narrowing their choices, but they're rounded little girls, maybe, whatever. But they are very conscious of the differences in the genders as much as boys are and 'That's girls' clothes', and 'Girls do that sort of thing'. And that's why I'm concerned, that they are actually perceiving it in some way that girls don't play with the blocks.
> **Glenda**: You can't understand why, can you? Given you're saying they are confident in other ways?
> **Edna**: They're confident and I can understand at one level if they're not wanting to take up the boys' space, but I've given them space, I've given them encouragement, I've given them reinforcement, I've given them everything, but they are not perceiving those blocks as being relevant to them.
> **Glenda**: Have you asked them why?
> **Edna**: No, I haven't.

Edna greeted my suggestion that she might ask the girls, 'Why?' with considerable discomfort. This was strongly conveyed through her body language and in her words:

> **Edna** (frowning and shifting in her seat): I don't quite feel confident about asking children, 'Why?' I don't

think, 'Why?' is very relevant to little children, or many people for that matter. 'Why do you do anything?' But if there's another way of phrasing that question . . . (fades).

Edna was not alone in her discomfort about asking young children 'Why?' My suggestion had been greeted in the meeting by an awkward silence. There were numerous suggestions offered to Edna about how to avoid the 'Why?' question. Suggestions included that she should ask the children the following questions, which all avoided 'Why?':

Would you go in the blocks if we did this?
Would you like me to add something?
What would you like to do?
Would you like me to take toys away, or would you prefer smaller blocks, or some people with it'?
What do you like best about it [blocks], or what don't you like about it [blocks], like the enclosed area.

The discussion soon shifted to another topic. Several months after this exchange we returned to the issue of asking children why they make the gendered choices that they do. During this discussion, Sally declared that she also felt uncomfortable about asking young children the question 'Why?'

Glenda: I come back to the question Sally raised—Why? Why the differences and what can we learn about that in terms of the teaching strategy that we use if we want to get them using the different equipment. You said something about asking the children 'Why?', and then you said . . . (fades).
Sally: I said I think I chickened out. I have chickened out in the past asking them 'Why?' Well, I think it's partly because you think it's too philosophical for kids of that age, and it's not really.

We talked in the group at some length about Sally's concern about asking children 'Why?' She struggled to articulate the reasons behind her hesitancy. She felt that the children 'might not be honest', that the boys might 'take off' and that the girls might 'be intimidated' by the boys. She also felt that her reluctance to pursue 'Why?' questions with children arose from what she learnt in her training about young children's intellectual capacities and their inability to think abstractly. During this discussion, several of the teachers nodded in knowing agreement with Sally.

Nellie was the only group member to express surprise at Sally's struggle to ask the children 'Why?' questions:

Nellie: But 'Why?' questions are one of the questions I ask my children all the time—as part of their language development.
Glenda: You are not really doing anything that's out of the ordinary.
Nellie: I'm not doing anything out of the ordinary. I'm just asking why they did that particular thing as I ask them why they've done something else.

However, Nellie did add that 'Why?' questions must be asked under very particular conditions: when the children raised the issue they were to be asked about. In her view it was very important that children raise the issue, not the adult. In this way, teachers would know that they were not imposing their concerns and issues on children. Guided by this rule, Nellie explored children's gender understandings. Her conversations with the children in her group showed clearly how children were actively 'in the know' about gender and how it structured their lives. She learnt that they had clear understandings about what girls and boys should do, what they should wear and who they should spend time with:

Home area—what you should do

Child (female to male): I'll do the washing up.
Teacher: *Why* do you want to do the washing up, Elaine?
Child: Because girls do the washing up.
Teacher: I think Mark could help with the washing up, or maybe he could do the next sinkful of washing up after you.

Do you know that sometimes the girls do the washing up and sometimes the boys do?
Child: My daddy doesn't, my mummy does.
Teacher: Dads and mums both do the washing up.
Child: No, they don't.
Teacher: Do you know that my dad does washing up, my mum does the cooking, and my dad does the cooking, too?

Home area—what you should wear

Child (female to male): You can't wear that, that's a skirt.
Teacher: *Why* can't Callum wear that, Jean?
Child: Because boys don't wear skirts.
Teacher: I think the skirt looks great on Callum. Do you know that Callum can wear skirts and pants? We can all wear any sort of clothes we like. Would you like to try these pants on, Jean?
Jean: No.

Indoors at fruit and milk—who you should be with

Child: This is the boys' table.
Teacher: *Why* is that, Tony? Why is this the boys' table?
Child: This is the boys' table because that's the girls' table.
Teacher: Did you know that we can sit anywhere at our kindergarten? All the children sit together or wherever they like, on any chair they like.

Nellie remained the only teacher in the group to use 'Why?' questions to uncover children's gender knowings.

Why did it happen as it did? Questioning children's knowing

Asking a child 'Why?' seemed a simple and obvious way for Edna and Sally to find out why the girls in their centres shunned block play. Yet the thought of doing so made them and other group members feel uncomfortable. Probing why this was so proved difficult. The teachers could not remember specific theories or theorists that shaped their views on questioning children or if any had. They had lost this detail in the years since their pre-service training. What had remained with them was the knowledge that, for some reason, asking children 'Why?' was inappropriate and therefore wrong.

Edna believed that young children didn't know why they did things. Sally held that young children couldn't deal with abstract questioning. Nellie felt that young children should only be questioned about their immediate interests. In slightly different ways, each teacher felt that it was developmentally inappropriate to ask 'Why?' of four- and five-year-old children. They saw developmental limits to what children knew about gender and/or limits to what and how they should be asked about it.

While it may be possible to trace these beliefs, acquired in their training, to specific developmental theorists, they also reflect a broader discourse in western society about childhood innocence. Cannella (1997) traced how this discourse has constructed a very particular pedagogy in early childhood:

> The discourse of innocence most obviously implies lack
> of knowledge or ignorance, as opposed to adults who
> are not innocent but intelligent . . . Knowledge is either
> considered non-existent or of poor quality. This
> innocence requires that access to additional knowledge
> be withheld or controlled with only 'safe' knowledge
> being allowed. Observation and supervision are
> required to insure this limited access. (pp. 35–6)

In other words, we need to closely observe and supervise children in order to control their access to the knowledge we consider safe for them. Cannella (1997) believed that developmental psychology is pivotal in this process. Its extensive and detailed knowledge base sees the child as different to the adult and in need of the adult's protection. It also justifies the protection of young children from particular types of knowledge on the grounds of the child's inability to understand this knowledge. It has achieved this outcome through the idea of the 'developing child'.

The developing child created through developmental psychology is understood as:

- distinct from adults in how they know, what they know and how they express their knowledge
- in need of special practices to support their expression and acquisition of knowledge.

The reasons for the group's reticence about asking children 'Why?' can be glimpsed in these truths of the developing child. Edna, Sally and Nellie each spoke of the child's difference from the adult and how this created the teachers' special questioning practices. These truths placed boundaries on what knowledge the teachers felt it was possible and permissible to seek from young children. The effect of this was to seriously limit children's ability to express their gender knowings (Edna and Sally) and the conditions under which it was allowed (Nellie). In the research group, we further silenced children's voices and privileged our own by using *our* observations and the published research of *others* to learn about *their* gender issues.

Our desires to do this can be explained if we note two canons of developmentally appropriate practice: observation is *the* basis for knowing the child; and scientific research about the child provides *the* rationale for how to act with the child. The teachers were following developmentally appropriate practice in observing children to uncover their gender knowing and in comparing this with scientific research. However, in doing so, they obscured a powerful source of gender knowledge: the children's voices. Silin's work suggests that we should not find this surprising. DAP's psychological base encourages teachers to put aside their moral and political decision-making:

> When teachers rely on psychologists for their
> knowledge base, they may be avoiding difficult

96

philosophical and social issues while believing themselves to be acting in a 'professional' manner. They also may be succumbing to a subtle, but nonetheless potent, form of technical mindedness because they are taking educational decision making out of the realm of moral and political consideration, where it more properly belongs. (Silin 1995, p. 92)

Alternative understanding of children's gender knowledge

When we use the idea of the developing child Cannella argued that children are 'denied the power to speak for themselves' (1997, p. 37) and Silin argued we avoid 'difficult philosophical and social issues' (1995, p. 92). If this is so, how else might we read the child? If we produce the child as 'gender innocent' through the discourse of the developing child, how might we produce the child as 'gender knowing'? Poststructuralist visions of subjectivity and how it is produced offer a beginning point.

In common usage 'subjectivity' refers to our individual consciousness or perception about action, events and ideas. Sometimes our understandings are referred to as subjective when they are distorted by our personal biases. In poststructuralism these meanings have been recast. Subjectivity describes our ways of knowing (emotionally and intellectually) about ourselves-in-our-world. It describes who we are and how we understand ourselves, consciously and unconsciously.

In poststructuralism, the individual is made subject (made knowing) by language (and hence discourse). So poststructuralists (along with many others) see language as the key to how we construct our subjectivity (our sense of ourself). Language is central in this process because it:

- constructs how we think, feel, act, desire and speak
- constitutes what we believe is normal, right and desirable.

97

To illustrate how subjectivity does this I'll draw on my conversations about gender with Chloe. She was a four-and-a-half year-old Anglo-Australian child in Carlie's kindergarten. In the following conversation we are discussing a videotape of her play with some boys at her centre.

> **Glenda**: You are playing with two boys here Chloe. Do you play with the boys a lot?
> **Chloe**: Yes, I normally do because the boys are really in the real game and there was only one girl.
> **Glenda**: Who was that?
> **Chloe**: The big boss April . . . I was really a girl. There was only one girl and I couldn't do anything.

However, life with the boys in the 'real' game rarely went smoothly. Chloe often felt frustrated and gave up when they resisted her efforts to lead them in new games. One such occasion centred on her attempts to initiate a Ghostbusters game:

> **Glenda**: Can you tell me about the game you are playing on this video?
> **Chloe**: It's just the idea of playing Ghostbusters. It was to be a new game.
> **Glenda**: Can you tell me what you were doing in the game?
> **Chloe**: Not very much.

Chloe's description of herself as doing 'not very much' seemed puzzling. She had initiated the game and worked hard to continue it. However, as usual the boys resisted these efforts and quickly began their own rough and tumble game. She was soon left standing alone doing not very much. Despite this, one of the boys, Charles, accused her of being bossy and of 'pulling and dragging' him:

> **Glenda**: Charles was saying that you were the bossy one in the game.
> **Charles** (interjecting forcefully): She was bossy to me. She pulled me and dragged me around the place.

Chloe: I did not!
Charles: Did so.
Chloe: Did not.
Charles: Did so.

Chloe quite rightly denied Charles's accusations. In revisiting the play recorded via videotape she was innocent of his charge. You might think that being rejected and facing such injustice might quell her desires to play with the boys. She certainly knew it was 'hard':

Chloe: Why are you taking pictures?
Glenda: I want to know more about how we can help boys and girls to play together.
Chloe: That'll be hard.

Despite the hardships, Chloe persevered. What pleasures did she experience in doing so? Carlie and I puzzled over this. However, Chloe's capacity to puzzle me didn't end here. A conversation between us some time later contradicted much of who she had struggled to be for months. She surprised me by declaring her desire to have tape-recorded *the* moment in which a boy had 'got her heart':

Chloe: Could you tape me today?
Glenda: I haven't got the video here today. I have just got my taperecorder. Why would you like me to record you?
Chloe: This is the first time a boy's got me in my heart.
Glenda: What does that mean?
Chloe: That means I'm feeling seasick (laughing).

Henry was the boy who had got her heart. I had seen Chloe talking and laughing with him behind the swings only moments ago. It was one of the few times I had seen her happy with the boys. She seemed jubilant as she ran back to Henry. She invited me to follow. When I commented on how happy she looked she surprised me once again:

Glenda: You look like you are enjoying yourself.
Chloe: I'm not.

Chloe looked very sad for a moment and then dashed back to Henry. Had she found a way to be with the boys that they accepted? She was sad, yet happy. I struggled to make sense of how Chloe could want to be the 'big boss' running Ghostbusters in one moment and then in another want me to record her 'losing her heart to a boy'.

We can use Davies (1989b) to trace how language was implicated in Chloe's decisions and how it formed her discourses of girlhood and in this her subjectivity—her knowings about herself-in-the-world. Davies argued that we form subjectivity in discourse through four processes:

- Learning to categorise people, including ourselves. For example, Chloe has learnt the categories of 'bossy' girl and 'girlfriend'. This learning formed the base from which she knew how to be with the boys.
- Participating in discourses and practices that give meanings to the categories we learn. Chloe participated in relationships and practices in which meanings have been given to 'bossy girls' and 'girlfriends'. For example, bossy girls are those who initiate games with the boys and they are girls with whom the boys don't play. Her relationship with Charles in their dramatic play and in their daily conversations form part of the practices through which she has learnt this meaning. In contrast, when girlfriends give their heart to boys they can spend time laughing and talking with them.
- Positioning oneself in a relationship to the categories and meanings given to them. In her relationship with Henry, Chloe had to decide how to position herself in relation to being a bossy girl. She decided on this occasion to be a girlfriend, not a bossy girl. She knew about both categories and the meanings that Henry and other boys gave to them.
- Recognising the position taken and emotionally investing in the position taken. Chloe recognised herself as a girlfriend because of desires created through recent events with Charles and other boys. The desires involved

significant emotional investment in not being ignored by the boys again. But did she also recognise the position because of her exposure to what it meant to be a girl in the 'real' game via the videos of Ninja Turtles and Ghostbusters that she knew so well. Had she come to understand more broadly that girls in the 'real' game are not only 'one' among the boys but they always 'lose their heart' to them in the end?

It was through these processes that Chloe came to know herself-in-her-world as she did. These understandings then constituted her learning in very specific ways in her play with other children, especially the boys.

If we use Davies (1989a) to think about Chloe's relationships with herself-in-her-world and her peers, we can:

- read them as relationships between language and power
- see the importance of storylines in children's play
- see how the peer group could constrain children's choices
- see that there were multiple ways of being masculine and feminine
- understand how Chloe is actively constructing herself as a gendered person in the world
- accept the idea that she is 'gender knowing'.

The power behind the meanings that Chloe gives to her relationships-in-her-world arise from her emotional investments in them. These investments make up her patterns of desires. Patterns of desire provide the power behind what is learnt via discourse about ourselves-in-the-world. Patterns of desire are themselves discursively constituted, as Davies (1993) explained:

> Within humanist conceptions of the person, desire signals the 'real', stable identity of any person. Because desire is understood as being constituted through discourse in poststructuralist theory, it is possible to see human subjects as not fixed but constantly in process, being constituted and reconstituted through

the discursive practices they have access to in their
daily lives. (p. 11)

Using these ideas we can see that Chloe was forming and
reforming herself as complex patterns of desire wove
through her daily life. Her desire to be a girl in the 'real'
game led Chloe to and through her frustrations and disap-
pointments. Chloe was negotiating her way through the
different ways to be a girl and through complex patterns
of desire within these. This complexity was part of who she
was. The other children, especially the boys, had tried to
keep her in a gender category that worked for them. I came
to know this through asking Chloe about her life with the
other children. Influenced by my readings of Davies, I
gained the desire and the confidence to ask her 'Why?' she
did what she did. She regularly gave complex and knowing
answers to my questions. Her request to me to capture her
heart going to Henry showed me how much she knew
about what I wanted to know from her.

If we analyse children's meaning-making through the
lens of feminist poststructuralism we can expand our
options for working with children by learning to privilege
their subjectivities. In particular, borrowing Davies' (1989a)
vision of how discourses form subjectivity we could do this
by:

- Seeking information from children about how they have
  categorised themselves and others and how gender is
  implicated in these categories
- Identifying the social practices through which children
  come to understand what is meant by the gender categories (e.g. girlfriend, mother, sister, etc.) that build
  their discourse
- Exploring the patterns of desire implicated in how children understand and 'do' gender.

An illustration from Chloe: Chloe had a variety of social
categories through which she could understand herself as
a girl in our society. For example, she could understand

herself as a bossy girl, tomboy or a girlfriend. Hence, while Chloe is formed subjectively in her discourses of girlhood, she has agency within this to reform her own subjectivity. Weedon (1987) put it this way:

> Although the subject in poststructuralism is socially constructed in discursive practices, she none the less exists as a thinking, feeling subject and social agent, capable of resistance and innovations produced out of the clash between contradictory subject positions and practices. (p. 125)

Conversations with children about their gender decisions and their gender knowledge offer one way for adults to gain insights into their discourses and their patterns of desire. Feminist poststructuralism thus suggests that there is a choice, albeit restricted, for Chloe about how to position herself as a girl in her day-to-day life. Each choice had emotional consequences because of her particular history of emotional investment in particular ways of being a girl. To understand these consequences for particular children we must invite them to talk with us about gender and listen to their knowings.

Chloe knew that rejection and loneliness was attached to being a girl who initiates and tries to manage games with boys. Chloe learnt that being a girlfriend and losing your heart reversed this. In my discussions with Chloe it was clear that she struggled with well-developed patterns of desire that constituted her as an initiator of play. However, the pleasures of this were constantly challenged in her play with boys. She was struggling to find a way of being a girl with the boys that was normal, right and the best way to be a girl. Her journey had just begun! She was struggling to find sufficient pleasure in her positioning as a girlfriend to override the emotional investment she had in being the leader. She needed to give up much of what she then enjoyed: playing exciting adventure games and thinking up new ideas. She would have to be prepared to be 'sad' to get it right with the boys.

To understand Chloe's gender discourses and how they influenced her decisions, we must focus on the moral systems (senses of what is right, normal and best) that constituted her patterns of desire. Conversations with children about what they see as gender right, gender normal and gender best can add to our sense of the strength of these patterns for them.

Chloe's moral system was complex. She was caught at the crossroads of contradictory patterns of desire. In accessing and analysing these patterns of desire through conversations with children, we can glimpse how discourses come to be so powerful in their learning. We can see how they form their choices about what they want to do and who they want to do it with.

Feminist poststructuralism suggests that children learn gender through their daily inscription in discourses and their active desire to make coherent and meaningful sense of themselves and others in, and via, these discourses. As Davies (1993) writes:

> . . . children must learn the ways of seeing made possible by the various discourses of social groups of which they are members. This is not simply a cognitive process of language learning, but also an ability to read and interpret the landscape of the social world, and to embody, to live, to experience, to know, to desire as one's own, to take pleasure in the world, as it is made knowable through the available discourses, social structures and practices. (p. 17)

Seeking children's gender meanings is a critical part of the context for understanding children's learning and for redefining them as gender knowing rather than as gender innocent. Feminist poststructuralism suggests that changing these gender meanings is difficult. It involves developing alternative discourses through which children can give meaning to their lives as girls or boys. We will find this hard if we do not explore what gives the children gender security and gender pleasure. We cannot do this without the children.

Chloe shows young children *do* know about gender. The discourse of the innocent, developing child risks silencing gender in children's lives. Yet, as the teachers in this project discovered, gender is highly complex and ever present in children's lives. If we are to take children's gender knowing seriously, we need a more complex image of what and how young children know about themselves-in-the-world. Thinking about how subjectivity is built may be part of provoking this complexity. Learning to ask children 'Why?' may be an important key to learning about their subjectivity. Conversations with them about gender certainly are.

Theory into practice

The teaching implications of using different theories of how children construct their gender meanings to read their play are illustrated below. As you read the vignette 'Pippa prefers home corner' reflect on these questions: How did she know gender? How did her gender knowing emerge? How might your preferred explanation of her gender knowing influence your teaching decisions about how to work with her?

Pippa prefers home corner

Glenda: Pippa, lots of the time I see the girls playing in the home corner. Is there some special reason for that?
Pippa: Yes, because they like playing mothers.
Glenda: What do they like about that?
Pippa: Well, I like going there and feeding the babies in the pram.
Glenda: What about the boys, do they ever play mothers?
Pippa: Sam always plays. He's always playing mum.
Glenda: Does he? . . . So do you play with Sam much?

Pippa: No
Glenda: Why not?
Pippa: I don't want to because I don't like him.
Glenda: Why don't you like him, Pippa?
Pippa: Because what he says to me.
Glenda: What does he say to you?
Pippa: He always says lots of hard things to me.

The 'hard things' that Pippa referred to were Sam's regular demands to be 'mum' in the home corner and to wear the glittery skirt that 'mum' did. He often told Pippa she was 'not fair'.

Later in the same conversation:

Glenda: Are there any places in the kindergarten that you don't play?
Pippa: I don't (fades) . . . . I don't like playing with them (pointing to the blocks).
Glenda: Do you know why?
Pippa: Because I like to go higher and higher but then they (pointing to the boys) smash down and hurt my ears.
Glenda: That must be very annoying. I don't think I'd like that either.

There was certainly videotaped footage of Pippa's block buildings crashing down with the help of two boys. That incident had occurred a month prior to my conversation with her. I didn't know if there had been similar occasions before or after the one I recorded.

A believer in children's gender innocence might read it this way: Pippa is becoming very much her own person. She loves playing in the home corner and is a confident block builder. However, she is experiencing some difficulty getting on with a child in the group called Sam. She really doesn't like him and has difficulty sharing with him. At four years of age, she can't yet explain clearly why she doesn't like him. I would like to ensure that this clash of personalities doesn't develop further. She has the skills to play cooperatively with other children. She just needs support to use these skills in her play with Sam.

The teacher might plan in this way: I would like to encourage Pippa to play co-operatively with Sam. To support her in this I will:

- ensure that Pippa has lots of opportunity to play alongside Sam
- model my own enjoyment in being with Sam
- encourage her to play with Sam
- positively reinforce her if she is voluntarily involved in play with Sam.

A poststructuralist feminist might read it this way: Pippa has developed clear gender categories about boyhood and girlhood. Her daily practices with Sam and her practice of block building with boys produced her meanings for these categories. Sam is challenging her right to be 'mum' and saying 'hard things' to her. When she builds with blocks the boys push over the tall buildings she loves to build. These practices are building the gender discourse that informs her choice of learning experiences and her choice of friends.

Her dislike of Sam and of block play choices are not based on her personality, her developmental immaturity, her individual whims or her personal preferences. They are located in the discourses through which she has learnt to understand girlhood and boyhood. She has learnt that she has most power over boys in the home corner and least when she is in the block corner. She has learnt that playing by herself in the home corner is more pleasurable than playing with Sam, as he tells her she's not fair. *The teacher might plan in this way:* I would like to expand Pippa's understandings of what it means to be male *and* female. In particular, I would like to show her alternative ways to experience power in her play with the boys and to help her find enjoyment in this. To support Pippa, I will first need to:

- understand more fully the categories she uses to make sense of gender and of gender relations
- observe the practices that continue to give meaning to her gender categories
- understand the patterns of desire that provide the power behind her categories
- reflect on their associated emotional benefits and costs for her
- create opportunities to talk with her about each of the above and then decide how her gender knowings might influence my program.

Feminist poststructuralist possibilities and provocations: a summary

Children are forming and reforming themselves using their gender knowings. The most potent source of information about young children's gender knowings are the children themselves. Accessing these knowings is the key to meaningful gender equity work with children. To explore this possibility teachers could:

- Find out which categories children use to understand gender
- Find out how children feel about gender and what ideas lie behind these feelings

- Reflect on the emotional costs and benefits for children of their gendered ways of being
- Use these reflections and children's gender knowings to decide how to work for gender equity with children.

Learning more about the debate

The following material should help you to understand better how children construct gender meanings in their lives and extend your understandings of the poststructuralist critiques of childhood innocence.

Further readings

Lloyd, B. & Duveen, G. 1992, *Gender Identities and Education: The Impact of Starting School*, Harvester Wheatsheaf, London. The authors use empirical research to show how young children negotiate gender identities in their first year of formal schooling. They provide an excellent overview of how this process has been theorised and offer an interesting counterpoint to the poststructuralist notion of multiple and shifting gender identities in young children in the latter part of the book (see pp. 178–83).

Silin, J. 1995, *Sex, Death and the Education of Children: Our Passion for Ignorance in the Age of AIDS*, Teacher's College Press, New York. Silin provides a compelling case for seeking children's meanings about life, living and dying, and shows what can be gained in our teaching through taking children's meanings seriously. In Chapter 4, Silin traces differences in how modernist and postmodernist theorists understand children and their capacity to make meanings.

Urwin, C. 1984, 'Power relations and the emergence of language', in J. Henriques, W. Holloway, C. Urwin, C. Venn, V. Walkerdine, *Changing the Subject*, (pp. 264–322), Methuen, London. This 'classic' chapter outlines the poststructuralist case for reimagining the individual and for reconceptualising subjectivity.

Yelland, N. (ed.) 1998, *Gender in Early Childhood*, Routledge, London. This book is an edited volume in which authors explore how gender operates in the lives of young children in the family, at home and at school. Several chapters offer excellent insights into how gender operates in young children's lives and how they make sense of this.

Professional development suggestions

- Talk with two colleagues about how they think that young children understand gender. What evidence do they offer to support their views? To what extent has the discourse of child innocence influenced their understandings? How do you think their views might influence their teaching decisions?

  Silin (1995 p. 134) wrote: 'Exploring the social definitions of children as ignorant and innocent and adults as knowledgeable, I have come to understand how these assumptions about knowing/not knowing structure our ability to hear children's questions' (p. 134).

  What might seeing the child as gender knowing/not knowing mean for how you would work with young children on gender issues?

- How would you explain the poststructuralist concept of subjectivity to someone unfamiliar with it? Reflect on the words you could use and the ideas that you would need to cover. How might you use Chloe or a child you know to help your explanation?

- Listen to and talk with a child you know to learn more about:

    the categories s/he uses to make sense of gender and gender relations

    the practices that have given meaning to her/his gender categories

    the emotional benefits and costs associated with them.

  What challenges did you face in this task? What might you change if you approached this task with another child?

6

We've been doing gender equity for years— what's new?

Tasha: What subject are you choosing for your elective?
Robert: Gender issues in early childhood education.
Tasha: That's a bit old hat isn't it? Very 1970s. We've been doing gender equity for years. Surely there's nothing new to say!
Robert: I thought it might help me rethink what I'm doing now. I'm really struggling to make gender equity a reality in my kindergarten group.

Tasha's reaction to gender equity programs is not unusual. Many early childhood educators share her view that 'it's all been done before'. Several members of the research group shared this view initially. However, after testing out familiar gender equity strategies, they changed their views. Like Robert, they often felt despondent about the difficulties of making gender equity a reality. This chapter uses their work in block play to show how what's 'been done before' often fails us. It also shows that the challenge to find new ways to achieve gender equity in the early years remains pressing and that innovation is possible.

The recent backlash against gender equity policies for the education of girls adds fresh impetus to the search for new ways of working for gender equity. In the late 1980s and early 1990s gender equity in education policies in several western countries were based on the assumption that a 'critical feminist mass' (30–40 per cent) in male domains would produce a cultural shift to 'gender inclusivity' (Blackmore, 1999, p. 90). The gender equity practices that have resulted from these policies and the policies themselves were heavily critiqued in the late 1990s for ignoring the educational needs of boys. In this critique it was assumed that those policies had successfully met the educational needs of girls (Lingard & Douglas 1999). This chapter takes issue with the idea that such success was achieved in early childhood education. It also takes issue with the idea that educational success is likely for girls when we rely on creating a critical mass for them in boys' domains in early childhood centres.

Debating teaching practices: When the old ways fail you

When members of the research group first observed children's play patterns in their centres they found several dynamics that surprised them:

- Boys and girls regularly chose to play in very different areas. Girls played in decorative, gentle, passive and domestic play areas. Boys' play was full of aggression, lots of action and lots of movement in areas such as construction and the sandpit.
- Boys and girls controlled the space they used differently. Boys controlled their space through physical aggression, girls through language. Girls avoided confrontation at all costs. Boys and girls also used physical and auditory space differently. Boys were more expansive and were louder in their use of space. If boys moved into a space and girls suspected a confrontation they would leave. Boys would move in and try to take over the space.
- Boys often demanded and received more teacher time.

They also used time differently. They were less persistent than girls, wanted more immediate results for their
efforts, changed direction often and, overall, concentrated for shorter periods of time.

The one activity area in which these patterns emerged most
starkly was block play. Groups of boys dominated this play
regularly in all but one centre. Often it was the same group
of boys. One teacher referred to them as the 'block corner
boys' and she and others described such boys as the more
macho boys within their group. These initial observations
uncovered three trends in the play dynamics between boys
and girls that were of concern for gender equity:

- boys regularly denied girls entry to the space
- boys constantly challenged girls' involvement in block
  play; many of these challenges were physical
- boys allowed girls into the play space only on the boys'
  terms.

Most of the research group were surprised by these patterns, all felt uncomfortable with them and all decided to
try to change them. They worked intensely to increase girls'
involvement in the blocks using strategies which have been
recommended in early childhood texts since the mid-1970s.
I have called these strategies: feminisation, separatism,
fusion and policing.

Feminisation involved placing in the block area materials that girls played with elsewhere, such as pieces of cloth,
tea sets, dolls and doll's houses. This did lure some girls
into block play. However, the strategy failed for one overriding reason: the boys often entered the block play space
first and, when they saw the girls' materials in the area,
moved them aside. As the girls moved towards the block
area they saw their 'feminine' materials being put aside by
the boys.

Separatism involved introducing girls-only days, or
girls-only time in block area. Excluding the boys in this
way removed the problem of them being first in the area.

Girls did get involved with blocks and their work indicated interest and skill in building with them. There were two difficulties with this strategy. Firstly, once girls-only time was stopped, the children reverted to their old patterns. Secondly, during girls-only times, some boys disrupted their play through what one person described as 'seek and destroy' missions. In these missions boys made swift forays into the girls' play and disrupted it using loud voices or aggressive actions. This often occurred at moments when the adults were occupied elsewhere.

Fusion involved combining the block and home corner areas. It is not a particularly new idea: Kilman (1978) suggested it as a strategy to reduce sexism in early childhood education. However, it was the most contentious option used. Teachers faced difficulties from their colleagues (see Chapter 8) and faced comments similar to those made by Cuffaro (1975):

> . . . it has been suggested on occasion that the two areas [blocks and housekeeping] be fused as a means of breaking down sex barriers. To do so would be to overlook the nature of each area and the particular learnings which each offers . . . fused they create confusion in the scale in which the child is working . . . (pp. 476–7)

The children's reactions to fusion were more complex but just as starkly gendered. When the two areas were fused, the boys' storylines either excluded the girls or the girls didn't see the storylines as interesting or comfortable. Without exception the boys' storylines derived from them constructing, exploring, creating, attacking and destroying someone or something. These storylines involved:

- solving problems via physical aggression
- killing and 'getting' the bad guys
- capturing space
- being loud
- physical contact with each other.

When the girls were in the fused area by themselves, they always initiated domestic play centred on the daily domestic tasks of being 'mums', such as cooking, cleaning, shopping, looking after 'baby' and having parties.

When the girls met the boys in the fused area, one of two things happened. Some girls moved elsewhere in the centre and then retreated into their domestic play. Talking with the girls about their retreat, it was clear their choice was based on a fear of the boys' destructive potential and on their own desire to continue with domestic play in a 'safe' space. A past history of unhappy incidents with specific boys positioned all boys as problematic, or potentially problematic. As Matti told me:

> Boys, they hurt you, they kill you, that's why no boys, no none here. They not play with us, do they Maddy?

The girls who stayed tried to position the boys in a non-disruptive role in their domestic play by suggesting that the boys be 'dad' or a pet. Each option worked slightly differently to 'quieten' the boys. For instance, 'dad' was sent to work, or sat at the table to wait for his dinner. Either way, he was less trouble because he either left the play area to 'go to work' or could be controlled as a pet. Making the boys pets allowed the girls (as 'mum') to boss the boys around and to tell them what to do, once again giving the girls some control over the boys.

From the boys' point of view, each of these positions was less than satisfactory. I was told that being 'dad' was 'boring' and being a pet was only fun if you were a 'naughty' pet. But if you did this you were generally punished or the game stopped.

Counting heads in the fused area showed boys and girls playing together but closer examination revealed they were regularly in very separate play worlds. The boys told me that they found the girls' play 'boring'. The girls were equally dismissive of the boys' storylines. They did not think that 'killing' was fun and they didn't enjoy loud, rough and tumble play.

Another way to increase girls' involvement in blocks is through the adult becoming more involved in blocks and carefully policing boys' interference with girls' play. This meant intervening every time the boys attempted to dominate, challenge or exclude the girls. Several group members did this. However, once again they found that this strategy only worked in the short term. The original play patterns reappeared when adults stopped creating special access to block play for girls. This remained a constant feature of the play in two groups for several months and meant that a considerable amount of adult time was needed within the block corner. Edna reported that she needed to be there constantly with the girls, questioning, commenting and generally extending their play in this area to protect the fragile relationships between girls and boys (see Chapter 2).

A flavour of this fragility can be gained from one particular observation taken when a girl was in block play. I shall call the girl Maria.

> Maria spent some time building a very complex and intricate building. She was on the edge of some very active 'boys' block play. Some of the boys had been watching her and seemed to want to enter her play. They brought a block over and put it by her building, just touching. She then walked around and took it away. Then one of the boys leant a block against her building. There was eye contact then he went away. When he did she went around and took it away. She constantly had her eye on the boys and on the teacher. The moment the teacher left to answer the telephone the girl left the blocks. The boys then moved in and started adding to her building.

In the different centres, girls and boys reacted quite differently to each of the strategies to increase girls' involvement in blocks. The boys resisted affirmative action to increase girls' involvement in blocks, disrupted their success in girls-only times and maintained a highly masculinist (macho) culture where rough and tumble and, at times, aggression was the norm. In contrast, girls avoided contact with boys to avoid conflict, attempted to incorporate boys in their play in non-disruptive roles and maintained a highly feminine culture in which domestic play and passive resistance were the norm.

So, the old strategies used to involve girls in block play had variable success. There were changes, but they were short-term and at times each was problematic for both boys and girls. Why was this so?

Why did it happen as it did: Challenging play patterns, challenging patriarchy

With hindsight, it is clear that the variable success of the research group's strategies derived from the implicit assumptions about gender relations upon which each was based. Approaches to gender equity which focus on making the curriculum more girl-friendly, such as feminisation, separatism and fusion, assume that girls don't play in specific areas due to lack of interest. So, if you can spark girls' interest, for example by giving them experience with the blocks or including materials of interest to them with the blocks, they will become involved. In other words, the problem is the nature of the materials and the girls. These approaches assume the cause of girls' non-involvement in blocks is the girls. In essence, they 'blame' the girls for not wanting to play with the materials, thus placing the responsibility for change with the girls. The girls need to change by developing an interest in the blocks. How this is accomplished differs slightly in each approach, but the implications are the same: the responsibility for change lies with the girls.

These approaches sit very comfortably with several DAP canons (see Chapter 3):

- Young children learn best when they make choices and follow their interests.

- Adults' responsibilities are to encourage and to expand children's interests so that their learning can be broad and balanced, but the ultimate choice must be the child's.
- To 'force' a choice or to 'control' children's choices is developmentally inappropriate.

From that DAP perspective, it is totally consistent to place responsibility for the girls' choices on the girls. As Cuffaro (1975) argued some time ago, 'stripping sexist connotations from the curriculum is not the primary focus of the teacher. The teacher's main concern is the total development of the child' (pp. 476–7).

Policing approaches to change involve slightly different assumptions about gender relations. The boys are implicitly defined as the problem. It is their fault that the girls don't enter the blocks area, so the adult needs to police the boys to stop them intimidating the girls. This strategy did increase girls' involvement in block play for periods of time, but there were also some difficulties within it. As it placed responsibility for the children's gender relationships firmly on the adult, she had to be present to control equitable gender relations. So, the adult needed to prioritise this aspect of their program and to risk jeopardising her responsibilities to provide a developmentally balanced curriculum.

The children's responses to these initial strategies to increase girls' involvement in block play suggest that none of these approaches, in and of itself, was sufficient to create lasting change. Each was based on a simplistic view of why boys and girls often prefer to live and play in quite separate worlds. In particular, they ignore how hard children work to behave, think and feel as a 'normal' female or male in the particular society into which they are born. They ignore the complex and powerful patterns of desire built up in this process.

Children spend considerable time trying to be a 'normal girl' or a 'normal boy' and trying to understand the 'proper' way to be masculine and feminine in their culture. To do this they must learn the dominant discourses of masculinity and femininity.

Discourses provide us with the frameworks through which we make sense of our social world (see Chapter 3). In children's play these frameworks help them make sense of their social world. In play they create and recreate their understandings of what they believe to be normal behaviour for boys and girls, women and men. They construct their play using what they have distilled from the adult world about normal gendered ways of being, thinking and acting.

As we watch children's play in western cultures we are involved in watching the recreation of patriarchy (Walkerdine 1981; Dunn & Morgan 1987; Davies 1989a; Danby 1998). Put simply, patriarchy is male dominance (Giddens 1991). There is overwhelming evidence that western societies are to varying degrees patriarchal and that patriarchy damages both men and women (Buchbinder 1994). In patriarchal societies children's play tests out what it means to live as male and female within patriarchy.

By saying that children learn to live as male and female within patriarchy, I mean that they learn what it means to be a female or male within a culture in which:

- masculinity is valued more highly than femininity
- particular ways of being masculine are valued more highly than others
- institutions and personal relationships maintain power relationships that benefit men and boys. These can be referred to as 'masculinist' power relations (Connell, 1995).

The research group found it difficult to escape the conclusion that the block play area was regularly constructed as a patriarchal space where masculinist (macho) ways of acting, being and feeling gave boys powerful access and involvement. Boys regularly gained and maintained block play as a space in which traditionally 'macho' ways predominated. In other words, block play was a space where male dominance was the norm: it was a masculinist space. This was clearly so when adults attempted to challenge the boys' dominance in block play through feminisation, separatism or fusion. Boys actively resisted the changes. But it was also evident in boys' and girls' reactions to adults policing their gender relations.

Many boys positioned themselves within traditional ways of being male ('macho' masculine discourses) and wanted to control girls' access to block play and the nature of girls' involvement in the area. As a result, girls rarely chose to be involved in block play when boys were present. Watching boys and girls playing in the block corner together, one could see why. The boys tried to gain and maintain their dominance. The girls, not surprisingly, resisted this but avoided confrontation at all costs.

For the boys and girls, in different ways, block play was about power relationships between them: Who got to do what, when and how? Who could exercise power in what ways? In this instance, the boys regularly exercised power physically and through the storylines they used. The effect was that they gained and maintained block play as a space in which particular ways of being male were dominant.

Both boys and girls exercised power but in different ways and with different effects for their block play. The girls preferred to play in ways and in spaces in which their ways of being, as girls, could dominate. Girls had the skills and the interest in blocks, but they were not interested in playing in an area in which 'macho' ways of being male were the dominant ways of being. They were not interested in patriarchal block play.

We need to understand how gender relations are constructed by the children to fully understand girls' curriculum choices and to develop appropriate responses to these choices. Approaches that see the boys or the girls as the problem do not create long-term change. This is what our old approaches have done and they have failed us and failed the children badly.

Alternative understandings for gender equity

Walkerdine (1981) offered help with thinking about power, children's play and gender relations:

> To understand power and resistance in the play of children we have to understand those practices that they are recreating in their play. These produce the children both as recreating the, often reactionary, discourses with which they are familiar, but also serve to constitute them as a multiplicity of contradictory positions of power and resistance.
>   . . . individuals are powerless or powerful depending upon which discursive practice they enter as subject . . . (p. 20)

If we consider these ideas a little further, we can redefine our teaching role in block play (and other curriculum areas). Walkerdine argued that children's play (e.g. block play) reproduces power relations based on dominant understandings of what it means to be a male and a female in our society. If we want to change these power relations, we have to change the discourses through which they make sense of themselves as masculine and feminine. We have to take them apart (deconstruct them) and remake them (reconstruct them). Each discourse through which we understand ourselves has specific effects on how we exercise power, what we enjoy doing and whether we are powerful or powerless in a given situation. How we exercise power and what we enjoy doing will be different for boys and girls, and each discourse will have different power effects for boys and girls.

By way of illustration: when boys understand themselves through 'macho' discourses, the most normal thing in the world is to be noisy, physical, involved in aggressive play and not defer to the girls. If boys see 'macho' ways of being as normal then they will enjoy exercising power in highly physical ways. In contrast, when girls understand themselves through traditional feminine discourses their

121

normality centres on being quiet, gentle, involved in domestic play and hating aggression. If girls see traditional femininity as normal, then they will avoid any confrontational exercise of power.

For boys and girls who understood their gendering through these traditional discourses, the effects in block play were simple. For the boys, exercising power physically and through their storylines excluded girls from the area and made them dominant in this area. They were extremely powerful. They used their understanding of what were normal ways of being, behaving and thinking as males to decide what to do and who could do it. However, if they entered the girls' storylines in block play they lost this dominance.

For the girls, there were several power effects of understanding themselves in traditionally female ways. It was extremely uncomfortable to stay in block play and to continue to act as 'normal' girls unless the boys entered their storylines as 'dads' or 'pets'. If they left block play, and continued to act as 'normal' girls, life was less problematic. So girls who understood themselves in traditional ways were cast as subordinate to the boys in the block play. They were powerless to do much other than leave or try to control the boys. This interpretation of children's play shifts the blame from the girls or the boys to the discourses through which they have learnt to understand what it means to be a boy or a girl.

We need to rethink why children act as they do in order to develop innovative ways of working with boys and girls. We need to understand how much of their play world is fundamentally about gender relations. They are learning through their play how to 'read and write human possibilities' (Haas Dyson 1994, p. 219). Nowhere is this process more intense than in their dramatic play. Through the storylines that weave through their dramatic play we can see how they are reading and writing their possibilities as gendered beings.

We can glimpse in these storylines the discourses through which they make sense of themselves and others. If changing the discourses through which children make sense of themselves and others may provoke a change in gender relations between them, then their storylines may hold the key to this change.

An obvious way to introduce children to new storylines is through books in the centre. Stories can be chosen which introduce boys and girls to the diverse ways it is possible to be, act, feel and experience as boys and girls. They can also be used to help children to discuss how sexism affects their play. This is one of the more traditional and popular ways to approach gender equity with young children.

However, most girls rarely pay attention to stories that they see as boys' stories, and vice versa (Davies 1989a). This means that teachers need to find alternative ways of integrating alternative gender storylines into children's play. Sally's approach to reconstructing children's storylines with children such as John (see Chapter 3) is one possible way to help children imagine new gender possibilities for themselves and for others. Teachers can also help children recreate their storylines by creating classroom communities in which children are in constant dialogue and in which multiple and conflicting voices are heard, are allowed and encouraged. For instance, teachers can encourage children to talk with each other about their storylines and the choices they are making within them about who and what they will play/work with. These discussions will inevitably raise issues of inclusion and exclusion, many of which pivot around gender. For instance, often boys will only choose boys to be in their story or the girls will only allow boys to be babies. When children have to talk about their choices with others they have to grapple with other children's responses to their choices. Boys may have to explain to girls why they never choose to play with girls or give them leadership roles in their play. Through such discussion teachers and children can raise issues of fairness and unfairness.

Creating dialogic classroom communities (Bakhtin 1981) offers the possibility for changing understandings (and, therefore, storylines) because in the moment of children experiencing difference, change becomes possible (Pinar et al. 1996). Moments in which multiple and conflicting children's voices flourish offer the possibility of hybridisation in which two or more understandings join to form something new (Bakhtin 1981; Kamboureli 1998). However, in the process of hybridisation of gendered meanings in children's storylines teachers must be alert to the power relations they create. They must be alert to where patriarchy lies within them.

Haas Dyson's (1994) study of the practice called 'The Author's Theatre' encouraged hybridisation. In this study she explored the 'cultural constraints and transformative power' of stories in young children's lives with a teacher who used the technique of 'The Author's Theatre'. This involved primary school children writing their own stories and then choosing friends with whom to act out their stories. At the end of this process, children had the opportunity to comment on the stories and to question each other about what was said and what happened.

Haas Dyson (1994) explained the consequences of this work in this way:

> . . . children's desires to be powerful in some way, to feel strong, and the ways in which simplistic definitions of power and of gender relationships put them at odds with each other and, indeed, with themselves can be brought out into the open. The dialogic process of exploring contradictions and conflicts, of grappling with issues of inclusion and exclusion, allow the stories of girls, boys, and powerful people to begin to be transformed. (p. 222)

'The Author's Theatre' is one way to encourage a dialogic process in which hybridisation and, therefore, changed understandings become possible. It was the very fact that issues of inclusion, exclusion and fairness surfaced and were discussed, debated and worried over that made it a transformative practice. Haas Dyson concluded that creating and interweaving alternative storylines through children's play works best when the following conditions are met:

- the storylines focus on children's own issues and respect their right to play
- routines are established which allow children to voice comments, raise questions as individuals and in groups about the storylines
- the process is carefully monitored by the teacher throughout
- the children have fun.

If these conditions enable children to explore and raise issues about power, exclusion/inclusion and gender, then they offer some guidance on how teachers might reimagine their role in children's play. When this reimagination centres on gender equity, then a teacher could:

- use children's storylines and play rituals to help the children see the gendered power effects of their gender discourses
- use open discussion of children's desires within their play to help them deconstruct and reconstruct their discourses of masculinity and femininity
- be more proactive in creating the space and the dialogue to challenge those discourses that create and recreate patriarchal power relations
- experiment with ways to expand children's repertoire of non-patriarchal storylines and play rituals.

By analysing who benefits from particular power dynamics in specific storylines, it becomes possible to rethink how to challenge sexist power relationships within them and to build feminist alternatives. To achieve this in practice teachers must shift from a focus on how many boys and girls are in block play to questions of how they are playing and who benefits from the play that takes place. Teachers will need to work hard to provide boys with understandings of masculinity in which dominance is not always seen as positive. They will need to work equally hard to provide girls with understandings of femininity that enable them to assert their rights and understandings within block play. They can do this through trying to remake their storylines. In doing so, teachers can remake their role in creating gender equity. Haas Dyson's work (1994) suggests that such work on children's storylines can help us to remake children's understandings and experiences of power in their play with each other. In doing so, we can help them to remake their gender relations with us and with each other.

Theory into practice

To see what it means to use different theories of how gender relations work in our gender equity teaching, let us look at a cameo from children's play with each other and reflect on how different theories might help us 'respond' to the children here.

Barbie's boobies

Several four- and five-year-old boys and girls are playing with Teacher Barbie and Olympic Barbie on a large mat inside a child care centre. Tim stands up and moves around, screaming loudly. He moves back to the girls, throws himself on the floor, stands up and moves towards Heather (the research assistant) with one of the Teacher Barbie blackboard pictures in his hand. He begins singing about the sky. He then tries to take the Teacher Barbie Blackboard from Sarah. Sarah grabs it back. He then picks up the trapeze. Sarah says very loudly, 'Hey, no.' Han, one of the other girls, goes to retrieve it. Tim then picks up the Olympic Barbie and touches its breasts before throwing it on the floor, standing up and moving towards the video with some packaging he picks up on the way. He then throws the packaging into the space where the girls are playing.

Throughout this time the girls are sitting playing with their Barbies. Tim calls to them, 'Hey, look Ballerina', as he shows the girls the written instructions which accompany Twirling Ballerina Barbie. He shouts, 'All here, all here.' The girls ignore him, remaining seated facing each other and looking at their Barbies as they have been throughout Tim's 'visit'. Mandy then calls to the research assistant and asks, 'Heather, Heather, why won't Tim shut up?'

Moments later Tim is pointing to the Olympic Barbie who is dressed in her tights and says to another boy, 'Take them off.' One of the boys starts stripping the Olympic Barbie. When it is naked Willie grabs it and begins to kiss it. He then holds her up to Jamie's lips and makes loud kissing sounds. There are lots of giggles between the boys at this. One of the boys then says, 'Boobies, she's got boobies.' This is followed by lots of collective laughter from the boys. Willie then says to the research assistant, 'Heather, look at this.' Heather is being invited by Willie to watch Tim press the naked Barbie's head to Jamie's lips. Jamie is being told by Willie to kiss the Barbie. The girls have taken their Barbies to another area of the room.

How did gender relations work for this group of children? How might our preferred explanation of why they acted as they did influence our teaching decisions about how to work with Tim and with the girls?

A person who thinks that the boys are the problem might read the cameo this way: The boys are making it extremely difficult for the girls to play with Barbie. It is their fault that the girls have left the area. They have harassed the girls and disrupted their play by being aggressive and by surrounding their play space. The boys' behaviour has meant that the girls have not had a 'fair go' in their play with Barbie. *The children's teacher might plan in this way:* To ensure that the girls get a 'fair go' in their Barbie play I will position myself alongside their play. I will intervene quickly if the boys disrupt the play and indicate my disapproval of their actions.

A poststructuralist feminist might read it this way: The boys are strongly positioned within 'macho' discourses of masculinity and of sexuality. These are evident in how they play with each other and in how they respond to Barbie. They are also evident in how they attempt to disrupt the girls' play with Barbie. The girls are equally strongly positioned within highly emphasised discourses of femininity. If I am to change their ways of responding to each other, I will need to work with them to remake these discourses.

The teacher might plan in this way: To ensure that the girls and the boys are able to experience pleasure in their play with each other and with Barbie I will need to expand their understandings of what it means to be male and female. I will try to show them that pleasure and power exist in exploring non-traditional ways of being masculine and feminine through encouraging dialogue with and between the children about these issues. As this will be a long-term project, I also will need to establish rules which stop the boys harassing or hurting the girls.

Feminist poststructuralist possibilities and provocations: a summary

Many of our traditional ways of achieving gender equity with young children have short-term success only. This is because they 'blame' the girls and/or the boys for gender inequities. Feminist poststructuralist theory suggests that we should blame the discourses of masculinity and femininity through which children makes sense of themselves, not the children. Long-term change in children's gendered behaviours is more likely to result from remaking their gender discourses. Creating dialogic communities in which children hybridise their gendered storylines offers one vehicle through which to do this. If teachers can remake the gendered possibilities within children's storylines they can, in part, remake their gendered discourses. Teachers could explore this possibility by:

- searching children's storylines to identify the discourses through which children are making sense of themselves and of others
- weaving alternative storylines into their play by taking children's gender issues seriously and having fun with them
- routinising opportunities for all children to comment on and question each others's storylines and the actions that flow from them
- committing themselves to long-term work with children on their storylines focusing on issues of power, inclusion/exclusion and gender.

Learning more about the debate

The following material explores how patriarchy and young children's lives intersect and how teachers might understand these intersections.

Further readings

Danby, S. 1998, 'The serious and playful work of gender: talk and social order in a preschool classroom', in N. Yelland (ed.), *Gender in Early Childhood*, Routledge, London, pp. 175–205. Danby details the nine phases of a local ritual of masculinity in the block play area of a preschool classroom. In showing how this local ritual is enacted she shows how the social order of gender is made in and through children's daily play with each other.

Gallas, K. 1998, *'Sometimes I can be anything': Power, Gender and Identity in a Primary Classroom*, Teachers College Press, New York. In this book Gallas shared her insights as a teacher researcher on how children live and give meaning to gender in her classroom. She studied the 'subtextual dynamics of classroom life' (p. 22) to illuminate the gendered 'undercurrents in the classroom' (p. 23). These undercurrents are vividly portrayed through vignettes of children's play and Gallas' reflections on the children's play. Chapter 3, 'Bad boys and their stories', and Chapter 5, 'Posing', are particularly relevant to questions of how patriarchy plays out in children's lives.

Professional development suggestions

- Talk with two colleagues about the children's play cameo of *Barbie's boobies*. How would they work with the children in the cameo? Would they agree that active and constant intervention in children's play is acceptable? How do they see their role in children's dramatic play? How might this influence their capacity to deconstruct and reconstruct storylines with children?
- Observe a group of children involved in dramatic play. To what extent are the 'gender politics' of the children's storylines patriarchal? If they are patriarchal, what alternative storylines could you introduce to the children that might help them remake their gendered power relations?
- How might you adapt the idea of 'The Author's Theatre' to work with preschool children? How might you use it with the children in the children's play cameo of *Barbie's boobies*?
- Danby (1998) details nine phases of what she terms a 'local ritual of hegemonic masculinity' (p. 179) in the

block play of preschool children. These phases describe how boys induct others into masculine rituals in the block play. They include boys protecting space, calling on reinforcements to support them and using verbal and physical resistance and threats. Danby argued that if teachers closely analyse children's everyday talk as they interact with each other they may see these and other gendered rituals that children play. How might close analysis of children inducting each other into gendered discourse help you to help them remake their gendered power relations?

7

What about the boys?

Allison: Did you see the article in yesterday's paper about girls in education? Apparently they're now more educationally successful than boys.

Joanne: It didn't ring true to me. I really wanted to look more closely at the statistics.

Amryl: It made me really angry. I think it's just part of the backlash against gender equity programs for girls.

Allison: I disagree. I think it had a point. Maybe we haven't been paying enough attention to the needs of boys.

Joanne: I agree that we need to think about our work with boys. Often boys undermine the work we are doing with girls. It's no good encouraging girls to be assertive and ambitious if their assertion and their ambition is met with boys' aggression and their 'put downs'.

Allison: But what about the under-achievement of boys? Maybe gender equity for girls does mean that the boys lose out.

Allison, Amryl and Joanne are debating how boys can, do and should fit into gender equity programs. Their debate was sparked by media coverage of the educational difficulties boys face. 1994 saw a flurry of media coverage in Australia on boys' educational 'woes', including poor literacy skills, behavioural problems in the classroom and poorer performance than girls in the Victorian Certificate of Education, in tertiary entrance scores (NSW) and in Year 11 subjects (South Australia) (see, for example, Arndt 1994; Heaney 1994; McIntyre 1994).

The concerns about boys and gender equity that surfaced in the mid-1990s revolved around questions such as:

- Are boys under-achieving in education?
- Is boys' under-achievement linked to gender equity programs?
- Are boys' 'needs' ignored in our current gender equity efforts?
- Do we need to do more for boys who are under-achieving?

Several teachers in the research group grappled with such questions. They were committed strongly to gender equity and in their teaching struggled continually to balance the needs of boys with those of the girls. Like Joanne, several teachers in the group felt that gender equity efforts for girls could not be divorced from boys' responses to them. Some also believed that the boys had special 'needs'. As Edna put it: 'It's a two way street. I want the girls to take up more space in the block corner, but I want the boys to do finer, more creative stuff in the creative area.'

What follows shows how teachers in the research group defined the 'needs' of the boys and the tensions and dilemmas that emerged for them in the process.

Debating teaching discourses: meeting the boys' needs?

One of the first and recurring dilemmas in the research group revolved around how boys fit into gender equity work. It surfaced when Sue sang the praises of 'girls-only' days in blocks:

> **Sue:** I used to have girls' days and boys' days with blocks just so the girls did—'Today, that's you'—that's

the only way I think that worked, and they knew and they loved it and they used to say 'Is it our day in the block corner?' And they loved it. They used to go in but they had the confidence. The boys would stand there and would say, 'How long will the girls be?' and I'd say, 'I'm sorry, they're going to be here the whole day today.' They accepted it, but they'd be threatening a little by standing right there and saying, 'What's going on?' Then I'd have to ferry them away again.

Sue was very clear that affirmative action for girls was her priority. In her view, the boys had to learn how to deal with affirmative action for girls. Others in the group were less certain. In the following conversation Carlie indicates her uncertainty about how fair this approach was for boys. As others joined the discussion, more dilemmas surfaced. I've headed their issues thematically to highlight the dilemmas the research group experienced in trying to find a comfortable space within their gender equity work for boys:

Is affirmative action for girls fair to boys?

Carlie: I've always felt guilty about doing that [girls-only spaces], but (fades)
Glenda: Have you? Why do you think you've felt guilty?
Carlie: Because being—trying to believe in equality of the sexes, because I feel for boys too, like you do in some ways, that the boys do miss out a little bit, and I try—I would like to think that everyone gets a fair share of everything, but in reality it doesn't work—so then I think well, that's fine, I'm doing it for the girls' sake, but the boys can do something else, but then I still feel that's dividing, and that's what we are trying not to do. We are trying to give girls a fair go, but to give boys a fair go too, sort of.
Nellie: It's almost reverse discrimination, in some ways, too.

Shouldn't we focus on extending the boy's experiences?

Edna: The point I was really making was that the boys also aren't experienced in certain things . . . we probably shouldn't make a value judgment that it's the girls that are missing out on the valuable experiences.

Sue: I guess in this whole thing I really—what Edna is talking about—I really kind of see that other side as just as important, if not even more important, to have the boys experience the dress ups and the beautiful creative dance clothes and things like that—I kind of consider that just as important as providing girls with that experience of being more expansive. I kind of see it as a two way thing, rather than providing these extra (hesitates and then stops).

Fay: Yes. But if you give the boys a fair go, you give them a chance to do some painting and some pasting and some other stuff—I mean you can make gender equity fair to them too.

Do boys need special conditions for learning?

Sue: I'm quite conscious of the fact that boys might feel too contained indoors and while you want to help them learn how to handle the sorts of things they find difficult to do, and many of those things you will find happen indoors, I'm conscious of that, but also maybe we can do it in a way that makes it easier—like, taking those things outdoors.

What do you do when boys' efforts are undermined by their peers?

Anne: It happened last year and the year before, when the kids were dressing up—some of the boys put on 'girl-type' clothes, for want of a better word, and the flack from the rest of the boys was just—had to be seen to be believed. 'He is wearing a girl's dress', 'He is wearing a girl's blouse', 'He looks silly', and the boys stopped doing it.

135

Should we make the boys 'do' things they don't want to?

> **Emma**: If you do that [make the boys sit quietly reading or doing collage] it just becomes a PR thing—that will keep them happy for a while.
> **Sally**: Or, 'She's watching, I'd better do it now'.

Is focusing on boys equally fair to girls?

> **Anne**: I'm very aware of that, so I'm trying to make that very even.
> **Edna**: We are still leaning in the direction of giving more to males, without even knowing it.

Is focusing on boys necessary?

> **Sue** felt that boys didn't need any special focus or consideration because: . . . they [the boys] are too busy setting the agenda, taking the control, the power and making people jump to their tune.

The research group often revisited these issues, puzzling over how best to answer questions such as:

- Should the boys' needs be prioritised?
- What are their needs?
- How do these fit with how we work with the girls?
- What do we do when the boys resist?

Each group member struggled to find answers to these questions. Their responses varied considerably:

- Sue remained firm that boys required no special consideration or attention.
- Edna vacillated between focusing on the needs of the boys and the needs of the girls.
- Fay and Nette worked hard to treat boys and girls identically.
- Carlie focused on supporting boys who were being undermined by their peers for crossing gender boundaries.

- Nellie tried to avoid 'giving more to males'. She felt the more aggressive and noisy boys in her group demanded her attention more than the girls did. To counter this she established rules to control the boys' behaviour.
- Sally settled on developing separate goals for girls and boys:

> I had the two goals running concurrently. I wanted the girls to use blocks more and make bigger buildings, not just their little fiddly things they do on one tiny corner of the block areas . . . to get the girls to use up a bit more space because we don't want the boys to hog it all.

Her goals for the boys were to:

> . . . give them the skills they lack, help them to play inclusively, to give them storylines for their play, and to help them to use non-sexist language.

Several months work with one boy led to a momentary victory:

> Well this day that John was building well with Kelly was the first time I haven't had to step in virtually every 30 seconds with him in the block corner.

However, Sally's work with the boys was seen as unfair to the boys by one parent. The parent argued that:

> The boys are really disadvantaged now because the girls get more than the boys do.

Why it happened as it did: meeting boys' needs?

Why did the research group find it so difficult to settle on a shared position on the needs of boys and their place within gender equity programs? Poststructuralist theory would suggest that their differences lay in the different discourses through which they understood what gender equity meant and what should be done to create it. In struggling with these issues, they were struggling with issues similar to those that feminist theorists and activists have struggled with across many generations. Like these feminists, they found different paths through their dilemma.

Sue's path echoed that of the radical feminists. At times, so did Edna's. Broadly defined, radical feminists believe that women's oppression by men is continuing, widespread, significant and evident in all aspects of our lives. This oppression means that women and men have distinct experiences, interests, desires, values and interpretations of the world. Radical feminists have detailed these differences in all aspects of women's lives, including childbearing and childrearing, work, sexuality and the experience of violence. They have detailed how 'men, rather than "society" or "conditions", have forced women into oppressive gender roles and sexual behaviour' (Tong 1989, p. 95). For radical feminists, challenging women's oppression requires us to develop a positive bias towards the feminine and to give validity to women's needs and concerns, more so than to men's. Many believe that avoiding involvement with men best does this. It has become a movement that celebrates women's differences from men and asserts their superiority to men (Jordon & Weedon 1995).

Sue's parallels with radical feminist discourses were several. She clearly felt that the girls were more disadvantaged than the boys and that because of this their needs, desires and values were distinct from the boys and to be prioritised. In addition, Sue, and at times Edna, felt that it was important to:

- ensure that time was spent on developing traditional feminine qualities in all children (caring and gentle boys and girls)
- ensure that their program enabled feminine skills to be acquired, practised and valued by all children (for example, all children learning to sew)

- encourage girls to be proud of being female rather than trying to be the same as boys
- prioritise the girls' needs to counter the boys' dominance within the program.

Fay's and Nette's emphasis on equal opportunities and equal treatment followed a path well worn by liberal feminists. Liberal feminism focuses on equal rights, status and opportunities for men and women, boys and girls. It assumes that inequalities between men and women are because women lack the same rights, status and opportunities as men, not because of any essential differences between them. The problem lies in how society is organised and structured. Once we reorganise social structures so that women have the same rights and opportunities as men then equality will be achieved. In education, equality will be achieved if girls:

- are given equal access to materials and space
- know they are as good as boys and that they can do anything boys can do.

Fay and Nette certainly worked hard to achieve these ends. However, they believed that boys were also disadvantaged by the current gender divisions and were keen to avoid any form of reverse discrimination. To this end they sought to make the boys and girls the same by ensuring that the best from each gender was experienced by the other. This strategy draws on the goal of androgyny that underpins some branches of liberal feminism. *Andro* forms the Greek words for male and *gyn* those for female. Tong (1989) explained how some liberal feminists draw on this concept to direct their work:

> It is in order to liberate women, and also men, from the culturally constructed cages of masculinity and femininity that many liberal feminists advocate the formation of androgynous personalities. Some liberal feminists favour . . . the development of a single, or

unitary, personality type that embodies the best of
prevailing masculine and feminine traits. (p. 31)

Sally, Carlie and Nellie each took a slightly different path
that blended aspects of radical feminism with sprinklings
of liberal feminism. (As we shall see shortly, their work was
also touched by poststructuralist feminism.) Sally worked
hard with individual boys and girls to offer them separate
but equal consideration. Carlie supported those boys and
girls showing signs of androgyny. Nellie focused on getting
rules in place to ensure that girls could exercise their rights
to equal opportunities.

Sally, Carlie and Nellie might have benefited from
having access to the debates, resources and professional
development on gender equity in the early years of school
that arose from the implementation of National Policy on
the Education of Girls (Commonwealth Schools Commission 1987). The work that flowed into schools from this
policy in the late 1980s and early 1990s provided teachers
with the opportunity to reflect critically on many aspects
of gender equity programs, including how boys might
be positioned within them. However, Sally, Carlie and
Nellie tackled their work with boys in a policy vacuum. In
the State of Victoria in which these teachers worked gender
equity policy for preschool children was non-existent. In
Lingard's terms, the 'policy culture' was silent on this issue
(see Lingard & Douglas 1999). Doing work within such
silence made it doubly difficult for these teachers to find
their way through this aspect of gender equity work.

Irrespective of how each teacher tried to find an appropriate space in their work for boys, each was touched by a
discourse that is central to liberal feminism and to early
childhood education: liberal humanism. Liberal humanism
is a way of thinking about the world that assumes that each
of us can take responsibility for our own actions (free will),
that we have the ability to exercise free will, that we should
and that we do. The individual is able to develop their
emotions, beliefs and capabilities in isolation from their

social context (Tong 1989). So, liberal humanism rests on the doctrine of individualism: a doctrine which emphasises the importance of the self and the development and achievement of the individual.

Within individualism, the needs and interests of the individual are paramount. Within liberal feminism, the needs and accomplishments of individual women are also paramount (Jordan & Weedon 1995). The belief that individual women do what they want if they are given equal opportunities derives from liberal humanism.

Individualism has direct comparisons to the goals of 'progressive' education. It emphasises the individual and their development (Pinar et al. 1998). 'Progressive' educators, many of whom have had a major influence on mainstream early childhood education, believe that the development of the individual was the goal of education and child-centred pedagogy was the educational method of choice (Alloway 1995b; Silin 1995).

The individual is paramount in liberal humanist thinking because it is assumed that individuals are the 'starting point and source of human action' (O'Sullivan et al. 1983, p. 114). Hence, in liberal feminism, individual children are the starting point for their own non-sexist identity formation. These ideas criss-crossed through the different paths each teacher took to find a space for boys in their gender equity work. They each placed a strong emphasis on the individual child's gender needs and interests and on how to work with individuals to produce greater gender equity.

Most teachers in the research group had trained as early childhood teachers at a time (1960s–1980s) when liberal humanism pervaded two core areas of mainstream early childhood knowledge: developmental psychology and progressive, child-centred education. With this background, it would be remarkable if they had not been influenced by liberal humanism; and it is not remarkable that their actions for gender equity often parallelled the path of liberal feminism. Liberal feminism with its roots in liberal humanism

141

sits comfortably with the child-centred pedagogy and individualism expressed in DAP.

Alternative understandings of boys' 'needs': the gender order and masculinity

What other paths might the teachers have followed? How else might we understand relations between women and men, girls and boys? Feminist poststructuralist critiques of early childhood pedagogies (e.g. Walkerdine 1981, 1984, 1990; Jordon 1995) offer some alternatives. They strongly suggest that our approaches to gendering in early childhood education have been severely limited by the particular modernist problematics informing them, including liberal feminist notions of the individual as fixed, rational, coherent and unitary.

Liberal feminism's view of the individual sees gender as a fixed, rational, coherent and unitary aspect of identity. The person's gendered self is seen as either traditionally or non-traditionally gendered. Hence strategies for feminist change focus on strategies for re-socialising the traditionally gendered individual (child or teacher) to become finally and coherently non-traditionally gendered. As Davies and Harre (1991/2) argue, such notions of pedagogical change place the responsibility for change on individuals rather than on social structures and discursive practices. In addition, such an approach to pedagogical change treats individuals as 'passive recipients of social structure' (Davies 1989b, p. 239).

Feminist poststructuralism has attempted to challenge these understandings by redefining the self: by reimagining our subjectivity and its multiple possibilities. As Davies explained in feminist poststructuralist analysis:

> We are . . . [understood as] multiple rather than
> unitary beings and our patterns of desire that we took
> to be fundamental indicators of our essential selves . . .

signify little more than the discourses, and the subject positions made available within them, that we may have access to. (Walkerdine & Lucey 1989, cited in Davies 1991, p. 43)

Two overriding factors limit our gender possibilities. Firstly, all western cultures have dominant ideas about the correct way to be male and female. These ideas order relations between genders, creating a particular gender order. Secondly, the traditional and current gender order in western cultures is patriarchal. A patriarchal gender order is characterised by 'emphasised femininity' and 'hegemonic masculinity' (Connell 1987, p. 183). Gilbert and Taylor (1991) draw on Connell to explain these terms:

Hegemonic masculinity is constructed in relations to the dominance of men over women, as well as over other forms of masculinity. It is heterosexual and technical competence. On the other hand, emphasised femininity, the form of femininity which complements hegemonic masculinity, is characterised by compliance with subordination and is oriented to accommodating the interests and desires of men. Associated with emphasised femininity are qualities of sociability, sexual passivity and acceptance of domesticity and motherhood.

A number of versions of femininity and masculinity are constructed in everyday social practices within institutions [such as early childhood centres] . . . Connell asserts that the forms of femininity and masculinity constructed at the ideological level tend to be 'stylized and impoverished', but that 'their interrelation is centred on a single structural fact, the global dominance of men over women'. (pp. 10–11)

Many feminist poststructuralists seek to disrupt the current patriarchal gender order with its rigid understandings of how to be male and to be female. Feminist poststructuralists see efforts to categorise us into male and female in the current gender order as problematic. Inequality will not disappear until we each desire and can

143

choose to be male and female in different ways at different times.

In the current gender order, it can be liberating for us to challenge the dominant way of understanding who we are and in doing so to create alternative and oppositional understandings of what it means to be male and female (Weedon 1997). Therefore, one educational task with boys could be to help them learn how to desire and to celebrate different, non-hegemonic ways of being masculine. Other tasks could include:

- talking about the things that girls and boys share, rather than only differences between them
- extending children's understanding of how to be male and female but ensure that we do not do so in ways that reinforce the existing gender order (male dominant, female submissive)
- encouraging boys to understand how their actions and reactions affect other children's power to do what they want and be who they want to be.

As Davies (1989a) argued, children:

> . . . need to have access to imaginary worlds in which new metaphors, new forms of social relations, new patterns of power and desire are explored. They need the freedom to position themselves in multiple ways, some of which will be recognisably 'feminine', some 'masculine' as we currently understand these terms . . . (p. 141)

Children need to work hard to resist dominant male or female desires. Adults can help them in this process:

> . . . even when [children] resist a particular . . . position . . . [they] cannot escape the implications of femininity [or masculinity]. Everything we do signifies compliance or resistance to dominant norms of what it is to be a woman [or a man]. (Weedon 1987, pp. 86–7)

Carlie and Sally each tried to work with children on their gendered desires. Carlie tried to support boys and girls who were investing in non-hegemonic masculinity and non-emphasised femininity. Her work with Peter captures how she tried to do this with the boys. She described Peter as having 'many feminine characteristics' and playing 'in non-traditional ways'. He was rarely challenged by other children but could be assertive if he was. She explained that Peter was 'not teased by the other children when he wore pink, or dressed up' (each occurred quite frequently) and to Carlie he was a 'non-sexist success'. However, she believed that he needed support to continue being non-sexist. In the following moment with Peter she tried to show she respected his enjoyment in dressing non-traditionally:

Peter was dressed in a bridal veil, skirt and net.

Carlie: You look wonderful, Peter.
Peter: Yes, I think so.
Carlie: Are you doing something special wearing those clothes?
Peter: Yes, I'm getting married.
Carlie: Where's your partner?
Peter: I can't find one.

Peter was confronting the implications of choosing to be masculine in a non-hegemonic way. Carlie tried to boost his enjoyment in this moment. However, he and she were both caught in the implications of his momentary difference from other boys in the group. After this conversation neither was sure what to do next. Each was learning that there are risks in even minor and momentary challenges to the gender order, the greatest of which is uncertainty. There are no well-worn paths to show us where to go next in such moments or how to shape them so that further disruptions occur.

Sally confronted a different risk in her efforts to have boys in her group 'do' non-hegemonic masculinity in their storylines. Starting with John, a boy who was strongly positioned within hegemonic ways of being masculine, made her task unlike Carlie's with Peter. What Sally risked

145

in striving to disrupt the current gender order was her relationship with John's mother. His mother disapproved of Sally's fleeting disruption to his position in the gender order, such as when he 'had a baby'. This reaction returned Sally to her initial dilemma: how should she create an appropriate place and space for boys in her gender equity work?

A growing literature on masculinities is entering into the debate about boys' place in gender equity. It walks a tenuous path through questions of how to create non-hegemonic masculinities and in doing so how to celebrate masculinity. Alongside this literature is a 'backlash' litera-ture which fulminates against the implications of feminist achievements for men and which has reasserted the value of traditional forms of masculinity. Faludi (1991) summarised the genesis and practice of this reassertion thus: 'A new "men's movement" drew tens of thousands of followers to all-male retreats, where they rooted out "feminized" tendencies and roused "the wild man within"' (p. 85).

A strong theme across most of the masculinities litera-ture is that masculinities are in crisis. As one male writer explained it: 'Often as white middle class heterosexual men we have grown up to feel self-assured, at least on the surface, for the modern world has been very much made in our image. Men often expected to be the centre of their social worlds. It can be hard to accept a period of uncer-tainty and change' (Seidler 1997, p. 1).

Several teachers in the research group were wary of the implications of moving boys from the centre of their social world. They knew that it meant uncertainty and change for the boys but didn't know how masculinity might be differ-ently imagined and practised by them. If we look to the current masculinities literature what guidance might it have offered these teachers and others now grappling with these issues? Buchbinder (1994) imagined that new masculinities might involve:

- men appreciating that differences exist between men and women without feeling that their biology is superior
- men not claiming power on the basis of physical size and strength
- men being attracted to men as just one of many ways to be masculine
- greater and more meaningful cooperation and care between men.

Central to these ideas is a call for men to rethink how they understand and live their masculinity. Buchbinder (1994) concentrated on men remaking their subjectivities to remake their sense of identity-as-male. Teachers heeding Buchbinder could work with boys to remake their subjectivities. The aim would be to help boys become more cooperative and caring with each other and to avoid claiming power physically. The aim would be also for boys to see themselves as different to girls but not superior to them and to avoid claiming power over girls physically.

In approaching this work there are several traps to be avoided (Fisher 1994, cited in Gilbert & Gilbert 1998). In summary, they include:

- Essentialising the differences between male and female by seeing them as biologically determined. The trap is that teachers do not feel they can change biology. (See Chapter 2.)
- Generalising that all boys and men are the same. The trap is that teachers develop general strategies for all boys that do not work because all boys are not the same. Class, ethnicity and regional location create some of these differences. (See Chapter 10.)
- Individualising the 'problem' and seeing the problem as belonging to individual boys rather than to masculinity. The trap is that nothing changes but some of the behaviour of one or two individual boys or that teachers focus on individual boys at the expense of other boys and of girls. (See Chapter 6.)
- Blaming the boys for the problem. The trap is that the

boys will feel resentful about being told they are wrong for doing what they see as 'normal'. Lots of teacher effort will go into 'changing' the boys or forcing them to do things against their will. (See Chapter 6.)

To avoid these traps teachers need to see masculinity as socially constructed and negotiated, and as multiple, to be able to problematise violent masculinities and to recognise that boys are emotionally and culturally invested in getting their masculinity right (Gilbert & Gilbert 1998).

Teachers also need to recognise the connections between masculinities and femininities. Poststructuralist theorists argue that emphasised femininity and hegemonic masculinity require each other to exist. One would not and could not exist without the other. The differences in what it means to be masculine and feminine are only possible because both exist. To be masculine is to be not feminine and vice versa.

In Jacques Derrida's terms, they form a binary opposition (Usher & Edwards 1994) in that each relies on the other for its meaning. Modernist thinking tends to seek final, fixed meanings for words (images, etc.) through these oppositions. We can finally fix the meaning of male because it is paired with female, it is the opposite of female and there are clearly known sharp divisions between them. Derrida argued that when we fix the meaning of words in this way a fixed and final 'Other' is created which has a negative, secondary and subordinate position in the pair. The existence of the 'Other' is necessary to define what is culturally positive and what should, therefore, be culturally privileged. For instance, in patriarchal cultures, in the binary opposition of man and woman, woman is defined negatively in relation to man and given the secondary and subordinate position. We socially determine and construct this gender order where woman is subordinate. This means that boys are learning to be male in a gender order in which men are seen as primary and dominant. Similarly, in the binary opposition of macho/sissy, sissy is defined negatively in relation to macho and thus macho is culturally privileged.

To unpack and remake the order between pairs requires an analytical process called deconstruction. The aim in deconstructing is to trace the relations of power between the binary oppositions and their meanings and to show 'that the privileged term derives its position from a suppression or curtailment of its opposite or other' (Grosz 1990, p. 95). Deconstructing binary oppositions is done by showing that each side depends on the other for its meaning. In doing so, the aim is to show that meanings are not fixed for all time but can be remade. The meaning of a particular word/text is multiple because we can socially determine and construct new meanings. This includes gender meanings. For instance, woman and man can have many meanings and not all of them need define woman negatively in relation to man. Jordon (1995) argued that in working with young boys the challenge is to find ways of beginning to remake the meanings of masculinity:

> Changing definitions of masculinity adopted by little boys in the early school years would not, of itself, destroy gender inequity, nor bring patriarchy tumbling down, but it could broaden the options for many boys and make school more tolerable for girls. Developing masculinities that do not use femininity as the subordinate term may seem a difficult task, but it should not, I believe, be impossible for charismatic and creative teachers (p. 83)

If we can deconstruct gendered binary oppositions with children, then new gender meanings become possible for them. For instance, if children see girl and boy as linked rather than opposite it then becomes possible for them to imagine a third gender of girl/boy. Young children could play with names for such a third gender. Or, if we turn the binary opposition on its head we could shift girl to a more advantaged meaning than boy. Hence, teachers would emphasise that it's great to be a girl and all about girlhood is positive and thus privileged. However, in working with boys it is important to understand that if this happens many boys face having their ways of being male challenged. If they see being a 'macho' male as a positive and culturally privileged way of being male then they will find it difficult to change this understanding.

Derrida believed that finding the 'Other' involves taking a particular word or concept and using reversal and/or displacement to create a new term which he called a 'hinge word' (Grosz 1990). A hinge word makes new meanings possible that can challenge the current relations of power in our ways of understanding the world. Kristeva (1981) pursued this idea to argue that the struggle for women's equality must contest the binary opposition of gender. Alloway (1995b) interpreted this to mean:

> While currently understood as categories with identifiable gender allegiances, qualities such as tenderness/strength, connectedness/separateness, interdependence/independence would cease to exist in everyday discourses as categories that identify gender. Rather than being coerced by predefined notions of gender, all social ways of being and relating would be available to all people. (p. 33)

To dismantle the gender order and the binary oppositions upon which it is based, teachers must work with each part of the opposition (male and female). In doing this, Alloway cautioned teachers against doing away with gender categories in their language without acknowledging, exposing and contesting the power relations these categories produce in the current gender order. For instance, calling boys and girls 'children' does not acknowledge, expose or contest the gendered power relations they live and practise in their daily lives with each other. Boys invested in violent masculinities will not act differently just because their teacher calls them children. For them to want a different way to be masculine, we must acknowledge, expose and contest the emotional investments they have in their current masculinities. We must deconstruct their gender politics before we can remake them. This involves:

- uncovering their gender meanings and patterns of desire
- exploring their gender assumptions and who benefits from these assumptions
- offering them alternative meanings in which they experience emotional pleasures.

The aim is to subvert children's taken-for-granted assumptions about gender and in so doing to acknowledge their emotional investments in them; and to work with children to make the current male and female dualism irrelevant for moments in their lives. Borrowing and reworking the ideas of Davies (1993), this has several practical implications for how teachers work with young children. They need to:

- Help young children see that they are involved in making and remaking meanings through their words, images, storylines, movements and songs. For instance, teachers can talk with children about how they know things, how they express these things, and what they do when they see new things.
- Show them how their daily experiences influence what meaning they give to words, images, storylines, movements and songs. For instance, teachers can talk with children about why they think what they do and what they have seen or done that makes them think in the ways that they do.

Drawing on feminist poststructuralist theory, Alloway and Gilbert (1997) offered several ways in which these ideas could be built on in work with boys. They suggest creating new possibilities for boys through 'problematising "masculinity"' (p. 99). This involves exposing boys to different images, words, performances and stories about masculinity (including other children's) and talking to them about:

- which ones they find desirable and why

- the dilemmas involved in different ways of being masculine
- when they have to make choices about how to be boys and how this feels.

It also involves teachers noting and curtailing those boys who use violence and aggression in their images, words, performances and stories.

Jordon (1995) also emphasised the importance of problematising masculinity for boys. Working within a feminist poststructuralist framework she argued that teachers need to work with boys to help them refuse dominant discourses of masculinity and to generate new ones. She described what this meant in practice when dealing with the violence of some young boys:

> . . . it should be possible to find ways of defining masculinity with the unacceptable aspects of fighting boys' behaviour being defined as the subordinate term, as characteristics of the weakling or the coward rather than the hero. Such discourses exist. I have seen a teacher catch and hold the attention of little boys who had become embroiled in an incident of escalating playground violence with the precept, 'A man can walk away from a fight.' . . . proposing the idea that true masculinity lies in self-control and moral courage . . . (p. 81)

Jordon (1995) offered several other definitions of non-violent masculinity that could be used to help young boys refuse dominant definitions. These included:

- presenting men as admirable and brave when they respond to community emergencies such as fighting bushfires, searching for people who are lost, rescuing people in danger, etc.
- presenting men as strong and admirable when they work with others for fairness and justice such as working in trade unions to make workplaces safer and

fairer, being involved in conservation and/or local
campaigns, etc.
- presenting men as admirable and likeable when they
care for other people such as being caring family members, child care workers, etc.

As Sally's work showed, when teachers participate in
remaking masculinities in these ways it is problematic on
three counts: it takes time and energy away from a focus
on the girls; boys resist; and there may be a backlash from
parents. Looking at how the backlash against feminism has
built and why might help teachers prepare for these reactions. When men's position within the gender order has
been challenged by feminists, they have reacted by:

- reviewing their own positions and assumptions
- seeking justifications for their actions
- feeling persecuted
- becoming angry and, at times, violent
- reimposing traditional controls on women
- trying to rediscover their essential masculinity
- accepting their unfairnesses towards women
- trying to recreate a new masculinity.
(Buchbinder 1994)

Teachers can draw two lessons from these responses. Firstly,
most men do not generously or easily give up their power
and position within the current gender order. Secondly,
many boys and others (e.g. parents and other boys)
invested in their hegemonic masculinities will probably
resist teachers' work. Teachers must expect and prepare for
these responses. In particular, they must acknowledge the
emotional investments that boys and others have made in
their masculinity and the patterns of desire these investments produce. In challenging constructions of masculinity
with boys and others, teachers must plan to work with their
fears, feelings and desires as well as with their ideas. For
instance, boys will want to feel liked, admired and comfortable in their masculinities. Teachers need to help them

redefine masculinity in ways that they and others can like, admire and feel comfortable with.

For early childhood teachers faced with boys who express their masculinity through being aggressive, anti-girl and harassing (like Reece and Bradley in the cameo below), there is little choice. They have to make the boys central to their gender equity work. If they do not, the girls face constant harassment. If they do not, boys risk harming themselves or others. Violent masculinity is dangerous. It is strongly linked to youth suicide, imprisonment and death for boys and men (Gilbert & Gilbert 1998). Working with boys is not a choice but a necessity for them and for girls.

Theory into practice

To see what it means to use these different theories of gender relations in teaching let's look at how one boy, his peers and his teacher interacted and how other teachers might respond. In this play cameo, all of the children are Anglo-Australian.

Reece, Bradley and the bouncing dolls

Reece and Bradley are jumping on a balancing board out-side. Nearby, Claire and Catherine are dressing two dolls in preparation for walking them in a pram. Suddenly Reece snatches the dolls from Claire and Catherine and puts them in the pram. He and Bradley race the pram past the girls and around the sandpit towards the outside shed. The boys are laughing and clearly enjoying themselves immensely. They race the pram back to the balancing board, onto which they place the dolls. Reece scrambles onto the climbing board and starts jumping. Each 'boing' of the board brings the dolls closer to its edge and closer to plummeting to the ground. Bradley giggles and watches in anticipation of the fall.

I watched a videotape of this episode with Bradley and

Reece. Here's how they recounted the events leading up to and immediately after this moment.

Reece: Now we've got the dollies.
Bradley: Now we've got the dollies.
Glenda: What were you going to do with them? Can you remember?
Reece: Play with them.
Glenda: Do you know what game you were going to play?
Bradley: Now that one was on the board and Reece jumped and it fell off, didn't it?

Reece and Bradley then swapped roles with Bradley jumping on the board in the hope that the doll would fall off. Claire and Catherine were nearby watching them. Reece and Bradley's comments on the next videotaped segment describe what unfolded next.

Reece: Wait a minute—make it [the video] noisy.
Bradley: We go up there and Reece was up there. He said, 'Want to swap?'
Glenda: Who wanted to swap?
Bradley: Oh, that's the girls.
Reece: I said to shut them up.
Glenda: What did you say?
Reece: Shut up to the girls.
Glenda: Why did you say that?
Reece: Because I was busy doing that [trying to make the dolls fall from the board again].
. . .
Glenda: Now what's happening here?
Reece: We are starting to jump. We put the baby down and then we jump. Go 'boing', 'boing', and it goes (at this point the dolls fall on the ground).
Bradley: Look at me—I'm looking at eyes.
Glenda: You are looking at the baby's eyes?
Glenda: What were you doing, Bradley?
Bradley: Looking at her eyes too.

155

Glenda: I think you were actually shampooing her hair there.
Bradley: Yes. I was looking in them too.
Reece: Oh, the girls hopped on.

At this point the girls sat on the bouncing board. Reece explained what occurred next:

Reece: The girls hopped on. They said, 'Boys' (laughter). Wow.
Bradley: We were 'boing', 'boing' and it was gone!
Reece: We changed it—we do this and I chucked it too.
Glenda: How do you think the girls liked that?
Bradley: You went 'boing', 'boing'.
Reece: There's me up the top—I walking up the top.
Glenda: The dolls are on the ground all by themselves now—how do you think they might feel?
Reece: Sad.

At the thought that the dolls might feel sad Bradley and Reece start giggling and explain that they threw the dolls from the top of the climbing board because they 'don't want them any more'. Reece then spots Claire and Catherine walking into the frame of the videorecording.

Reece (shouts): I hate her.
Glenda: Which person?
Reece: I hate that Claire.
Glenda: Do you? What does that mean?
Reece: It means she barks too loud.
Bradley: It means she always knocks me out of their play.
Glenda: Does she? How does she do that?
Reece: She sends me out. That's what she does. Then she chopped my head off.

How did masculinity work for these boys? How might our preferred explanation of the gender order and of gender relations influence our teaching decisions about how to work with these moments?

A radical feminist might read it this way: Bradley and Reece are acting in very traditionally 'macho' ways. They have used aggression and rough and tumble play to take over the climbing area and the dolls and prams. In doing so, they have sidelined the girls' opportunities to be involved in this play. Their actions are based clearly on a deep dislike of the girls and of what the girls like doing and playing. *The children's teacher might plan in this way:* The boys need to learn traditional feminine qualities of caring and of being gentle with the dolls. I will set up a variety of activities to encourage these qualities in them. However, as the girls were clearly disadvantaged in their exchanges with Bradley and Reece I will prioritise spending time with the girls, reinforcing their positive caring and gentle dispositions. I will also plan a series of stories and experiences that help the group as a whole to celebrate the feminine.

A liberal humanist might read it this way: Reece and Bradley have each developed their own ways of being male. Each is adventurous, active and enjoys rough and tumble play. This tendency has made them a little over enthusiastic at times and the aggression that results needs to be reined in. *The teacher might plan in this way:* The key to changing Reece's and Bradley's aggressive streak is to work closely with them as individuals. I need to work with them one on one so that I can reinforce their behaviour when it is positive. I will also model positive and appropriate behaviours for them when they are playing with the dolls.

A poststructuralist feminist might read it this way: Reece and Bradley are positioning themselves inside hegemonic masculinity. They experience considerable pleasure in this positioning and through it place themselves in direct opposition to girls and feminine toys and ways of being.

The teacher might plan in this way: In my interactions with Reece and Bradley I will need to think about how I can revisit this play with them to disrupt their understandings of the gender order. To do this I will use story, drama, discussion and informal interactions to:

- explore the similarities and differences between boys and girls and between boys and boys by talking with them
- help them understand their gender position in the current gender order and its implications for the girls by looking at what is fair and unfair in their relations with each other
- challenge dominant masculine ways of being by playing with definitions of masculinity that emphasise cooperation and caring as representing strength and courage
- offer strong support for other ways of being gendered through my comments, my stories, my discussions with children.

Feminist poststructuralist possibilities and provocations: a summary

There are many ways to be masculine. The dominant and therefore more desirable ways to be masculine include being aggressive and violent. Many teachers have to negotiate aggressive and violent masculinities in their work with young children because boys have learnt to desire these ways of being masculine and to see them as positive. To unpack and remake these understandings with boys teachers could:

- expose boys to different images, words, performances and stories about masculinity (including other children's)
- talk with boys about which masculinities they find desirable and why
- explore with the boys the dilemmas involved in different ways of being masculine
- expose the times when boys make choices about how to be boys and the implications of the choices they make
- develop definitions of masculinity that redefine what it means to be strong, courageous, likeable, admired by others, etc.
- note and curtail those boys who are violent and aggressive in their images, words, performances and stories
- offer strong support to boys who are non-violent.

Learning more about the debate

The following material focuses on how the current gender order operates in our lives and how it might be deconstructed. Part of this information touches on the current debate about boys' educational disadvantage.

Further readings

Alloway, N. and Gilbert, P. (eds) 1997, *Boys and Literacy: Professional Development Units*, Curriculum Corporation, Melbourne. This publication includes seven professional development units teachers can use to work through a number of issues about boys and literacy. It provides a general framework for working with boys and includes an extensive bibliography on approaches to working with boys.

Gilbert, R. and Gilbert, P. 1998, *Masculinity Goes to School*, Allen & Unwin, Sydney. The first two chapters provide an accessible and thorough overview of the debates about masculinities and boys' school experiences. The discussion in Chapter 2 of different theories of schooling and masculinity offers a useful basis for rethinking approaches to work with boys in early childhood education.

Kenway, J.,Willis, S., Blackmore, J. & Rennie, L. 1997, *Answering Back: Girls, Boys and Feminism in Schools*, Allen & Unwin, Sydney. Pages 47–61 critically explore the contention that boys are the educationally disadvantaged gender.

Lingard, B. & Douglas, P. 1999, *Men Engaging Feminisms: Prof-feminism, Backlashes and Schooling*, Open University Press, Milton Keynes. Chapter 4 offers a very helpful analysis of the statistics behind the concerns about boys' performance in education that shows that media representations of these statistics have been over-simplistic and therefore misleading.

MacNaughton, G. & Williams, G. 1998, *Techniques for Teaching Young Children: Options in Theory and Practice*, Addison Wesley Longman, Melbourne. Chapter 19, 'Deconstructing', explores the theory and practice of using deconstruction as a teaching technique. Many of the practical examples in the chapter relate directly to gender and young children.

Professional development suggestions

- Talk with two colleagues about the extent to which they think that boys are missing out in gender equity programs. What evidence do they offer to support their views? How do you think their views would influence their support of gender equity for girls? How would Kenway & Willis (1997) respond to their comments?

  Alloway (1995b) wrote: 'To focus only on the girls is to assume that the boys have got it right, that there is no need to challenge boys' ideas of what it means to be a male in relation to a female' (p. 102).

  What might Alloway's view mean for your work with boys in a gender equity program? How does her view relate to those of Kristeva and of Buchbinder?

- A number of educational writers, policy makers and journalists have begun to argue that the educational needs of males need to be addressed in gender equity programs. How would you define boys' current educational? To what extent are these 'needs' produced through their positions within the current gender order?

- To what extent do you believe that resources and time need to be given to boys' special educational needs?

8

If it matters that much, just do it yourself

Robin: I'm having a difficult time with my co-worker Rosemary at the moment. She goes silent every time I talk to her about getting new curtains and bedding for the home corner.

Meera: What's the problem with what's there at the moment?

Robin: The material is dreadful. It's pale pink with mauve hearts. I really hate it. I'd like something more gender-neutral for the area.

Meera: If Rosemary's so difficult about it, maybe you should just leave it be.

Robin: But, it's really important to me and it's such a small thing for us to change. I'm not sure why she is so bothered by it. I don't want to face the 'silent treatment' again.

Meera: Well, if it matters that much to you, just do it yourself.

For Robin, changing the design and colour of material in a play area seemed a small and simple change to make. For her colleague Rosemary it was not so simple and tension was developing between them over the issue. In the research group, Nette experienced similar tension in her relationship with colleagues over her decision to reorganise her block play and home corner areas. In this chapter, we look at how these tensions surfaced and why teachers can find changes in the mundane and everyday business of teaching the hardest to make.

Debating teaching practices: Reorganising equipment, reforming gender

Nette wanted to disrupt the idea that blocks were for boys and home corner was for girls. To do this she reorganised the children's inside play area by bringing outside blocks inside and combining these with home corner equipment. As she explained to the research group:

> My current aim is to present kindergarten equipment
> to children in a manner which discourages gender
> bias. Blocks, dolls and dramatic play combined play
> with this equipment by both girls and boys, thus
> challenging some of the stereotypical use of these items.

Nette worked part-time in two kindergartens, sharing each with another teacher. Consequently, she had to negotiate her decision to alter equipment positionings with these teachers. One teacher told her she was 'crazy'. The other teacher 'just couldn't accept it' and found it impossible to work with outdoor blocks inside. Consequently, for seven weeks Nette had to reposition *all* indoor and outdoor blocks twice a week to ensure that the room organisation was back to 'normal' for this teacher.

A little later in the year, Nette did gain agreement from one teacher to reorganise block play and home corner for a special project. It went extremely well, with boys and girls each playing in the redesigned area in constructive and collaborative ways for much of the time. Nette decided that she wanted the change to remain once the project was completed. Her colleague was 'surprised by the fact that I wasn't going to put it all back at the end of the term'. This was despite a discussion in which her colleague admitted that she found the 'set-up easier to use with the group of children she'd got'. Summarising the reactions of several of her colleagues to the changes she had made, Nette said:

> Discussions with colleagues about my concerns over the different ways boys and girls are treated in many kindergartens has resulted in me being labelled a radical feminist by some or as worrying about something that doesn't exist.

In the research group there was considerable uncertainty about whether Nette's reorganisation was appropriate. For instance, Edna argued that the kindergarten room should be set up with separate spaces for home corner and blocks because each offered specific and distinctive learning opportunities for the children. As she explained to the group:

> It gives a sense of order and categories for the children . . . These are expectations of us from our training and because we are preparing the children for the next step. It's why we are doing it. But whether it's the right thing to do . . . We would have to look very closely to justify ourselves if we were doing it differently. If we had everything down one end of the room and the children just went and got what they wanted to use where ever and however they wanted . . . (fades). I know of a lot of teachers who would get very upset if children moved the equipment together.

Matti, another member of the group, felt concerned about how the Children's Services Adviser in her area would react if she did such a thing, while a third member just felt it 'was wrong'. She couldn't explain why. She just knew it was. Another wondered 'what College would say' and yet another felt the parents in her centre would be 'dead against it because it wouldn't look like a normal kindergarten'.

A simple change in room organisation based on a desire for greater gender equity in children's play choices had led to Nette being seen by several of her colleagues as a 'crazy' and a 'radical feminist'. In particular, she was seen to be acting in ways that went against what had been learnt 'at college' and went against normal practice as defined by several colleagues and parents. They made it difficult to continue with her work. 'Getting on with it by herself' meant being strong, being determined and being prepared to risk being marginalised professionally.

Why it happened as it did: DAP pedagogy and the will to truth

Michel Foucault argued that we learn most about our social institutions and the exercise of power within them through studying the mundane, ordinary, daily decisions and practices of people (Foucault 1977a & b, 1978, 1982). In doing so, we also learn about the possibilities and challenges of creating social change such as that demanded by gender reform (Weedon 1997).

Foucault believed that all social institutions in the modern world survive and thrive through creating and maintaining 'regimes of truth' about how we should think, act and feel towards ourselves and others (Foucault 1977a & b, 1978, 1982). For instance, educational institutions such as early childhood centres survive and thrive through creating and maintaining a set of truths about how we should think, act and feel towards ourselves as early childhood professionals and towards children, parents and colleagues. These truths are woven together into a regime (or system of management) that governs what are seen to be normal and desirable ways of thinking, acting and feeling in all early childhood institutions. In doing so, they create and maintain a system of morality that says what is a 'good', 'true' way to be an early childhood professional and what is not.

This system of morality rests on three propositions about the relationships between knowledge and modern organisations examined in other chapters in this book. Exploring how these propositions intertwine can help us understand why Nette's seemingly mundane decision to reorganise equipment produced such strong reactions from her colleagues.

The first of these propositions, explored in Chapter 2, is that different interpretations of our social world compete for the status of truth. Foucault shared with other postmodernist theorists, such as Derrida and Lyotard, the belief that nothing is inherently true, that within any field of knowledge (e.g. child development, early childhood education) there are many different interpretations of our social world that compete for the status of truth. Some gain that status by reaching a point where they appear to be right, correct and immutable—true—but are not. They are just one of the many possible versions of truth about any social phenomenon. They are seen as truth because they have successfully competed to achieve this status.

For instance, we could use Foucault to argue that there is no one right or true way to offer blocks and home corner, as some of Nette's colleagues believed. There are many ways. Nette had one truth about how to offer blocks and home corner, her colleagues had different truths. Nette interpreted what was the right and correct (or true) way differently to her other colleagues. However, that there are different ways of interpreting the world is not Foucault's key point. His point is that some are seen to be more true than others.

So, from a Foucauldian perspective, Nette faced such opposition to her changes because particular ways of organising space and materials in the early childhood curriculum had triumphed over others to gain the status of truths. Particular approaches to room organisation had become normal, accepted, taken-for-granted, not in need of questioning. In Nette's local area, the idea of having separate spaces for blocks and home corner had achieved the status of a truth for many of her colleagues. It was right and it should not—indeed, need not—be questioned. They believed their way to be normal, correct and, therefore, the true way. To borrow a now infamous phrase from a former

Australian Prime Minister, Paul Keating—having separate spaces for blocks and home corner was the practice of 'the true believers'.

The second of Foucault's propositions about knowledge and power we met in Chapters 2 and 4. This is the idea that ways of being and acting in our social world stand out as truths not because of any inherent truth within them but because they have institutional and personal support. The institutional support Foucault called 'the political substance of a regime of truth'. The personal support he called 'the ethical substance of a regime of truth'. Individuals support particular regimes of truth about how we should think and behave towards ourselves and others because all regimes of truth about our social world and social relationships institutionalise particular systems of morality (Davies 1993; Gore 1993) and constitute particular ways of being as normal, right and therefore desirable.

These systems of morality tell us how we should act, feel and think if we want to be seen as normal. To be normal we have to learn to tame, create or style ourselves in ways that ensure we look and sound normal to others and feel and sound normal to ourselves. Most of us try be normal because only individuals who act normally gain institutional backing and support. In doing so, the ethical, personal substance becomes integrated with the political, institutional substance of the regime.

In Nette's story, the political substance of the regime was evident in the power of the academy to construct notions of good teaching in pre-service training. For instance, Nette's colleagues' beliefs about room organisation had the status of truth for them because they had been articulated and circulated by 'College'—the very institution that certifies who is competent to practise as an early childhood teacher. Colleagues such as Edna regarded Nette's work as odd and different because of what they had learnt at college. They used college to provide a powerful institutional justification for their truth that blocks and home corner should be provided separately. Nette had no comparable institutional knowledge base with which to defend her decisions and so they became questionable and therefore problematic for her. While this did not stop Nette's work, it required her to be prepared to regard herself as 'radical', to accept what she did as odd and different to the norm and to be totally committed to her project.

The personal substance of the regime was evident in how Nette's colleagues wove together their personal power to sanction changes at the local level and to tame difference. Nette's colleagues used their personal power of sanction to marginalise her approach to organising space and materials and to maintain their own way of organising them as pre-eminent. One colleague directly blocked her work and the other colleague tolerated it, rather than supported it.

The third proposition that weaves through Foucault's work on power and knowledge is that we can learn what ideas have the status of truths by looking at who and what is seen as 'Other' to the normal. The creation of 'Others' allows us to define what is normal and positive and, therefore, to be privileged. This idea was canvassed in detail in Chapter 7. Nette was clearly seen as 'Other' to the norm for her views on block play organisation. Hence, the majority, in this instance, regarded working for gender equity and experimenting with the organisation of space and materials as not normal. In this instance, the norms, the truths, about early childhood curriculum worked against experimentation and against working for gender equity. In other words, it is not normal to experiment and it is not normal to work for gender equity. Neither has a place in dominant understandings of good practice. Hence, the current regime of truth implicitly condones the status quo in gender relations. It does this through marginalising those who work for greater gender equity in the early childhood field.

In summary, Foucault argued that we live in a world in which there is no one inherent truth, but many competing truths. Of the many truths that circulate in a given field of knowledge, for example in early childhood education, some gain the status of truths and create a regime of truth that governs our ideas and practices. This regime is held in place by complex webs of power between the ethical (personal) and political institutional substance of a regime. (See for example, Dreyfus & Rabinow 1982; Gore 1993; Rabinow 1997; Weedon 1997). It is these webs of power that wind through the mundane and everyday business of teaching and make it a site of struggle. In Nette's case, the everyday business of teaching was a site of struggle over the gendered meanings and normal practices of block play in early childhood settings.

Alternative understandings of everyday teaching decisions

Room organisation is not the only area of early childhood practice that has acquired the status of a truth that cannot and should not be questioned. Other areas include how children should be assessed, how teachers should relate to children and how children should be taught (see Davies 1988, 1989a; Walkerdine 1989, 1990, 1992). Alloway (1995a) has argued that:

> . . . all early childhood educators . . . observe a common language, a common set of beliefs that are elevated to the status of 'truths' about child development . . . [and are] articulated in a shared language, in immediately identifiable terms such as: child development, developmental stages, development of the 'whole child', developmentally appropriate practice, integrated curriculum, children's interest driven programs, individual needs, individual readiness, individual planning, close observation of the individual child's development. (pp. 2–3)

These beliefs regulate the practice of early childhood staff on a daily basis. More recently, Cannella (1997) has shown how these truths rest on an equally powerful set of truths about childhood in which the child is always seen as 'Other' to the adult. This position of 'Other' allows the adult to measure, regulate and control the child. It also allows the adult to disqualify the child from serious and fair participation in decisions about their lives because the child is seen as insufficiently competent to take decisions. Developmental psychologists and early childhood professionals are two groups of adults who directly benefit from constructing childhood and children in this way.

The elevation of particular early childhood discourses to the status of truths makes it hard to innovate in early childhood education. In particular, it has marginalised gender equity work by defining it as different and 'Other' to the mainstream. In Nette's project, a set of truths about how and why to organise space and materials in particular ways marginalised her efforts to rethink these truths in the name of gender equity. She was marginalised as her actions and her ideas were defined by colleagues as different and 'Other' to the mainstream.

In this instance, and in many others, our truths produce and maintain a highly 'parochial professionalism' (Williams 1997, p. 59). We limit the object of our work, our practices and boundaries in ways that close us off from 'interdisciplinary as well as larger world concerns' (Williams 1997, p. 58). When we believe we have the truth about children and pedagogy we attempt to codify and to institutionalise it. We close ranks around these truths and use them to induct new teachers into the profession (Lubeck 1998). This provides early childhood teachers with great certainty that inductees are learning the normal and proper ways to think and to practise as early childhood teachers and it provides certainty to already qualified teachers about their practices. However, our parochialism and our certainties come at a price. In a social world in which inequalities and injustices flourish, the truths of mainstream early childhood education help the early childhood field evade questions such as:

- In whose interests do we educate and care for children?
- How do we contribute to greater social justice and equity?

To understand what early childhood truths mean for selection of resources, teaching practices, understandings of child development and assessment of children's learning we must understand how particular discourses gain and maintain ascendancy and reach the status of truths. Foucault argued that this occurs through how the political and ethical substances of a regime of truth operate (Gore 1993; Rabinow 1997). To understand how truths are produced in any field of knowledge, including early childhood education, we must map its ethics and its politics. The remainder of this chapter will use Foucault's work to map the ethics of the early childhood field.

Foucault saw ethics as the personal relationship to the self: how we should discipline and style ourselves to create and maintain certain ways of being as normal and true and to establish that we are normal and correct in how we are acting and feeling (Gore 1993; Rabinow 1997). In other words, our ethics flow from the question, 'How should we act and feel to ensure that we are true to ourselves as teachers and to prove to ourselves and others that we are true believers?' To map the ethics of a field of knowledge we need to ask these questions of ourselves.

Walkerdine (1990, 1992) has powerfully documented the Foucauldian sense of ethics in early childhood education. She argued that the child-centred pedagogies which are at the heart of early childhood education and constitute its current regime of truth are based on an ethics of individualism and on the 'dream of democratic harmony' (Walkerdine 1992, p. 22).

If we return to Nette's story, we can see that an ethic of individualism made her gender equity work problematic in three ways. Firstly, traditions about how to offer materials and equipment could remain unquestioned by individual staff, and colleagues reinforced them. Going against tradition to achieve gender equity goals was not seen as innovation but as abnormal. Whether things should/could be done differently is a key question in any process of change, but it did not arise until teachers began debating their decisions in the research group with other teachers. The catalyst for change was not just any group of teachers. It was a group that had as its *raison d'être* the changing of gender relations. Without this catalyst, traditions that inadvertently contributed to sexism between children would have remained unchallenged.

Secondly, working for gender equity was problematic because knowledge learnt in pre-service training was constructed and reconstructed as truth. 'College' was seen as the holder of truths about what constitutes good and normal practice. Going against 'college', irrespective of what was taught there, individuals saw as problematic. In this instance, working for gender equity clashed with what 'college' taught. If pre-service training has ignored issues of social justice and equity, then how can individuals reconstruct their knowledge and practices to support progressive social visions and practices? Who gives permission to construct new truths about good practice? The occasional one-off inservice session that constitutes most professional development in the field is unlikely to challenge fundamental truths from 'college'.

Thirdly, to publicly own and advocate a vision of progressive social change was to be odd, abnormal and wrong. As long as individual early childhood staff articulate their social vision in isolation from others, such marginalisation is likely to confront other committed and motivated staff working for progressive social change (see, for example, Kenway et al. 1994).

The professional limits and boundaries in early childhood education, embedded in the truths of individualism, prevent us from acknowledging the political and ethical nature of our educational work (Silin 1995; Lubeck 1998). This is because they focus attention on the developmental needs and interests of individual children and take it away

171

from their political needs and interests and our ethical stance on these.

When gender equity work tests the professional limits and boundaries of early childhood education then tensions arise between those who strive to maintain them and those who do not. The tensions often arise over everyday teaching because it is in the close-up of the everyday that we live the politics and ethics of our field. For instance:

- how Nette positioned blocks directly related to her commitment to increasing girls' involvement in blocks;
- how Nette's colleagues positioned blocks directly related to their lack of commitment to gender equity.

When the everyday business of teaching is challenged so too are our personal and professional politics and ethics.

If the ethics of individualism within DAP is problematic for gender equity then it needs to be challenged by those concerned with gender equity. It should be replaced with an ethics of collectivism in which early childhood teachers collectively form visions about the processes and content of early childhood curriculum. Feminists and those concerned with social justice should embed progressive social visions such as gender reform within their ethics.

The research group and how it operated provides some insights into how such collaboration might begin and what an alternative ethic of the self might look like for feminists in early childhood education. During the research project individuals changed many of their beliefs and practices about early childhood. For instance, Nellie and Sally reshaped their views on free play and Anne rethought her approach to observation. To do so they shifted their relationship with the knowledge they used for teaching decisions. This shift occurred along several dimensions, which were implicated in restyling (retraining) themselves as early childhood teachers. One of the key dimensions was to change from individual responsibility for teaching knowledge to collective responsibility for critiquing and developing this knowledge. This required that they reflect on their own and other teachers' practices in collaboration with others. This occurred because the research group required that each person regularly discuss their individual teaching decisions across a range of practices with others in the group. It also meant that the gendering implications of these decisions were explored with others.

This process of group sharing and exploration challenged the view that early childhood teaching is an individual responsibility and an individual negotiation with the self. It suggested that how teachers worked for gender equity was in part the research group's responsibility and that individual teachers should negotiate ways forward within the research group. Therefore it challenged the view that knowledge of the individual child is and should be the sole knowledge required for curriculum planning. Individual research group members now had to include what others in the group felt was appropriate or not from a gender equity perspective. Through this there was an addition to what Foucault called the disciplinary gaze to which group participants were prepared to subject themselves.

Orner (1992, p. 83) described the disciplinary gaze as one in which the 'regulation of the self [occurs] through the internalization of the regulation of others'. All project members, including myself, had always given a privileged position to the disciplinary gaze of college. Project members had unquestioningly remembered and acted upon the pedagogic truths of their pre-service training, over many years. Membership of the research group offered the opportunity for an additional disciplinary gaze into the equation of the self as a teacher. It required that the research group members expose and negotiate pedagogic truths with others, including me, someone from college. As individuals they had to take account of gender issues and negotiation with the group, as well as college, when they took their curriculum decisions. This often led to conflicts between different truths about what can and should be done. For instance, whether children should be questioned about their gender knowledge and how this might occur (see Chapter 3).

These conflicts, traced in other chapters in this book, went beyond the reorganisation of space and materials to questions of:

- if, how and when to intervene in children's play
- how to question children
- how to observe and evaluate children's learning
- what could and should be the goals of gender equity in early childhood curriculum work?

To act and think as early childhood teachers for gender equity, we had to learn to open ourselves to collective critique of our curriculum visions and practices and to see such critique as necessary and positive. We also had to take this back into our daily practice. In Foucault's language we needed to 'style' (train) ourselves as people willing, and able, to do this, and as people prepared to think of how we might collectively determine our relationships with our pedagogic knowledge. We had to be prepared to subject ourselves to the gaze of others. We had to be prepared to be more reflexive in relation to our knowledges of the child and how to be with the child as early childhood teachers. We had to reconstruct our ethical relationships with our selves so that we no longer relied on an ethics of individualism to direct our decisions. We also had to take on the progressive gaze of others in that we had to listen to how others saw our work.

Through our work together for gender equity, we developed an ethic of the self that was based on the research group as a collective and on critical engagement with it in two ways. Firstly, we 'collected' with others who embodied visions and aspirations for gender equity. Secondly, in coming together in the research group we opened our curriculum decisions and the knowledge of the child upon which they are based to radical critique from the group (or collective).

To build from this work others could open their

pedagogies to the 'possibilities for indeterminacy, multiple voices, multiple knowledges and multidirectionality' (Cannella 1997, p. 100). Such collectivity is essential to political change. People working with others and among others can displace individualism and the limitations it places on how early childhood teachers are with young children.

In displacing individualism, teachers will need to search for answers to questions such as:

- How do we decide between competing truth claims about what is in the best interests of children?
- How do we decide what knowledge should underpin our curriculum decisions?
- Whose version of the truth about what is appropriate for young children do we privilege?

As mentioned in Chapter 3, Foucault argued that we must judge the validity of knowledge through reference to other than 'truth claims' (see Weedon 1997). In his view we need to judge such claims politically and ethically, and we can do this through asking:

- What is this truth?
- Who benefits from this truth?
- In whose interest is this truth?
- Who gains power through this truth?
- In whose interest should I invest?

These questions require us to recognise the different and competing power effects of these truths and to decide whose interests we want to support. Those committed to greater equity and social justice will privilege the truths that support greater equity for women and girls and work against patriarchy. As Nette's story showed, traditional ways of organising space and materials very often benefit boys and reinforce patriarchal ways of being masculine and feminine. As a person committed to gender reform, Nette chose to privilege the truth that traditional ways of organising space and materials are problematic for gender equity and reject the truth that 'separation is best'.

Until early childhood teachers can decide between competing pedagogical truths more collectively and can share this responsibility more widely, we will continue to exact a high personal and professional price from those working for progressive social changes such as greater gender equity. Like Nette, they may face isolation, ridicule and derision for daring to rethink the mundane, ordinary, daily decisions and practices of being an early childhood teacher that derive from and form our *telos* (goals). They may also be silenced by the assumption that there is a right and true way to 'do' early childhood education (Lubeck 1998).

An individual working in a field of true believers has little chance of:

- convincing others to break with traditions
- effectively challenging colleagues about their social visions and educational practices
- going against, or reassembling, knowledge learnt in pre-service training
- discussing and negotiating their educational visions and practices with others committed to progressive social change.

Each of those actions could counteract the individualism within early childhood education. They could allow us to shape an ethic of the self based on what I have called critical collectivism (MacNaughton 1996). This ethic of the self would involve early childhood teachers in:

- privileging the use of dialogue in assessing knowledge claims
- recognising and assessing the political implications in all that is done and said
- producing diverse visions and practices of early childhood education and how it can contribute to progressive social change.

The will to knowledge arises when people are willing to and able to reflect critically on themselves and the knowledges they produce. Privileging dialogue in assessing knowledge claims allows collectivity rather than individualism to be privileged in producing knowledge: 'A primary epistemological assumption underlying the use of dialogue in assessing knowledge claims is that connectedness rather than separation is an essential component of the knowledge-validation process' (Collins 1989, p. 763).

'Connectedness' relies on an ethic of caring infusing the dialogue so that each individual is be valued, their voice heard, emotions accepted/expected and empathy developed. Dialogue in which there are many voices allows differences to emerge and understandings to be negotiated and critiqued with others and 'can lead to more sophisticated forms of interaction and community' (Maher & Tetreault 1993, p. 126). Dialogue creates this possibility because in the moment of experiencing difference change becomes possible (Pinar et al. 1996). In moments in which multiple and conflicting teacher's voices flourish, hybridisation occurs. Hybridisation is the process in which two or more understandings join to form something new (Bakhtin 1981; Kamboureli 1998). However, as argued in Chapter 6, in the process of hybridisation of meanings teachers must be alert to the power relations they create. Teachers concerned with feminist changes must be alert to if and where patriarchy lies within their newly hybridised meanings.

These dialogic practices of knowledge validation offer one way of imagining how critical collectivism might work between groups of teachers and those who work with them. However, in the research group we glimpsed the limits of dialogue as well as its possibilities. At times, dialogue merely recycled our existing meanings. It only became part of the process of change when we accessed new meanings through it. This happened at points in the research group's life when we encountered unfamiliar discourses of teaching and learning through reading and through new people entering the group.

Critical collectivism might offer teachers greater choices about their ways of being and ways of working with young children if it uses dialogue informed by a constant search for different ways of understanding pedagogies and their place in young children's lives. If the early childhood field remains wrapped in an ethics of individualism, which insulates it from critiques of its traditions, our practices and our goals, it will be insulated from change. This is a real possibility. As Weedon (1997) reminds us, the discourses that support the status quo are likely to dismiss other discourses as marginal or bad. For instance, in the wider educational field in Australia Kenway and her colleagues (1994) found that:

> The dominant discourses are those associated with the profession and culture of teaching, and with the changing demands of governments and educational bureaucracies . . . these revolve around excellence and standards, and efficiency and effectiveness. Gender reform is subordinate within both discursive regimes. (p. 191)

Who will lose and who will win if individualism remains the ethical truth of early childhood education?

Theory into practice

To compare what it means for teachers to use different ethics to guide their work, let us start with a conversation between three participants in the research group and imagine how teachers using different ethics might continue the conversation.

The daffodil curriculum

Nette: I tried to get gender up and running as an issue for our [the regional teachers' network] conference in a couple of weeks but no-one else in the meeting would be in it.
Glenda: How many other teachers were there, Nette?
Nette: . . . nine. So nine people, eight others rejected it or saw it as not an issue.

Carlie (speaking with considerable anger): It's not an issue. Other things are seen as just so much more important.
Glenda: Like what?
Nette: Curriculum.
Glenda: But, isn't gender part of the curriculum?
Nette: Oh, no, not according to them!
Carlie: To me gender is part of the curriculum.
Glenda: What sort of things are part of curriculum . . .?
Carlie: Oh, whether you have playdough before milk and fruit, or after.
Glenda. You sceptic!
Sue: And, whether you have pink or green.
Nette: Should you have cutters and things with the dough, or should you just let them manipulate it? Actually, the letter that's just gone out just—a brief information thing about the conference—has got in one part of that—'we are making daffodils today—everybody's going to make a daffodil'—so that's the sort of thing the conference is going to be about. Well, that's what they're labelling curriculum . . . Anyway I was fighting a losing battle there so I gave up in the end. It was just not an issue.

A teacher using an individualistic ethics of the self might continue the conversation in this way: Nette has a personal interest in gender issues but it's important that people's personal concerns don't distract us. We need to focus on ensuring that other teachers understand how to present materials such as playdough to the children correctly. I was taught in my training that how we present materials to children is important. It gives children a sense of order and it provides them with categories for making sense of their world. I'm really against adding any cutters to the dough. Young children go through a period of

179

manipulation and exploration of materials to find out what they can do with them. If you add cutters and rolling pins too early you stop this process and stop them fully exploring its properties. I see so many young teachers in my region doing this. I really worry about what it does to young children's creativity. I'd really like to focus on this issue in our curriculum inservice.

The teacher would argue for her inservice topic by calling on traditions learnt in college to establish the idea that there are normal and correct ways to be as a teacher. She would be concerned that others share her norms and would see any deviations from them as problematic. She would not see her own ideas on curriculum as personal but as professional truths. She would see them as normal and correct.

A teacher using a critically collective ethics of the self might continue the conversation in this way: Nette has a strong interest in gender issues. It's important that the teachers' group explore how these interests might contribute to our understandings of our work with children. We need to ensure that other teachers have the opportunity to engage with her ideas and the opportunity to debate them and their own social visions. While I was taught in my training that how we present materials to children is crucial, I think it is important to open myself up to different ways of thinking about curriculum. It's important for me and for the children. If my work contributes to gender inequality I'd like to know about it and to think about how to change my practices accordingly. I'd really like to focus on how we might do this in our curriculum inservice using Nette's gender interests.

The teacher would argue for the inservice on gender by stressing that traditions learnt in college need to be questioned and that there is no normal and correct way to be as a teacher. She would be open to discussing her views with others and would see the possibility for challenging her norms as exciting and as important for the children she works with. She would think it important to be with others who can challenge her practices and who can help her think about how she might sustain inequalities through them.

Feminist poststructuralist possibilities and provocations: a summary

Early childhood education is highly resistant to pedagogical innovation because it rests on the ethics of individualism. This ethics of individualism is apparent in how teachers use knowledge of the individual child gathered by individual teachers to take their teaching decisions. The effect of building teaching practices through an ethics of individualism is that political concerns such as gender reform are marginalised within it. This makes changing pedagogies in the interests of gender reform difficult. Teachers could innovate more effectively if they moved to an ethics of critical collectivism. This would mean:

- discussing and critiquing with others daily teaching decisions and the knowledge upon which they are based
- exploring with others the gendered power implications of daily teaching decisions and knowledges
- experimenting with gender reform pedagogies and reflecting on these experiments with others.

Learning more about the debate

The following material provides extended reading on Foucault's work and shows how other writers have used his work to take a critical stance on educational knowledge and processes.

Further readings

Gore, J. 1993, *The Struggle for Pedagogies: Critical and Feminist Discourses as Regimes of Truth*, Routledge, New York. Chapter 3, 'Regimes of Truth', details how Foucault constructed and used the idea of regimes of truth and outlines ways to analyse them.

Gore, J. 1997, 'Who has the authority to speak about practice and how does it influence educational inquiry?', paper presented at the *Annual Conference of the Australian Association for Research in Education*, 30 Nov.–4 Dec., Brisbane. Gore uses Foucault's work on power and knowledge to explore how power operates in practice and in theory in educational settings.

Pinar, W., Reynolds, W., Slattery, P. and Taubman, P. 1996, *Understanding Curriculum*, Peter Lang Publishers, New York. Chapter 9, 'Understanding curriculum as poststructuralist, deconstructed, postmodern text', provides a useful overview of how a variety of postmodern and poststructuralist ideas has been taken up and used in curriculum theory and practice. Pages 450–65 contextualise Foucault's contribution to this work.

Usher, R. & Edwards, R. 1994, *Postmodernism and Education*, Routledge, London. Chapter 4, 'Subject disciplines and the disciplining subjects', provides a good introduction to Foucault's work on power and knowledge and shows how it can be used to take a critical stance on modern educational institutions and to teaching and learning within them.

Professional development suggestions

- Describe Nette's experiences to two colleagues. How do they see Nette's work? To what extent do they draw on pedagogical truths to assess Nette's work?
- What pedagogical truths guide your work with young children? Whose interests are served by these truths? Which truths would you find it hardest to rethink?
- Design an inservice day for early childhood teachers that could encourage them to develop an ethics of critical collectivism in their work.

9

But what about the parents?

Keith: I'm struggling to convince Craig that it's okay for him to play with our new dolls. I see him looking at the dolls but he won't touch them.
Monique: I wouldn't dare try. Craig's dad thinks that boys should be boys. He'd be really unhappy if he knew that you were trying to encourage Craig to play with girls' toys.
Keith: Maybe I should talk with him about it.
Monique: I wouldn't bother, you won't change his views. I'd steer clear of it if I were you.

It's not surprising that Monique is hesitant to talk to parents about gender issues. Many early childhood staff find that building strong partnerships with parents in their gender equity work is tricky. Many writers call for staff to seek such partnerships (e.g. Browne & France 1986; Perrett 1988; MacNaughton 1993; King 1994), but offer little guidance on how to achieve them.

Research on this aspect of gender equity work is sorely lacking. There is considerable research evidence about how parental attitudes to gender equity influence children's gender development (e.g. Brenes, Eisenberg & Helmstadter 1985; Logan 1988; Walkerdine & Lucey 1989; Perry & Morgan 1993; Bower 1998; Grieshaber 1998). However, there is little research evidence on parent attitudes to gender equity programs or on how to build their support for them. This leaves staff reinventing the wheel each time they attempt to build parental support for their gender equity programs.

Members of the research group invented very diverse wheels in working on gender equity with parents. This chapter charts this diversity, the influences on it and how parents responded to it. It also explores why some parents support gender equity programs and why some do not and how selected poststructuralist ideas might help staff work productively with this diversity.

Debating pedagogies: building partnerships with parents

Several teachers in the research group had to negotiate their way through parental support, resistance, vacillation and indifference to their gender equity intentions. Carlie's and Sally's work with parents typifies these reactions and the contexts that produced them. We shall look at their work in turn.

Firstly, Carlie's work. Her work with Peter and Sam illustrates how two mothers with very similar sons can respond to a teacher's gender equity intentions in very dissimilar ways. At four years of age, Peter often involved himself in non-traditional activities and often wore non-traditional clothes. Peter's mother interested herself in what he was doing and felt very comfortable with him dressing up, wearing bows and trying on traditionally female clothes. His difference from the majority of boys in the group meant that he gained special interest and attention from Carlie and myself. We were intrigued to know how and why Peter was so confident and positive in his non-traditional ways of being masculine.

Peter's mother became aware of our special interest in her son through our informal conversations with her. She was delighted by our interest and invited me to her home to study her son more closely. Peter's mother talked at length about how different she felt her son was from many of the more 'macho' boys at the centre and how pleased she was with his differences. She was especially delighted that his strong and active imagination allowed him to imagine many ways of being masculine and enabled him to develop a wide variety of interests and skills. She was also pleased that he was in a centre that actively encouraged and supported him in his difference to other boys. She also told me that her husband felt the same way about Peter's way of being masculine. However, she was concerned about whether it would be possible to find a school that allowed him to continue to 'be himself'.

Sam was another boy in Carlie's group who had a constant interest in playing in home corner, regularly sought out one of the sparkly home corner skirts to wear, loved to bring his pink, cuddly toys from home and was a very gentle, quiet child. He told me that he didn't like being a boy because 'boys are noisy and hurt people' and that he regularly avoided areas where the more 'macho' boys were playing. These boys also avoided playing with him, and the girls regularly told him he couldn't play in the home corner and that boys didn't wear skirts.

Sam's mother became aware of his differences from other boys through observing him and other boys when she was on 'milk and fruit' duty at the centre; and from other parents' comments. She was both fascinated by and concerned with the differences she (and others) saw. She wanted Sam to be non-sexist but realised that other adults watched Sam because of his difference. For instance, other adults often commented on Sam's joy in wearing the sparkly skirt and his pink 'teddy'. Sam's mother also saw that other girls and boys rejected Sam because of his difference. Sam regularly told his mother he had no 'real' friends at kindergarten. He told me similar things. Like Peter, Sam's 'non-sexist' moments also meant that he gained a special interest and support from Carlie and myself. Sam's mother increasingly saw this as problematic, despite her intentions to raise a 'non-sexist' son. She was particularly worried about suggestions from her husband and her relatives that Sam was not acting normally for a boy and that he needed to 'get it right' before entering school. The unspoken but heavily hinted fear was that he could end up gay. Sam's mother found this a distressing thought. She became unhappy about Carlie's support for Sam's difference and asked Carlie to rethink her work with him.

Sally also experienced parental concerns with her gender equity program. She had anticipated some of these concerns and strove to draw more parental support for her gender equity work by:

- involving parents in researching and documenting gender dynamics in her program
- showing parents videotaped footage of children's play in which gender dynamics were prominent
- sharing information with parents in informal discussions and in the centre newsletter about how gender influences children's lives
- talking to parents during pre-enrolment interviews about her gender equity policies.

Each of these strategies was intended to provoke discussion among the parents about gender issues—and each did. In one parent meeting I attended we showed the parents some videotaped footage of the gender dynamics between children in the block play area. One mother, after watching a segment in which her son had just hit a girl, said, 'Boys need to learn to be aggressive, because they need to be aggressive to succeed in the world of business.' Sally described to the rest of the research group what happened next:

> **Sally**: Actually I was really quite pleased that at least most of the parents indicated to her, without us having to say anything, that it's better to be assertive than aggressive. I think they were all thinking of darling

little John and how their children come home whingeing about what he has done to them . . .

And we were able to lead on then as to how important it is for girls to be assertive, too, so I think if they got nothing else out of the night, at least his parents realised that aggressiveness and violent behaviour isn't really the way to go . . .

Well, since the discussion, particularly, I've been able to talk to mums on duty, because it is mainly mums that I have, not that dads aren't welcome, and show them instances of children playing well together, and they can see the advantages now, whereas before they would have looked at children playing in blocks. They wouldn't have even looked at the fact that it was boys and girls playing well together, or that all the boys were dominating there and all the girls were dominating there.

Despite such events, Sally often felt daunted by talking with parents about gender issues:

I am about to tackle a discussion with the parents of John, a most angry, aggressive and sexist boy about whom I am very concerned. His father is an army officer and the child has a lot of war toys and also swears like a trooper. I think I am going to be battling to get the message across to his parents, but at least I am game enough to try now.

Sally's intended message for John's parents was that she wanted their help in her efforts to reduce John's sexist behaviour. She felt that long-term changes within John's behaviour would be more likely if she had their support and understanding of what she was doing. However, John's parents indicated that they were not totally comfortable with her approach because they felt that 'the boys are really disadvantaged now because the girls get more than the boys do'. Despite their response to her work with John, Sally persevered with it.

Sally and Carlie each came to learn that when you raise gender issues with parents and/or their children, you should expect parental reactions that range from support and/or uncertainty through to antagonism. The consequences of this diversity in response for members of the research group came to the fore in a conversation Carlie initiated:

> **Carlie**: They [other teachers] are worried about parents' expectations, and being challenged by parents about their program, more so now, because twenty years ago what the teacher did with the kindergarten children was gospel and no-one challenged them and that's why I think I really admire people like you and Sally who have really taken the bull by the horns and gone in there.
> **Sally**: There's horns involved in it, believe me, because I've had a few parents who don't like it.

As the conversation continued others in the research group said that they feared the 'horns' and so had taken gender equity 'underground' in their centres:

> **Nellie**: I've been a bit of a chicken and not saying, doing that subtly under the carpet.
> **Glenda**: A bit like Matti at the first meeting—'I want to do all this, but I don't want to tell the parents'.
> **Anne**: I felt exactly the same.

Going underground might seem to some a drastic or a cowardly thing to do. But as the conversation continued it was clear the teachers had good reason for their decisions:

> **Carlie**: Well, I think there are a lot of people out there in the field that are worried about what the parents think, because it's a numbers game. You've got to keep your kids at this kinder, because it's going to lose its subsidy.
> **Nellie**: And if you are too radical you lose them.
> **Lee**: And you've got pressure from the committee to be normal so that you'll keep your kids.
> **Rhona**: Then sometimes, people would be attracted to you if you are in the right area but you are a bit radical.

Sally: I don't think it would keep you open, the number that would be attracted.

The 'numbers game' to which Carlie referred was a funding policy in which kindergartens in the Australian State of Victoria were funded on child attendance numbers. To receive a State operating grant each centre had to reach and maintain a particular number of children enrolled. As this operational funding paid the teachers' salaries, its loss meant loss of their jobs. These teachers clearly felt that their child attendance numbers could be adversely affected if they actively pursued a gender equity policy. Yet the State of Victoria in which the teachers worked had just released curriculum guidelines that promoted gender equity (MacNaughton 1993). In this context, why did these teachers feel so vulnerable and why was their work with parents on gender equity so daunting?

Why it happened as it did: The parents with and without 'horns'

To understand why teachers often feel daunted by working with parents on gender equity it is necessary to see how parent involvement is understood in early childhood education. Mainstream early childhood texts and policy documents promote parent involvement in early childhood services. Parent involvement could mean any one of the following:

- centre fundraising
- helping with snack times
- contributing to the management committee
- assisting with centre excursions
- distributing newsletters
- as visitors sharing a special skill or interest with the children. (Hughes & MacNaughton 1999)

Parent involvement is believed to increase children's educational success and positively influence their cognitive and social development (Endsley et al. 1993; Studer 1993/4; Laloumi-Vidali 1997). Parents are also seen to benefit from involvement in their children's services, becoming empowered to make informed choices about their children's education and care.

However, as Usher & Edwards (1998) pointed out, recent moves by the State to formalise and increase parent involvement in education has been associated with the rise of the New Right. Governments have 'developed an apparatus of power-knowledge that sought to establish the boundaries within which "normal, moral and socially responsible" education is defined and outside of which all else may be regarded as deviant' (Kenway 1990, p. 170). Parents are charged with patrolling the boundaries and with watching for practices and policies that break through them. Usher and Edwards (1998) explained how this shift in educational accountability supported New Right practices in schools:

> Parents are deployed to observe and judge schools
> although their actual presence is irrelevant to the
> pressures felt by the schools themselves. In panopticon
> fashion, they must act as though the parents are
> observing and judging them whether or not they are.
> In this sense disciplinary power is not simply exercised
> through modern institutions but also over them . . .
> (p. 114)

Members of the research group were not working in schools, but they were working in educational institutions in which parental oversight of their work was pervasive. Parents were their employers and parental choice directly affected centre enrolment numbers and therefore teachers' job security. Conversations within the research group showed that teachers acted as if the parents were 'observing and judging them' and that they regulated their gender equity practices as a consequence of the parental surveillance (imagined or real). Parental surveillance established boundaries about normal early childhood goals and practices that marginalised teachers' work for gender equity.

These boundaries were built from three sources. Firstly, they came from how early childhood teachers position themselves in relation to parents. The current dominant discourses of parent involvement regularly position parents and teachers as competitors over children's 'best interests'. Often parents' ways of knowing and acting are seen as 'Other' to those of teachers and, within this difference, are subordinate. The person who knows the child is the teacher, the parent is unknowing, misguided and often wrong (Cannella 1997).

Strongly implicated in this positioning of parent as 'Other' to the teacher are the discourses of developmental psychology and of professionalism in the early childhood field. Each discourse places the early childhood professional in the position of the knowing expert. Early childhood staff practise according to the standards of good practice promoted by the early childhood profession. These standards are embedded in DAP and promoted via professional codes of ethics of associations such as the Australian Early Childhood Association and the National Association for the Education of Young Children in the USA. Those who challenge these codes or the developmental knowledge upon which they are based are deemed to be unprofessional (Cannella 1997). Within each discourse, parents' knowledge is secondary to that of professionals, undermining parents' rights to decide what is in the best interests of their children.

The boundaries created by parental surveillance of teachers' work were also built because of the marginalisation of feminist discourses. This marginalisation has been widely documented (see Faludi 1991).

Thirdly, teachers' work was bounded because DAP discourses of normal early childhood goals and practices had dominated the field, marginalising feminist gender equity discourses. This is most obvious in the texts of the early childhood academy. Feminist understandings of the child do not have a traditional institutional base within these texts. The academy had a key role in circulating feminist discourses of the child for Sally and Sue, but each had encountered them outside of the specific part of the academy responsible for early childhood education. Sally had met them while studying in a gender and education course and Sue while studying history. In contrast, academic training of early childhood teachers institutionalises specific 'DAP truths of the child' by providing the discursive formation through which DAP customs and traditions about good teaching are created and maintained. Each member of the research group had been touched by this discursive formation during their pre-service training. Understandings of the child they learnt in this training were shared, powerful and, without exception, premised on modernist developmental discourses. As I argued in Chapter 4, these discourses exclude gender issues. Consequently, they offer teachers only a limited knowledge base from which to talk with parents about their children's gendering.

When members of the research group developed knowledge of gendering and young children, they became unusual within their region. Their colleagues (like them) had been trained via DAP views of the child. Feminist discourses had no established presence. Hence, their colleagues would be unlikely to promulgate feminist readings of the child or to argue with parents that gender equity is and should be a concern within their work with young children. The organisation of physical space in early childhood centres further institutionalised DAP discourses. Early childhood centres are designed according to very strict guidelines that regulate the balance between indoor and outdoor space, the amount of space per child, the height of windows and the equipment that should be available within a given space. The space is partly designed to maximise the physical safety of the child (*Australian Standards for Playgrounds* AS 2155) and partly to maximise the development of the child (*The Victorian Children's Services Regulations* 1988). While these safety concerns are clearly important, the resulting openness of the space also means that the teachers are open to the public gaze of parents.

This public gaze re-institutionalised as the norm what had gone before, such as DAP practices. This, in turn, led some teachers in the group to self-discipline/censor their own gender equity work. So 'going underground' appeared to be the only reasonable and safe option for some teachers for three intersecting reasons:

- an increased and highly public and conservative parental gaze on their work
- the then current discourses of parent involvement in services
- the marginalised position of feminist gender equity discourses in the early childhood field in particular and in society more broadly.

The dual marginalisation of feminist gender equity discourses meant that teachers in the research group often experienced the parental gaze as restrictive rather than supportive. Hence, working with parents by necessity will often involve fighting the marginalisation of gender equity discourses both in early childhood and more broadly. In particular, at a time when there has been a strong backlash against feminist gains for women (see Faludi 1991), many teachers are likely to meet parents for whom feminist approaches to gender equity are 'radical' and as such problematic. For this reason, work for gender equity with parents is inevitably political work. It involves creating political allies of those who are on side and working with them to reform how other parents see gender equity work.

Alternative understandings of parents, gender equity and defensible teaching goals

For several teachers in the research group, the public gaze of parents regulated and restricted their gender equity work. This gaze made some of them work underground rather than with parents. How could they rethink this approach to gender equity work with parents? Cannella (1997) suggests that teachers should seek radical politicised partnerships with parents in which they struggle with parents for social justice and equity. She explained her suggestions this way: 'We would become partners with younger human beings, their families and their communities in establishing goals for action that included recognition, decolonisation, the struggle for justice, and the creation of caring communities in which all are justly perceived' (p. 163).

Others in early childhood education have also called for a shift from parent involvement to parent partnership. In partnerships with parents, staff relate to them as co-learners, advocates and decision-makers in children's services (Wright Sexton 1996). Interwoven through this approach to working with parents is a call for a commitment by early childhood teachers to advocacy for children's rights and social justice (Hughes & MacNaughton 1999).

Will a partnership model guarantee that teachers don't need or want to take gender equity underground? Feminist poststructuralism would suggest not. It suggests instead that the conflicts, differences and parental uncertainties encountered during the research project are an inevitable consequence of the existence of different discourses of masculinity and femininity that structure ourselves and our institutions. Such differences will produce competition for dominance and therefore conflict and uncertainty about what is normal and correct will be inevitable.

Drawing on Foucault's work on knowledge–power relations, Davies (1993) argued that in any society at any point of time, a limited range of discourses of masculinity and femininity circulate. Each gender discourse constitutes different culturally- and historically-specific power relationships.

Thus it is not surprising that:

- Parents' attitudes to their children's gendering are

194

diverse. In particular, it's not surprising that dominant discourses of gender prevail among many parents.

- John's parents were in conflict with the other parents over the most desirable way to be male. Such conflict is inevitable when different discourses are in circulation.
- Sam's mother experienced uncertainty about the desirablity of having a non-sexist son. Traditional discourses of masculinity have more power and more currency at this point in time.

Feminist poststructuralists would also argue that, as Peter's mother showed, some parents reject and object to dominant understandings of what is normal. Moreover, some parents see non-traditional ways of being masculine and feminine as normal and desirable ways of being. When this happens greater gender equity becomes possible in educational settings (Davies 1989; Alloway 1995; MacNaughton 1995; Kenway, Willis, Blackmore & Rennie 1997).

Parent reactions to their children's involvement in the gender equity research project suggest that we need to recognise and plan for the complexity and for the conflicts they may generate. Staff cannot assume all parents will automatically be against, or for, their work. Staff in the research group encountered strong support through comments such as:

- Doesn't it make you mad when you see girls doing that? (Giving in to one of the boy's demands). She's got to learn to stand up for herself.
- I've taught my daughter that girls and women can do anything. It's really important to me.

They also encountered hostility and contradictions:

- It won't make my boy a sissy will it? I like him the way he is, strong and a go-getter. I don't believe in all this being equal stuff.
- Boys shouldn't cry. I don't want no poofter son you know.
- I want my daughter to do, to be, you know, anything

she wants later. I want her to learn how to take good care of her husband, though, be a good wife.

- How can you stop him not liking the girls? I hate that. He needs to learn respect. He's such a typical boy. Still that's how it's got to be isn't it?

What is clear from these reactions and from the research group's experiences is that staff face a tricky task in their gender equity work with parents. Drawing on feminist poststructuralist theories of change, staff may improve their ability to gain parental support for their gender equity programs if they can:

- identify the various discourses of masculinity and femininity circulating in the centre
- ensure that non-traditional discourses circulate
- show that non-traditional discourses are not marginalised or seen as abnormal by them
- ensure that parents understand that there is support for non-traditional ways of being masculine and feminine.

These goals can be achieved by creating open and ongoing opportunities for parents and colleagues to discuss gendering. Sally and Carlie did this by:

- Making the most of informal discussions with parents. Sally and Carlie each created regular times and places that allowed them to informally discuss gender with parents. This drew parents into staff's concerns (and discourses) and drew staff into parents' concerns, especially their puzzlement about their own children's gendered behaviour. Sally and Carlie sought to use the discussions to show their acceptance of non-traditional ways of being masculine and feminine, highlighting the positives for the child.
- Organising parents' meetings with a focus on gender. Carlie found parents were reassured by discussions at one parent meeting about the idea that there are lots of ways to be masculine and feminine. The meeting had also helped them understand how their children were

being supported in their differences. Staff sought to ensure they had others present during these meetings (parents, other staff, etc.) who would confidently artic-ulate non-traditional discourses.

- Writing articles for newsletters. Sally included items about non-traditional ways of being masculine and fem-inine and the developmental advantages that staff (or others) saw in this for children.
- Doing research and sharing it with parents. Sally, Carlie and I talked with the girls and the boys in their centres about why they didn't regularly play with each other. The girls regularly gave boys' aggression as a reason for avoiding certain play areas. When the parents learnt how gender issues were affecting their children's learn-ing and development, they became more interested in working with staff on ways of resolving it.
- Involving parents in special projects. Sally asked parents to help monitor children's use of different play areas and children's leadership styles within the play. After closely watching the gender dynamics of the play several parents become strong advocates for gender equity programs.

Using these opportunities may allow staff and parents to expand the discursive repertoire of the parents in the group to ensure that non-traditional understandings of gender are in circulation. They can also challenge the idea that there is only one normal way to be male (traditional macho ways) and only one normal way to be female (traditional passive ways). To achieve these outcomes, staff need to explore with parents how gender discourses limit their children's ways of being and their ways of learning.

One hope for doing this could lie in staff and parents generating what Lyotard, a French theorist of postmodern-ity, called 'little narratives' (Usher & Edwards 1994, p. 181). Lyotard was especially interested in language and what he called the 'game rules' of language. He believed that those rules and the accounts of the world (narratives) we produce using them helped to limit our understandings of our world and of our possibilities for being within it. Little narratives are stories/accounts about what is happening in a local area that produce a 'constant and localised questioning of knowledge' (Usher & Edwards 1994, p. 182). The aim is to generate new questions, new rules, new ideas, new imaginations about the issues/topic under narration.

Applied to work with parents for gender equity, the aim would be to tell local stories (little narratives) that capture parent, staff and child knowledge about gender. These stories would be used to generate new questions, rules, ideas and imaginations about gender. They could allow parents, staff and children to voice their understandings, desires and feelings about gender. They could show how different children, staff and parents see the effects of gender on children's lives differently, how they see gender normality and how they see non-traditional gendering.

If staff and parents produce little narratives about gendering in children's lives, this could change the relationships between them from ones in which staff (as the gender experts) tell parents (the non-experts) about gender to ones in which staff and parents co-construct narratives about gender that arise in and through their daily lives with children. Centre newsletters, staff-parent discussions and group meetings would provide the space in which the little narratives and the questions, rules, ideas and imaginations they contain about gender could be shared.

Lyotard believed that emancipation and thus greater equity is created in dissensus not consensus. It is when we disagree rather than agree that hope for change happens. In our disagreements (dissensus), dominant norms and values are questioned and re-created, leading to the possibility of greater justice for those involved (Bertens 1995).

Thus, the little narratives staff and parents co-construct should not aim to create or reflect consensus. They should produce dissensus if they are to produce changed and more equitable and just ways of understanding children's gendering. Dissensus can produce change through producing debate and questioning of what we take to be truths in our world. Little narratives about how children learn, what they learn and how gender can and should influence this could produce questions such as:

- Do we want early childhood education to produce children who conform to the status quo?
- Do we want it to focus on the personal development of the individual and to promote individualism?
- Do we want early childhood education to transform society?

The potential to produce change through local little narratives arises from their capacity to dislodge certainties, such as gender certainties, and in doing so to challenge metanarrratives. 'Metanarratives' are those philosophical and social theories that provide the western world with its universal truths and legitimise it. They 'explain phenomena metaphorically by placing them within stories—narratives—of humanity's gradual and sometimes uneven progress . . . towards an unspecified destination or telos' (Hughes 1994, p. 77). Metanarratives tell stories of how humanity can progress towards some goal, some 'epic purpose' (Usher & Edwards 1994, p. 180). Examples of metanarratives include feminism, liberalism, Marxism, science and philosophy. To illustrate:

- Feminism tells stories of how humanity can progress towards equity for women.
- Liberalism tells stories of how humanity can progress towards liberty for the individual.
- Marxism tells stories of how humanity can progress towards communism and equity for all.
- Science tells stories of how humanity can progress towards the control of nature. In the case of human sciences, such as psychology, it tells stories of how humanity can progress towards the control of human nature.

- Philosophy tells stories of how humanity can progress towards truth.

For Lyotard, the stories that are told about how humanity might progress towards a given goal both limit and are limited by the culture of which they are part. Metanarratives 'define what has the right to be said and done in the culture in question, and since they are themselves a part of that culture, they are legitimated by the simple fact that they do what they do' (Bertens 1995, p. 124). What they 'do' is shape our understandings and our imaginations about what is possible for humanity and how humanity might achieve these possibilities. In this process of shaping human possibilities the founding assumption within all metanarratives is that they provide the total picture of what is possible in a particular arena of human endeavour. For instance, Christianity's founding assumption is that its story (narrative) of how humanity can achieve salvation offers us a total picture of what salvation is and how it might be achieved. Similarly, the founding assumption of science is that it offers the total picture of how to control nature. Lyotard saw just social change arising from challenging the totality of metanarratives (Lyotard 1989) and the limits that this totality imposes on what goals we imagine to be possible for humanity and how we might reach those goals.

We have touched elsewhere on how individualism and developmentalism constrain work for gender equity. Each of these discourses derives from the metanarratives of science and liberalism. Liberalism sees human progress being achieved through methods of government that ensure liberty (freedom) for individuals. Individualism is foundational to this pursuit. The human sciences, such as psychology, see control of human nature being achieved through methods of education that produce the rational, self-governing individual. As Walkerdine (1998) explained: 'The liberal order of choice and free will had to be created by inventing a natural childhood which could be produced and regulated in the most invisible of ways' (p. 212).

Developmentalism is foundational to this pursuit. Its stories produce a child who develops according to nature's template and who only requires conditions that support this natural phenomenon to achieve her/his full potential as an individual. Hence, developmentalism and individualism link to privilege a child-centred pedagogy in which the natural, individual child is enabled.

The fate of gender equity work in early childhood education is tied to our capacity to challenge these two ideas embedded in the metanarratives of liberalism and science. They serve to legitimise conservative ideas about the aims of early childhood education, its pedagogies and what place concerns such as gender equity should have within it. For instance, they legitimise a focus on the individual, developing child as part of governing for liberty and of educating for rationality. Individualism and developmentalism go to the heart of what teachers can and will defend in their work. Creating dissensus about them through producing little narratives that question their rules, their imaginations and their questions might be one way to reposition gender issues in early childhood. However, as feminists have pointed out, this needs to be done in the context of feminist goals (Usher & Edwards 1994). In other words, it is only possible to have feminist change if we hold onto the goals of the metanarrative of feminism—equity for women. To this extent, I am suggesting a feminist twist to Lyotard's approach to change—holding onto the metanarrative of feminism while challenging other metanarratives.

This approach traverses a tricky road. It requires that we recognise the complexities of being women and girls in all our differences from each other and claiming that common pro-feminist causes are possible within and across these differences. As Blackmore (1999) explained: 'The ongoing strategic problem for feminism as a political movement is the sameness/difference issue. Feminist claims

201

have wavered between sameness and difference, between the gender-neutral "I" of universal man and the "we" of the collectivity of women' (p. 217).

In holding onto the metanarrative of feminism we are in danger of holding onto an essentialising narrative of gender. Blackmore (1999) argued that this strategic problem is best dealt with by a 'feminist postmasculinist politics' (p. 218) that acknowledges the politics of difference and the politics of privilege. To do this means that feminists need to be alert to the common experiences of marginalisation and silencing in masculinist cultures of women as a group, but we also need to see and hear the different ways in which different women and men and boys are touched by this. Unless we can balance this strategic need for essentialism against the politics of difference then feminist narratives will produce 'cultural explanations that silence others' (Spivak, 1990, p. 33).

Applied to the aims of early childhood education, this means that we need to look at how a focus on the individual, developing child impacts on girls and on boys as groups. We need to look for the gendered power effects of the metanarratives of liberalism and science. However, we also need to look at the politics of difference within this. What are the power effects of these narratives on girls and boys of different classes, abilities and races and their experiences of each other? This need links strongly to issues of how we work with boys as well as girls (see Chapter 7). As Lingard and Douglas (1999) argued:

> The poststructuralist move of strategic essentialism that Spivak (1992), for instance, argues for has obvious advantages for certain feminist arguments. However, strategic essentialism cuts both ways in the context of the 'What about the boys debate?' and in masculinity politics more generally . . . it is not possible on the one hand to deny the recuperative masculinists' claims to boys as a single category and on the other hand allow for its use for pro-feminist arguments. (p. 151)

So a feminist quest for dissensus in early childhood education needs to take into account the tricky nature of the gendered politics of privilege and of difference and their intersections.

Dissensus about the goals and role of early childhood education is not new. Its goals and its roles have varied through time and within and between countries: 'Early childhood education has, at various times, been seen as a means of social reform; as a facilitator of children's natural development; and as a preparation for later schooling' (Jipson 1998, p. 222).

Early childhood teachers committed to gender equity must decide how to produce this dissensus in ways that recast their relationships with parents and reposition gender equity work in early childhood education. Two poststructuralist ideas affirm that little narratives might be a fruitful point from which to start this work. Firstly, Foucault's argument that no 'local centre', no 'pattern of transformation' could function if, through a series of sequences, it did not eventually enter into an over-all [sic] strategy. Foucault (1978, p. 99) suggested that local practices provide a way of illuminating how the gendering of power operates locally at specific moments through the discourses in circulation. For instance, we can identify through the children's local gendering practices their gendering resistances, challenges and transformations.

Secondly, local narratives allow parents', staff's and children's subjectivities to be explored and their feelings, desires, actions and experiences to be taken seriously. To do this, local little narratives must allow all voices to be heard and questioned. They must produce many and varied readings of children's gendering. They must encourage dissensus, that is, competition between discourses to emerge because, as Weedon (1987) explained, this is how understandings become changed: 'It is the conflict between these discourses which created the possibility of new ways of thinking and new forms of subjectivity' (p. 139).

Staff will need to work with some parents' subjectivities

to actively promote positive attitudes to non-hegemonic ways of being male and female and they must be prepared to grapple the 'horns' that might charge them. Some of these horns might include persistent re-emergence of hegemonic gendering. Local little narratives might produce some non-hegemonic views of gender but it will be difficult to do this when hegemonic views persist because they are seen as natural and normal. Little narratives might also offer one way of recasting relationships between parents and early childhood staff. However, the horns of gender equity work will remain unless staff develop diverse and ongoing strategies to gain parental support for their work.

Theory into practice

To see what it means to use different theories of how to work with parents in our gender equity teaching let's look at how different theories might help us respond to this conversation. The conversation took place while I was setting up to watch some videotaped play with Tim.

Boys are mean

Glenda: What one of the girls said to me was that sometimes the boys are mean to the girls. Do you think that they are?
Tim: Yes. I am. So are my friends.
Glenda: How are you mean to the girls, what things do you do?
Tim: What I do is chase them.
Some moments later, the videotape begins.
Tim: There's me!
Glenda: And what are you doing there?
Tim: I'm throwing mud pies.
Glenda: Who at?
Tim: The girls.

How did gender relations work for Tim? How might our

preferred explanation of work with parents influence our teaching decisions about how to approach Tim's parents?

A teacher who sees parents as competitors might read it in this way: Tim has very strong and traditional views about gender relations. He has probably learnt these from his parents. I will need to go carefully in anything that I do to encourage him to play more constructively with the girls.

The teacher might plan in this way: I think the best way to work with Tim is to take a softly, softly approach, especially when his mother is on milk and fruit duty. If she learns about what I am doing, she may not like it.

A poststructuralist feminist might read it this way: Tim is strongly positioned within macho discourses of masculinity. The girls are equally strongly positioned within highly feminine discourses of femininity. If I am to change their ways of responding to each other I will need to work with them and their parents to change the discourses they use. I should identify the various discourses of masculinity and femininity circulating in the centre before deciding how best to build a partnership with parents on gender issues.

The teacher might plan in this way: It will be important to find out how parents feel about the issues raised in this conversation. To find out what discourses of gendering circulate among the parents, I will create some opportunities with parents to discuss gendering. I will start by sharing this conversation with parents in the newsletter and ask them for comments. Then I will think about how I might involve them in finding out how the girls and boys in the centre see each other and use this information in a meeting with parents about the implications.

Learning more about the debate

The following material offers ways to understand how gender operates in parents' lives and in and their relationships with early childhood staff.

Further readings

Goldstein, L. 1997, *Teaching with Love: A Feminist Approach to Early Childhood Education*, Peter Lang Publishing, New York. Chapter 4; 'Mothers and Teachers', explores the gendered nature of complex relationships between mothers and teachers. It focuses on tensions and alliances within mother/teacher relationships and how an 'ethic of care' might help us to understand them.

Woollett, A. & Phoenix, A. 1996, 'Motherhood as pedagogy: developmental psychology and the accounts of mothers of young children', in C. Luke (ed.) *Feminisms and Pedagogies of Everyday Life*, pp. 80–102, State University of New York Press, New York. This chapter takes up several themes touched on elsewhere in this book about how developmentalism limits how we see the child and discusses how it also limits how we see parents and their place in children's gendering.

Kenway, J., Willis, S., Blackmore, J. & Rennie, L. 1997, *Answering Back: Girls, Boys and Feminism in Schools*, Allen & Unwin, Sydney. Pages 9–10 provide a brief but powerful description of how one teacher strove and eventually succeeded in gaining acceptance from parents for her gender equity work.

Professional development suggestions

- Ask two colleagues how comfortable they feel about talking with parents about gender issues. To what extent do they attempt to homogenise parental views on gender equity? To what extent do they position parents as 'Other' to themselves?

- How might you discuss Tim's behaviour with his parents?
- Hoy Crawford (1994) writes: 'Because gender concepts strike an emotional chord in many people, this issue is often perceived as one best left alone, unless parents raise the topic' (p. 152).

To what extent do you agree?

- Write a little narrative about how Sally or Carlie works with the parents in their centre. What gender questions, rules, imaginations and ideas are provoked in your narrative? Now try to rewrite it as if you were Goldstein or Woollett & Phoenix (see readings above). How do the questions, rules, imaginations and ideas change? Which version offers you the most innovative reading to guide your relationships with parents?

10

But it clashes with my multicultural program, doesn't it?

Sue: Now you are working in a culturally diverse centre, how is your gender equity work going?

Leonie: I've been trying really hard to find good non-sexist children's books that show cultural diversity. Do you know of any?

Sue: No, but are you sure that your views on gender equity are culturally relevant to the families you work with?

Leonie: I'm struggling to think that through. I am worried about imposing my cultural values on them. But I do feel really strongly about gender equity.

Sue: I know what you mean. I find it really hard to know how to talk about gender equity with the parents in my centre. Their cultures are so different from ours. I feel that if I do I'm not respecting their cultural views on gender relations.

Sue and Leonie were two Anglo-Australian teachers each committed to gender equity for young children. They were also committed to multicultural perspectives in their work with families and young children. Like many other early childhood staff, they were struggling to find an appropriate way to mesh these commitments. There were fleeting moments in the research group where we attempted this but failed. More often we were silent about the intersections between gender, culture and ethnicity. This chapter explores the material, discursive and political dynamics of this silencing. It also examines how Sue's and Leonie's dilemmas might be resolved.

Debating teaching practices: gender equity and cultural diversity

In the research group's first meeting, each person shared their reasons for joining. Emma linked her reasons tightly to several gender issues that had arisen in her work with Jewish boys and girls in a Jewish kindergarten. She had several general concerns about gender dynamics in block play and home corner, but she also had 'another sort of interest in terms of the religious'. Emma explained this way:

> . . . we have a very formal and high priority religious studies program within the school so that the children at 3, as soon as they start with me, they start off with a very formal religious program and a Hebrew language program as well, and the Jewish religion is quite—there are different roles for men and different roles for women . . . and just a quick example, we have a morning prayer session every day, and we always choose a boy to come up to be the leader, to be the Cantor in the Synagogue—there's always a Rabbi or a Cantor who leads the congregation in the singing, so the boy comes up and he wears the prayer shawl and that's what he does, and so we are also allowed to call up a girl to be a leader as well, but she's not allowed to wear the prayer shawl, because that's something that only men do in the Orthodox Jewish tradition.

Emma went on to explain that she was interested to see whether or not the girls were excluding themselves, or were being excluded, from particular points in the program, and how that might tie in to the religious ceremony.

209

In subsequent meetings she shared her observations of gendered dynamics between the boys and girls in her group, but we never returned to the issue of how her work with the children linked with their Jewish culture and its place in her centre.

A similar pattern occurred with Nellie. She was an Italian-Australian and worked in a lower middle class and ethnically diverse suburb. Children in her centre came from a number of cultural backgrounds, including Turkish-Australian, Greek-Australian, Anglo-Australian and Vietnamese-Australian. In her first group meeting, she shared her observations about how gender and cultural identity mixed in her centre.

> It doesn't seem to matter where the girls go in the centre, they are ostracised by the boys. For instance, one Turkish boy said to this little girl who doesn't use English a lot, even though she can speak it quite well, she's Arabic, 'Don't sit next to me.' It was a clear 'girl–boy' situation. Another Turkish boy won't let any girl sit near him at milk and fruit time. The other boys from different backgrounds join in when he does this.

Others in the group listened attentively to her observation at the time. But, once again, we never returned to a discussion about how the children's cultural diversity influenced the gendered patterns of behaviour she observed and influenced her work.

In Sally's first meeting she placed cultural diversity and gender firmly on the agenda. She explained to the group that she worked in 'a very multicultural centre' and 'this seemed to be a factor' in her gender observations. Sally explained that she had been monitoring children's play patterns in the home corner. She had 'timed the amount of time each child spent in the home corner and averaged this over a week'. Sally found that 'NESB girls spent less time than other girls and than the boys' and 'they seemed to be less assertive than anyone else in the group'. The girls were mainly from a Greek-speaking background and their parents had helped Sally to collect the data. The results surprised Sally and disappointed the girls' parents.

Once again, we listened attentively to her observation but we never used it in our discussions about children's gendering. Why was this? Why did we only fleetingly explore links between gender and cultural diversity?

Why it happened as it did: When gender equity and multicultural perspectives meet

Looking back on these silences, it is possible to see material and discursive reasons for them. One obvious material factor was our class and ethnic homogeneity. We were all white and middle-class. (Nellie was the only non-Anglo-Australian. She was second generation Italian-Australian who saw herself as more Australian than Italian and had rejected much of traditional Italian culture because of its sexism.) We did not experience the intersections between class, gender and ethnicity as problematic and, in this regard, our history resembled that of many white, western, middle class feminist projects which have silenced the specificities of class and ethnicity. However, my awareness of this history and my desire to be involved in a feminism that was not exclusive make my omissions particularly painful to recall.

We worked in a discursive context in which literature on how class, gender and ethnicity intersect in early childhood was virtually non-existent. In a review of Australian early childhood curriculum texts and policy documents from the early 1980s, gender was visible in only 16 per cent of the documents on multiculturalism (MacNaughton 1998a) and multiculturalism was absent in the literature on gender (MacNaughton 1995). Walkerdine (1989) was the exception to this in relation to gender and class. In this context, our reading on gender in early childhood compounded the silences on ethnicity produced by the group's cultural homogeneity.

These silences were further compounded by my role within the group. I was struggling to 'own' the feminist politics underpinning the project, and even making gender problematic in early childhood pedagogies felt an enormous task. Ethnicity and class were lost in these struggles and when they did surface I felt unclear about how to take the issues forward. In my determination to focus on gender, I regularly 'forgot' to look for and, therefore, to see the specificities of class and ethnicity. My 'forgetting' was in part made possible because these dimensions of gendering were not made problematic by others in the group or in literature we explored.

Alternative understandings of gender equity in culturally diverse contexts

How might such silences be challenged in the future? How do and how should discourses of gender equity intersect with discourses of multiculturalism? Early childhood texts that discuss gender equity and multiculturalism offer three alternatives: tokenism, homogeneity (sameness) and alterity ('otherness') (MacNaughton, 1998a).

I shall look in turn at how each of these alternatives imagines the relationships between gender and culture and their potential to challenge silences on these relationships.

Firstly, tokenism. The *Concise Oxford Dictionary* defines tokenism as 'the principle or practice of granting minimum concessions, especially to appease radical demands'.

Tokenism is a superficial recognition that an issue exists but there is expenditure of only minimal effort to try to resolve it. Tokenism occurs in curriculum discourses of gender and multiculturalism when gender is recognised as an issue but when only minimal time or effort is given over to exploring why it is an issue, or how it might influence teaching within a multicultural curriculum, or vice versa.

In a multicultural curriculum, tokenism results in gender equity being mentioned as a goal within the overall context of developing multicultural perspectives in early childhood programs, but without elaborating what this entails. Tokenistic texts and policy documents generally only contain one reference to the inclusion of non-sexist perspectives in the program. Or, conversely in the overall context of gender reform, multicultural issues are mentioned but without any elaboration. In gender texts and policy documents, this discourse can be recognised by the fact that there is generally only one reference to the inclusion of multicultural perspectives in the program. Of one hundred policy documents and texts written on multiculturalism in early childhood in the past twenty years (MacNaughton 1998a) gender tokenism was evident in 27 per cent of them. Typically, these texts and policy documents contained one line or a sentence that stated that non-sexist education is an important component within multicultural programs. They did not develop this in any way by discussing why or how it might be achieved within a multicultural program. The majority of the documents dealing with gender/multicultural intersections in a tokenistic way were written in the early- to mid-1990s. There is now an awareness that gender is relevant to curriculum discourses of multiculturalism and vice versa but uncertainty about its precise relevance.

The second approach to linking gender equity with multiculturalism I have called 'gender homogeneity'. If you consume milk regularly you will have a passing knowledge of what homogenisation means. To homogenise milk is, according to the *Concise Oxford Dictionary*, to 'treat [milk] so that the fat droplets are emulsified and the cream does not separate'.

To homogenise gender in discourses of multiculturalism is to treat gender so that the gender differences between and within cultures are emulsified and the cultural groups are not separated. All cultural groups are treated as if the same gender goals do, can and should apply to all children, irrespective of their particular ethnic or cultural heritage. Gender homogeneity as a curriculum discourse often has one or more of the following features:

213

- gender will be mentioned as a issue
- there will be several references to gender equity as a goal within multicultural and/or anti-discriminatory programs
- a commonality of gender equity goals across all cultures will be assumed or implied (Benisom 1992)
- there will be no mention of possible dilemmas or challenges involved in implementing the same gender equity goals in all cultural groups.

While this approach to gender was evident in approximately 5 per cent of the texts I examined, they were some of the more recent texts. This suggests that this approach to gender presence is new but has increasing adherents.

The third and final approach to linking gender equity discourses with those of multiculturalism I call 'alterity'. Alterity is the 'other-ness' of something. I borrow from Ashcroft et al. (1998) to explain its derivation: 'Alterity is derived from the Latin *alteritas*, meaning "that state of being other or different: diversity, otherness" (p. 11).

In relation to gender in a multicultural context, alterity involves treating 'other' cultural groups as if *they* are the ones who have difficulty with gender equity. We glimpsed this in action in the conversation between Sue and Leonie that opened this chapter. Each teacher assumed that gender equity was problematic in her multicultural settings. Sue and Leonie as Anglo-Australians saw non-Anglo parents' culture as *the* overriding problem in working for gender equity.

Alterity as a curriculum discourse on gender and multiculturalism often has the following features:

- Relationships between gender equity and multicultural perspectives are explored
- It is assumed that 'other' cultures may find gender equity problematic and it is stated or strongly implied in conversations and in documents that there is a need to be aware of this potential conflict. People may or may not discuss how to resolve the dilemmas involved.

By implication, gender is normalised and naturalised in the dominant culture (Pettman 1992), thus presenting the dominant culture as gender-neutral. In Australia, the dominant culture is Anglo-Australian and its approach to gender is seen as normal and natural. It is the other cultures that do things such as 'treat their women badly' or 'overemphasise boys being macho'. The dominant and the other culture(s) are assumed to have gender discourses that are homogeneous within themselves, but different between each other. Hence, all Anglo-Australians are seen to share the same approaches to gender and these are different from the approaches of Chinese groups, Greek groups, etc.

Tokenism, homogeneity or alterity approaches to meshing gender equity and multiculturalism are each inherently problematic. Tokenism has been widely discredited as an approach to social justice issues by several writers in early childhood (e.g. Dermon-Sparks 1989; Siraj-Blatchford 1994) and beyond (e.g. McConnochie, Hollingsworth & Pettman 1988). Actions and policies based on tokenism are superficial, minimalist and rarely followed through and, therefore, do not lead to any real change in relations of inequality.

For instance, one picture representing Vietnamese-Australian families in a display of Australian family diversity would be tokenistic because it would provide children with minimal information about Vietnamese-Australian families. One image cannot convey the diversity and complexity of family life in Vietnamese-Australian families. It could tend to reinforce their pre-existing stereotypes by suggesting that all Vietnamese-Australian families live in the ways depicted in the picture.

Children cannot develop the necessary depth of knowledge or complexity of understanding if they are presented with a single image, story or learning experience. How can they learn that there are just as many ways to be a Vietnamese-Australian girl as there are to be an Anglo-Australian girl if only superficial or minimum time is spent exploring gender in multicultural contexts?

Homogeneity is problematic because it assumes a

215

consensus over gender equity values where consensus cannot and should not be assumed (Pettman 1988). For instance, homogeneity assumes a consensus within each cultural group in Australia about gender relations. To take up this discourse in relation to culture and gender equity in the 1990s seems not only inappropriate but also outmoded. As Benisom (1992) forcefully reminded us: 'Feminist theorists have exploded the idea of a common culture. For example, Iris Young (1990), calls attention to the ideal of commonality as a totalizing force that gives rise to racism, ethnic chauvinism, class devaluation, homophobia, sexism' (p. 9).

Do early childhood teachers want to be understood as racist, ethnically chauvinist, devaluers of class, homophobic and sexist? If not, they must challenge discourses of gender homogeneity in their work.

My reason for arguing that alterity approaches are problematic derives from the work of Ralph Pettman. Pettman (1992) writes that alterity discourses 'are based on deterministic notions of culture, which constitute "the other" who is not "us" in essentialist ways. They construct categories [such as Muslim women or Turkish men] that exclude or entrap whole groups of people, and construct differences in value or entitlement in society' (p. 56).

I'll draw on comments I have heard numerous Anglo-Australian early childhood students make to illustrate what such 'entrapment' means. When they first think about gender equity issues in early childhood settings they have remarked that 'Turkish people don't like their boys to play with dolls' and 'Greek boys always get their own way at home'. Such comments mean that the problem of gender equity is constructed as residing in cultures other to the dominant Anglo-Australian culture. In making these comments the Anglo-Australian students deny the problematic and sexist nature of Anglo-Australian society. For instance, many Anglo-Australian fathers don't like their boys to play with dolls, but this is seen as them just·being 'typical dads' wanting 'real little Aussie boys'. What Anglo-Australians do is natural and normal, what others do is inherently sexist and problematic. These understandings are racist because they prejudge the other as the problem.

Alterity discourses of culture and gender rely on and build from homogeneous discourses of culture and gender which assume all people in a given culture share common values about, for example, gender; and that the other cultures do not, and cannot, change over time. Pettman (1988) suggested that this is most likely to occur when assumptions are made firstly about what is 'authentic' and/or 'traditional' within a particular culture and then that this is the dominant attitude or value throughout that culture. For instance, when a person assumes that all Muslim women believe in being veiled in public, or that all Latino men believe in 'machismo', they homogenise the 'different experiences, identities and social interests' (Pettman 1988, p. 18) of individuals and groups within each culture.

This is both simplistic and inaccurate. All cultures are dynamic because there is always conflict over core social values and relationships. For instance, Ganguly-Scrase and Julian (1997) recently documented this dynamism and how it produces complex but highly gendered ethnic identities among Hmong refugees to Australia when there is conflict over core values within the group. Furthermore, some feminist writing (e.g. Said Khan 1992; hooks 1995) indicates considerable conflict over gender relations in many cultures now and over time. This has led to strong and active feminist political groups in countries as diverse as France (Tong 1989), Turkey, Egypt, Iran, India, Sri Lanka, Indonesia, the Philippines, China, Vietnam, Korea, Japan (Jayawardena 1986), Australia (Pettman 1992), the Caribbean (Tang Nain 1991) and the United States (Tong 1989).

Those Anglo-Australians who continue to assume that gender issues are a problem in other cultures open themselves to criticisms that their understandings of culture are trivial and depoliticised (Pettman 1988). How might they overcome these difficulties?

While an obvious solution for Anglo teachers might be for them to work with groups of teachers and parents in which there is ethnic and class diversity, this should not be seen as the only way forward. Relying on black and working-class women to do the work on gender, ethnicity and class has three major problematics. It can:

- Reinforce racism and classism because black and working class women are yet again servicing the needs (in this case the knowledge needs) of white, middle-class women. As hooks (1989, p .47) argued, when black women are 'called upon to take primary responsibility for sharing experiences, ideas and information [this] places black people once again in a service position, meeting the needs of whites'. In addition, it can reinforce racism and classism because it can position white, middle-class women as unable to speak on issues of race and class. This can produce theoretical inaction on issues of race and class by white women, and as hooks (1989, p. 47) argued it reinforces racism by suggesting that black women's experiences are 'so removed from that of white women that they cannot address such work critically and analytically'.
- Ghettoise class and race perspectives because it assumes the issues of class, ethnicity and gender relate only to black and working class women. It denies the relationships and relevance of black and working-class women's experiences to those of white, middle-class women and thus denies the relationships of oppression between them. As Gorelick (1991) wrote: 'We must trace how these processes—of racism, imperialism, class and national, religious and sexual oppression—are connected to each other and determine, in very different patterns, the lives of all and each of us' (p. 473).
- Produce apolitical views of black and working-class perspectives because it assumes that membership of ethnic minority and working-class groups is a sufficient qualification for examining racism and classism. However, as Siraj-Blatchford (1994b) indicated this is not so:

218

> . . . not all people from ethnic minority groups are
> anti-racist, and while membership of an ethnic
> minority group may, however unpalatable a fact this
> may be to a majority of professional researchers, be a
> necessary qualification for the adequate study of that
> same group's reality, it is not *sufficient* in studying
> racism and sexism . . . while our ethnic group
> background or gender status may provide a
> qualification the arguments presented so far do not
> suggest that this would represent a *necessary* or
> *sufficient* quality in its own right. (p. 35, Original
> emphasis)

Feminist literature, and especially the feminist postcolonial
and poststructuralist literature, offers some alternative
ways forward for Anglo teachers wanting to rethink their
approach to race-culture-gender in children's lives. 'Post-
colonial' has many meanings but broadly it identifies the
new relations of power that form after decolonisation and
the effects of colonisation on societies. Decolonisation
marks the point at which there is:

> . . . independence from direct colonial rule, the
> formation of new nation states, forms of economic
> development dominated by the growth of indigenous
> capital and their relations of neo-colonial dependency
> on the developed capitalist world, the politics which
> arise from emergence of powerful local elites managing
> the contradictory effects of under-development. (Hall
> 1996, p. 248)

Many postcolonial theorists seek to map and express 'the
reconstitution of subjectivities across national boundaries'
(Hall 1996, p. 257) and their discursive constitution. To this
extent, much postcolonial theory is poststructuralist and,
within this, deconstructive (Dirik 1992). The aim of
postcolonial deconstruction is to show the 'relationships
between imperialism and subjectivity' (Brooks 1997, p. 105).
Postcolonial theory with its interests in how subjectivity is
remade within and across national borders has led to
debates about national identity and pointed to the multiple

ways of constructing and living a national identity. In doing so, it has shown the fragility of fixed cultural identities, highlighting instead how cultural identities shift and slide as people experience new languages, experiences and understandings (Gandhi 1998).

The concerns and interests of postcolonial theorists intersect with those of poststructuralists, feminists and anti-racists. Each contributes to a picture of how multiple forms of oppression operate and to a call for 'a politics of difference to incorporate the voices of the displaced, marginalised, exploited and oppressed black people' (Brooks 1997, p. 108). Each does this by showing the limits to and oppressive effects of discourses of cultural difference based on tokenism, homogeneity and alterity.

From within this body of theory we can find possibilities for reconceptualising the intersections between gender, race and culture in our work with young children. This theory suggests that reconceptualisation involves meshing cultural issues with gender and vice versa by:

- finding and naming common projects within which to create greater cultural and gender equity through . . .
- deconstructing the gender/culture dualism and repositioning of the other.

However, in meshing issues of gender and culture the aim is not to produce a homogenised, single understanding of gender equity and its possibilities. There are many possibilities because of the ways in which race, gender, class and sexual orientation intersect in and construct our lives. It is important to remember that: 'The categories of race, gender, class, and sexual orientation are abstractions. No one is just a woman, for example, or just a rich person, or just a white person, or just a bisexual. Real people occupy many roles and identities simultaneously' (Zack, Shrage & Sartwell 1998, p. 327).

The aim in meshing work on issues of race, culture and gender in early childhood education is to produce complex understandings of the shifting struggles, tensions and possibilities in the lived experiences of race-gender-culture in children's and parents' lives. These complexities will vary from area to area and from centre to centre as the lived experiences of children and parents will differ. However, in any work for gender equity there would always be recognition of the simultaneous ways in which race, gender and culture construct lived experiences.

Finding and naming 'situated' common projects

Searches for common projects in local early childhood centres can begin by drawing on the rich and complex feminist literature on gender in multicultural, multiracial contexts (e.g. Collins 1989; Caraway 1991; Tang Nain 1991; Benisom 1992; Brady 1993; Tsolidis 1993; Siraj-Blatchford 1994a; Brewer, 1997). For instance, Benisom argued that feminism and multiculturalism share three common concerns/projects:

> moving differences from the margin to the centre
> recovering silenced histories, lifestyles, etc.
> exposing oppressive, non-democratic practices.

(I will return to these projects in more detail later.) Benisom argued that these projects require us to challenge those discourses of ethnicity, race and gender which create and maintain the idea that work for gender equity is distinct and separate from multicultural/anti-racist work. In early childhood, this would require teachers to challenge discourses of gender invisibility which imply that gender equity work is not relevant to multiculturalism and vice versa, and also to challenge discourses of alterity which see gender equity work as problematic for other cultures.

It would also involve problematising the dominating effects of white cultures and how these silence the possibility of common projects. In part, common projects arise from serious exploration of how sexism is situated in each culture and how this affects women within and across cultures in different situations (e.g. in the workplace, in their local area and in the family). Understanding the specific situations in which women and girls experience sexism leads to common projects based on 'situational anti-sexism' (Spivak 1990, p. 58) rather than on some general view of what is in the interests of all women or of all girls.

Deconstructing the gender/culture dualism and moving to 'simultaneity'

Benisom (1992) argued that we need to challenge discourses that place us in the position of choosing whether gender or race/ethnicity should be privileged in our educational and political work. She proposed that deconstructionist feminist theory could be to used to 'defy the dominant view of differences that are posed as oppositional and hierarchical dualisms or binarisms' (Benisom 1992, p. 7) and could, therefore, challenge dualistic thinking which privileges *either* gender *or* race/ethnicity. She is supported in this position by the work of Black feminist theorists in the United States who see race, class and gender as 'simultaneous forces' (Brewer 1997, p. 238) inextricably threading through who we are.

Challenging dualistic thinking is part of deconstruction. As discussed in Chapter 7, deconstructive reading of a particular issue involves critically taking apart ideas, practices, structures and language and allows the 'unthinkable, unthought' (Cixous & Clement 1986, cited in Tong 1989, p. 224) to emerge. Kenway and Willis (1997, p. 210) have described deconstruction as a process that can help teachers to explore 'the cultural excuses which are used to justify the status quo'. Many of our 'cultural excuses' are seen to build from how dualistic thinking contributes to 'the making of social hierarchies' (Siedman 1995, p. 125). This is because social hierarchies rely to a large extent on social categories for their continuation.

Deconstruction can highlight the 'cultural excuses' in our curriculum work by forcing us to see that by thinking dualistically we see gender and multiculturalism as separate, and privilege one above the other in our work with young children. We provide ourselves with cultural excuses for maintaining the status quo when we come to think that it is too hard to work on both, or that it is not necessary to. This leaves gender and/or race/ethnicity untouched in our curriculum work.

Deconstructing the dualism between gender and race/ethnicity involves seeing and analysing how it creates our cultural excuses for maintaining the status quo. We can often see how our cultural excuses work by imagining what alliances there might be between each part of the dualism. So, rather than thinking about what separates them we re-imagine their relationships to each other by asking what binds them or how they work together to produce experience. What alliances can we imagine despite the differences between them? How might they permeate each other? Such questions can form the basis for reconceptualising intersections between gender/race/culture. In this instance, what might gender and multiculturalism share in common as curriculum discourses?

We can see how this might work if we return to the conversation between Sue and Leonie that opened this chapter. Thinking dualistically about culture and gender does, in this instance, create a problem that leads Sue to temporarily suspend her gender-equity work.

How might thinking deconstructively help Sue to move beyond her problem? To think deconstructively, Sue would first need to identify the dualisms she had created between gender and culture in her thinking about the parents and the children. She would then need to re-think the possible boundaries and alliances between Anglo-Australian and non-Anglo parents in her gender equity work. She would have to re-imagine what binds them, how gender permeates their cultures and how culture permeates their gender. What common projects might she search for which enable their differences and their similarities to emerge and be respected?

Such thinking moves beyond alterity discourses and towards an understanding of how gender-equity issues might permeate all cultures, including the Anglo-Australian, not just the other. When we re-imagine how each part of a dualism such as gender and culture might be permeable to each other and allied, we re-position the other. For instance, before Sue could extend her equity work across and through the gender/culture dualism, she would need to re-position the non-Anglo parents so that they were not seen as other to Anglo parents but as within the same group. Such re-positioning is tricky because of the power relations between Anglo-Australians and other Australians. In Australia, upper-class and middle-class Anglo-Australians are politically and economically more powerful than any other group (Stratton & Ang 1998). Consequently, there is a danger that decisions about what binds people will be taken by the dominant group, thus reinforcing the dominant view about what the gender issues can be, are and should be in a multicultural context.

To avoid this, repositioning/rethinking the other should acknowledge the relationships of power, oppression and discrimination which maintain the status quo; should acknowledge our own positions within these relationships (Maher et al. 1993); and should actively challenge them. Hence, an anti-racist stance is implicit within a repositioning of the other. In practice, an anti-racist stance on repositioning the other would involve creating curriculum documents, texts and/or materials that make visible the power relations between different cultural groups and the current beneficiaries of these power relationships. In early childhood curriculum discourses, it would also be clear that there are power relations between genders and it would be clear which gender benefited most from those power relationships at different points in time.

These questions of power and of repositioning the other to find common projects/causes relate directly to work with children. Children can be encouraged to think about what is fair or unfair in how gender is practised within their own and other people's cultures. They can also be encouraged to think about what is fair and unfair in the relationships between their own culture and other cultures.

In addition, we could see gender identity and racial/ethnic identity as dynamic and mutually constitutive (Walby 1992). Each identity is constantly in the process of forming; each identity informs and forms the other. In other words, a girl is always in the process of learning what it means to be a girl, because each of us is always in the process of forming and re-forming our gender identity. The same is true of our ethnic identity. How girls learn to be a girl and what they learn about being a girl is informed by their ethnicity and vice versa. Our ethnic identity is formed and informed by our gender. A new discourse would acknowledge this inter-relationship and would regard it as essential to explore in any discussion of multiculturalism. For instance, within such a discourse, it would be impossible to learn about Greek-Australian culture without looking at how being Greek-Australian is informed by, and forms, gender identities for Greek-Australians.

We could recognise that identities are formed in a time of 'flexible citizenship' (Chambers 1996, p. 53) in which our cultural pasts and presents intersect. All women form identity from their cultural past and from their cultural present, so their identity is not 'firmly located in any one culture, place or position' (ibid., p. 53). We could also recognise the poststructuralist work on identity that argues that our identity is never finally formed but always 'open to change, to transformation, to realignment' (McRobbie 1996, p. 42). There is, for example, never one final and fixed way to be a female Greek-Australian.

Benisom (1992) offers us a practical way to reposition the other in an anti-racist way. She identified three concerns common to anti-racists and feminists that could inform attempts at meshing gender/culture/race. I mentioned them previously—moving differences from the margin to the centre; recovering silenced histories, lives, etc.; and exposing oppressive, non-democratic practices.

Moving differences from the margin to the centre

In practice, moving differences from the margin to the centre would create a focus on the gender differences within and between cultures. Teachers could develop resources and experiences that would introduce children to these differences. Children could be encouraged to think critically about their own and others' culture and gender and how each forms and informs identity. They could be encouraged to learn about the complexities of who we are rather than about superficial emblems of culture, such as particular foods or dances.

Recovering silenced histories and lives

Recovering silenced histories, lives, etc. could involve children learning about those gender and culture histories and lifestyles that are not normally found within mainstream texts, stories and curriculum materials. For instance, teachers could actively learn about and encourage children to seek the histories and lifestyles of women from a diversity of culture backgrounds who were public achievers, heroines, adventurers or rebels. This may help us to understand the commonalities and differences between us. Hoy Crawford (1996, p. 193) produced an extensive list of what she calls 'Famous Women in History' that describes the accomplishments through history of women from a variety of cultural backgrounds. Staff could research these women and share their stories with the children.

Children could also learn that particular ways of living and practising gender vary in cultures across time. Hoy Crawford (1996) suggested that we tell children that, for instance:

> . . . in China, it once was the fashion for affluent men to grow long fingernails. Or that men once wore wigs, curls, ruffles, and silk stockings. Or that in the sixteenth century, only men wore high heels. Or that women in history have led men into battle. Or that in the agrarian society before the Industrial Revolution, men were mostly at home on family farms and participated more in the raising of their children. (p. 123)

Such discussions could allow children to explore not only the cultural specificity of gender and identity but also their changing natures.

Exposing oppressive, non-democratic practices

Exposing oppressive, non-democratic practices could involve children learning about fairness and unfairness such as racism and sexism; and how to recognise these forms of unfairness in their relationships with each other and from texts. Dermon-Sparks argued that young children gain, 'the intellectual and emotional ability to confront oppression and work together to create a more just society' (Dermon-Sparks 1989, p. 5). To enable them to do so, staff can:

- help children to feel good about themselves
- build children's capacity to participate in the curriculum to their full potential
- build children's ability to have positive relationships with others
- teach children to decide what is fair and unfair in their day-to-day relationships with each other
- help children to learn to stand up for themselves and for others who are treated unfairly
- build children's capacity to think critically.

Hence, in a curriculum focused on the simultaneity of gender, race and culture issues, children would gain those intellectual and emotional skills which will help them confront both sexism and racism in their daily lives. Finding ways to achieve this is an urgent challenge for all in early childhood who are committed to greater equity and social justice for all children. Otherwise they leave themselves open to the criticisms that they are:

- Using simplistic and inaccurate understandings of culture and cultural identity to inform their work
- Ignoring the mounting research evidence about the fundamentally gendered nature of learning for all children, irrespective of cultural background.

Do teachers want to be seen as simplistic, inaccurate and ignorant?

Theory into practice

To see what it means to use these different understandings of gender/culture/race intersections let us look at a dispute between Riad, a Turkish-Australian boy, and Elizabeth, an Anglo-Australian girl, and some alternative ways to 'read' it.

My traffic lights

Riad walks over to a set of wooden traffic lights that are placed near a wooden steering wheel. Tina and John are sitting beside each other on a wooden plank immediately behind the steering wheel. John is holding the steering and taking Tina for a drive. She is telling him to 'beep the horn'. At this point Riad changes the traffic lights from green to red. John refuses to beep the horn and Tina wanders away to the climbing frame. Nellie, the teacher, approaches Riad and moves him away from the traffic lights so that she can discuss an incident in which he hit someone in the sandpit. As Nellie is talking with Riad, Elizabeth runs up to the traffic lights and stands behind them. Riad returns and a tussle begins between them about who is 'running' the traffic lights. Eventually Riad pushes Elizabeth aside and she leaves the area. She joins Tina who is jumping on a trampoline nearby.

A teacher using a tokenistic understanding of gender and culture might read it this way: Riad and Elizabeth are struggling to resolve their dispute over who should play with the traffic lights. It's good to see them beginning to play with each other, given their different cultural backgrounds and their different genders. However, I need to think about how to help them get on better with each other. I will need to encourage them to develop better conflict resolution skills.

The teacher might plan in this way: To develop the children's conflict resolution skills I will encourage them to use their words more with each other. I will talk about this with the children in a group and remind them about the need to use their words whenever there is a dispute between them.

A teacher using a homogenising understanding of gender and culture might read it this way: Riad and Elizabeth are struggling to resolve a dispute over who should play with the traffic lights. It's good to see the children mixing so well with each other, given their different cultural backgrounds and genders. However, I need to think about how to help the girls and boys get on better with each other. I need to help Riad understand that girls can direct traffic as well as boys can and to help Elizabeth to be more assertive when he challenges her right to direct traffic. I need to encourage John to listen more to Tina when they are playing together.

The teacher might plan in this way: To help the girls

and boys from different cultures play together more positively I will:

- positively reinforce them in the times when they do play positively
- read them some stories about girls and boys from different cultures playing cooperatively
- put up some posters that show girls and boys from different cultures playing cooperatively in a variety of settings.

A teacher using an alterity understanding of gender and culture might read it this way: Riad and Elizabeth are struggling to resolve a dispute over who should play with the traffic lights. It's good to see Riad mixing with girls at all, given his cultural background. He is so used to being 'macho' at home and getting his own way as a boy. He often refuses to play with the girls. I don't like to challenge his cultural beliefs but I am concerned about how he treats the girls.

The teacher might plan in this way: I will have a general discussion with the children about respecting each other's play space and about using our words when we are unhappy. Over the next few days, I will position myself by Riad and reinforce this idea as necessary. I will try to remind him that we all play together in this kindergarten, that we are all friends. I'm not sure I can or should do more than reinforce our general group rules about caring for others.

Feminist poststructuralist provocations and possibilities: a summary

Meshing work for gender equity with work for respecting cultural diversity is tricky. The current approaches to doing this in early childhood education such as tokenism, alterity and homogeneity are problematic because they are conceptually simplistic and outmoded and because they lead to minimal change in relations between genders and between cultural groups. Feminist poststructuralist/postcolonial theory suggests that to move beyond current approaches teachers could:

- Build a much more complex understandings of the intersections between race, gender and culture in children's lives by searching for the simultaneity of race, gender and cultures in constructing children's identities
- Find and name common projects for race-gender-culture equity that are situated in issues in their local area and situated in dialogue with others
- Reposition the other in their local area by moving race-gender-culture differences from the margin to the centre; recovering silenced histories, lives, etc.; and, exposing oppressive, non-democratic practices.

Learning more about the debate

The following material explores how gender and ethnicity intersects in people's lives. It raises questions about how staff could take these intersections in work with young children.

Further readings

Brewer, R. 1997, 'Theorising race, class and gender: the new scholarship of Black feminist intellectuals and Black women's labour', in R. Hennessy and C. Ingraham (eds), *Materialist Feminism: A Reader in Class, Difference, and Women's Lives*, pp. 236–47, Routledge, London. In this chapter

231

Brewer presents a strong theoretical and political case for paying attention to the relationships between gender, race and class in people's lives. While she does not deal with children or early childhood education she presents useful ways of thinking about gender in culturally/racially diverse settings.

Spivak, G. C. 1990, 'Postmarked Calcutta, India', in S. Harasym (ed.), *The Post-Colonial Critic: Interviews, Strategies, Dialogues*, pp. 75–94, Routledge, London. This chapter is based on an interview with the feminist postcolonial theorist Gayatri Chakravorty Spivak. Through talking about her as an Indian woman traversing cultures she theorises how class, race, culture, geography, gender, work and politics intersect in her life. She shares her life story to show that subjectivities are complex, in process and involve negotiating our cultural pasts and presents, and discusses the complexities of herself.

hooks, b. 1995, *Killing Rage: Ending Racism*, Owl Books, New York. Pages 86–97 detail how feminism is a Black concern and strongly debunk the myth that feminist concerns are only the concerns of the white and middle-class.

Brown, B. 1998, *Unlearning Discrimination in the Early Years*, Trentham Books, London. This book, based on recent research about children and discrimination, offers strong practical advice to early childhood staff on how to talk with young children about issues of discrimination. Chapter 1, 'Not too young to learn', traces the intersections between race and gender in young children's learning.

Professional development suggestions

- Ask two colleagues how they would implement gender equity goals in a culturally diverse setting. Which approaches to gender and cultural diversity are represented in their views?
- How could you actively learn about and encourage children to seek the histories and lifestyles of women from a diversity of culture backgrounds who were public achievers, heroines, adventurers and rebels?
- To what extent do you agree with the following statement about cultural dominance and subjectivity? How might it apply to your approach to gender and cultural diversity in early childhood?

  Members of dominant groups have always defined their subjectivity as mobile, changing, flexible, complex and problematic—in other words, 'safe for democracy'—whereas the subjectivity of their others remains uncomplicated, unsophisticated, unproblematic, verifiable and unknowable, that is, incapable or undeserving of 'democracy'. (Minh-ha 1996, p. 15)

- How do gender, class and race intersect in your life? How do they form/inform your identities? How 'mobile, changing, flexible, complex and problematic' have they been in making your identities?

11

Reconceptualising early childhood pedagogies

I began this book with the aim of unsettling several myths that make gender equity and traditional early childhood education unlikely and uncomfortable allies. These myths are that:

- Gender is biologically fixed and immutable
- Good early childhood practice inherently produces equitable outcomes for all children
- Gender is not an issue in early childhood settings
- Young children don't know or care about gender
- Early childhood teachers solved the problems of how to work for gender equity years ago
- Boys miss out in gender equity programs
- Individual teachers are free to pursue gender equity if they want to
- Parents cannot be allies in gender equity programs
- Gender equity and multiculturalism do not and should not mix.

In unsettling these myths, I have scrutinised the practices and theories of early childhood education and of specific early childhood teachers. This scrutiny has often shown the teachers and the theories of early childhood education to be lacking when it comes to gender equity. My intention was and is not to blame individual early childhood teachers for the lack of progress so far towards gender reform in the early years of education. Instead, I have tried to show how, at every twist and turn, traditional early childhood discourses mitigate against gender equity in early childhood education. Within the research group, individual teachers who understood and practised teaching from within traditional discourses struggled with gender equity across several dimensions. They struggled to see gender equity as an issue, they struggled to see how to practise it and they struggled to find allies in their work for it. Their struggles exposed the myths that constrain work for gender equity in early childhood. They showed how these myths were intimately connected to their truths about the developing child and about what and how the developing child could and should learn. These truths were regularly constructed at these sites through:

- the teacher's pedagogical gaze
- the teacher's reading of the child
- the teacher's strategies, including organisation of space and materials
- the colleague's gaze
- the academy's gaze
- the parents' gaze
- the teachers' self gaze.

If early childhood pedagogies are to be reformed with feminist intent then their reformation must take place at each of these sites. The previous chapters have offered feminist poststructuralist provocations and possibilities about how this might happen. In this chapter I draw these together to suggest a way of understanding and practising early childhood teaching that could reform it and revitalise work for gender equity.

Reconceptualising the pedagogical gaze: wearing multiple lenses

Early childhood teachers gaze at children for many reasons. A good early childhood teacher knows how to gaze artfully through the lens of developmental psychology. DAP pedagogy requires this of her/him. This gaze creates the knowledge of children that teachers use to plan for children's learning. Anne's story in Chapter 4 pointed to gender weaknesses in this lens. Teachers' pedagogic interventions in gendering were intimately linked with how specific gendering discourses informed their understandings of the child and therefore, who the object of the gaze should be. Creating a gaze with gender as its object is central to reconceptualising ways of working for gender equity in early childhood.

A reconceptualised gaze in early childhood could be built from multiple lenses, each with the power to see gender from many perspectives. Each lens could bring gender into focus in different ways. The artful early childhood teacher could have a wide repertoire of lenses that were put on, used and discarded as more powerful ones became available. Options for building this repertoire explored in this book include:

- A multiracial feminist lens that brings into focus the intersections between gender, race, class, ability and sexuality
- A storyline lens that sharpens the focus on how children construct and experience gendered power relationships in their play with each other
- An ethics of the self lens that brings into sharper relief children's ways of transforming themselves into correctly gendered people
- A radical feminist lens that throws light on the positive attributes of femininity
- A masculinities lens that intensifies awareness of

the different ways in which boys live and practise masculinity.

Combining, shifting and changing these lenses and searching for new ones could revitalise how teachers see and work with gender in children's everyday lives.

Reconceptualising readings of the child: privileging feminist knowledge(s)

Imagining an early childhood pre-service course devoid of child development theory is difficult. Imagining an early childhood pre-service infused with feminist poststructuralist theory is equally difficult. However, if early childhood education is to take gender equity seriously, teachers' knowledge base needs to be expanded. To do this, the privilege regularly offered to developmental psychology should be revoked. Feminist knowledge is not the only knowledge that should gain in this process. There should be gains for those producing knowledge about the politics of everyday life as they pertain to ethnicity, sexuality, disability, class, geographical location and age. At times these knowledges should be privileged and at times feminist knowledge should have a privileged place. For example, early childhood teachers could gain new pedagogical insights from developing an indepth understanding of feminist poststructuralist concepts such as 'discourse', 'subjectivity' and 'power'. Through these concepts they could see:

- How children and teachers position themselves within gendering discourses
- How these positionings are implicated in power relations between children and between children and teachers
- How power relations have shifting gendering effects for teachers and children.

237

Using these feminist poststructuralist concepts of discourse, power and subjectivity it is possible to move beyond essentialist accounts of gendering. For instance, the social *meanings* of being masculine and feminine can become, as they did in the research group, a point for challenge by teachers. In addition, teachers can debate and take action about how these meanings are implicated in gender relations. This is because the concepts of discourse, power and subjectivity presuppose that gender is a social construct, not an essential biological process (nor a by-product of social practices).

Essentialist accounts of the child silence gender as a category and favour accounts of the gender-neutral child that lead to pedagogies that contribute to patriarchal gender relations. It is critical for feminist praxis for teachers to have accounts of gendering that challenge gender as a 'natural' fact of life and which emphasise the categories of male and female, boys and girls. Such accounts are intimately related to teachers' desires to actively challenge traditional gendering and to work against sexism. Therefore, it seems critical to find ways to privilege gender differences as a critical point of analysis in early childhood training and professional development because, as Fenby (1991) wrote, 'Within the patriarchy, "the issue of difference is undeniably political"' (Taylor 1987, cited in Fenby 1991, p. 28).

Reconceptualising teaching strategies: exercising power and seeking subjectivities

The repertoire of strategies offered to teachers seeking gender equity has been extremely limited for some time. As several of the stories in this book show, the strategies have also been flawed. Creating gender equity with young children is more unsettling and more complex than modelling non-sexist behaviours and encouraging boys and girls to play non-stereotypically. It involves:

- struggling with gendered power relations
- exercising adult power for girls and against boys
- stopping sexism between children
- making children alert to adult surveillance of sexism
- increasing children's discursive repertoires
- understanding the pleasures and benefits children find in traditional gendering
- disrupting the demarcation lines between genders
- intervening in, and extending, children's storylines
- challenging category-maintenance work on less traditionally-gendered children
- exercising pedagogical power with feminist intent(s).

These actions can help interrupt the gender boundaries between young children. To maintain the effects of this interruption teachers need to privilege children's subjectivities to better understand how silences, actions and speaking help girls and boys to resist or reinforce patriarchal gendering; the dangers and possibilities they see within such resistances; and the reasons for the choices they make in different situations. Through such understandings teachers can use their pedagogic power with a clearer understanding of how it may be liberatory or subjugatory (Lewis 1993) for particular children at particular moments in time. Teachers may learn how boys and girls refuse and/or take up discourses and how children's silences, actions and non-actions can be differentially powerful or dangerous resistance strategies for girls and boys. For instance, girls may remain silent in spaces where patriarchal ways of being (such as block play) dominate to avoid violence: speaking up or acting in this space may be perceived as dangerous unless the teacher is present.

Recognising these dangers provides options for how teachers might then choose to use their pedagogic power and how they might deal with girls' silences in play when boys are present. Alloway (1995) demonstrated that young girls in early childhood education can refuse gendered discourses and practices but teachers need to recognise that such refusal might be constituted as dangerous by some girls. As Lewis (1993) highlighted, adult women can experience challenging gendered discourses as dangerous. Young girls have fewer verbal, cognitive, political and experiential resources to draw on when constituting their resistances. How teachers ask girls to resist patriarchal gendering must be cognisant of the differences constituted by age. Teachers should also reflect on how young girls may read the dangers and possibilities within the demands we make of them. Otherwise, we risk turning girls away from the struggle to articulate and practise their own interests and thus put at risk the potential of 'interrupting patriarchy' (Lewis 1992, p. 167).

This book provides glimpses of how to take more account of children as active subjects. At the very least, this involves:

- talking to the children about why we want to watch their play (e.g. to find out more about how boys and girls play together and why it is they sometimes do, and sometimes don't)
- asking them what they know about gender relations
- finding out how children feel about gender and why
- inviting children to ask us questions
- discussing children's play with them
- seeking children's understandings of specific gender incidents.

Teachers can help children to recognise how gender shapes their and other children's desires, understandings and actions and to examine the gendered power implications of these. Children as young as three years of age can understand what is 'fair' and what is not (Brown 1998). Through examining the gender-fairness of particular desires, understandings and actions, teachers can introduce young children to embryonic processes of deconstruction. This can be then used by teachers and children to engage in 'a collective process of re-naming, re-writing and re-positioning' (Davies 1993, p. 199) gender relations in and

240

through children's imaginative play. How this might happen, and the feminist potentials within it, offer exciting territory through which to teach with children as active subjects.

Reconceptualising relationships with colleagues, parents and the academy: challenging 'truths' and being critically collective

For the DAP-styled early childhood teacher, the gaze, readings of the self and the child, teaching methods and the organisation of space and materials are detailed at length within the texts of the academy. They are effectively transmitted to, and through, students learning to be early childhood teachers within the academy. In the previous chapters I have documented how these techniques worked through specific teachers in the research group. Within the research group, progress for gender equity was most visible in the moments in which people went against their usual practices and, in doing so, questioned the truths of their training.

If teachers see what they learnt in college as *the* truth and thus correct and immutable, then little will change in how they practise gender equity. To progress towards gender equity in early childhood education teachers need to heed Foucault's warning that everything, including the truths of early childhood education, is dangerous, and then be prepared to challenge these truths.

If early childhood educators take action for gender equity and draw on feminist readings of the child they will inevitably need to question the DAP rationalisations that normally underpin and regulate their work. They will need also to transform their existing knowledge base and to elaborate alternatives to it. Broadly, individual research group members needed to transform their knowledge about:

- How to teach, specifically the appropriateness of child choice and adult intervention in play.
- What to teach, specifically moving to a gendering curriculum that included developing an ethics of care, expanding girls' and boys' discursive repertoires, challenging violence and sexual harassment, and supporting differences in masculinities and femininities.
- How to organise materials, space and time.

However, transforming knowledge and practice is difficult. Chapters 2 through 10 indicated the power of DAP truths gained via pre-service training and how difficult it was for specific research group members to rethink these.

In the research group rethinking was possible once a new relationship with our truths was established by holding them up to critical reflection with others. If early childhood pedagogies are to be reconceptualised with feminist intent(s) then it will be critical for this to be done with others. It will be essential that it is done with a strong commitment to the hard intellectual and political work of questioning the truths of existing knowledges and practices. It will also be important that this questioning is based on the lived experiences of teaching and learning in early childhood settings. Teachers, children and parents have much to tell each other about the political implications of current truths of teaching and learning and of gender. They also have much to offer the process of reconceptualising these with feminist intent(s).

Developing an ethics of critical collectivism (Chapter 7) informed by collaborative dialogue (Chapter 9) offers teachers a way to reform their relationships with parents, policy makers, colleagues and the academy. Ethics, in Foucault's sense of the term, are independent of moral codes '. . . because ethics operate somewhat independently of moral codes, we are dealing not with duties but with *choices*; choices about the ways in which we act on ourselves, about the relationships we form with ourselves' (Gore 1993, p. 129) (Original emphasis).

This distinction enables us to make choices about how we operate ethically on ourselves even if moral codes within pedagogies remain stable. Thus we have choices, irrespective of the specific moral codes guiding our pedagogies, to self-style as anti-racist, feminist teachers or not, and to develop a *telos* that is anti-racist and feminist or not. The stories in this book show that there are material, discursive and institutional limitations (including policy frameworks) on these choices, but there are, nevertheless, choices. Engaging in critical reflection with others about how we are constituted ethically as pedagogues enables different choices to be shared and debated. If this involves critical reflection on personal ethics and care of the self, then a space is created in which to choose anew our 'technologies of the self' as a teacher.

Gore (1993) believed that such processes of debating the ethics of the self represent working with a 'will to knowledge', rather than a 'will to truth'. Gore explained: '[Foucault saw] the will to knowledge as the general desire to know, and the will to truth as the desire to know the difference between truth and falsity in particular disciplines or discourses' (p. 10).

In line with Foucault (1977a, cited in Gore 1993), Gore argued that intellectuals could/should constantly question one's truth and work for the more general 'will to know'. The intellectual search should be for knowledge, not for truth. However, over time the academy has established many powerful early childhood pedagogical and gendering truths. Questioning these truths and moving towards a will to know involves risking our pedagogic reputations. Collaborating with others who also risk their reputations as pedagogues can make the risk feel positive and necessary and the consequences as something to be challenged rather than endured.

Critical reflection must occur within the bounds of our existing discursive resources with which we make sense of and debate our pedagogical world. Therefore the extent to which we can restyle will also be constituted within the knowledge-power relations of the discursive field in which we operate. It will also be constituted within the bounds of our own gendered, classed, racialised and sexualised identities.

Teachers forming new relationships with colleagues and parents could remake the knowledge-power relations of early childhood education by seeking to:

- explore multiple ways of creating dialogue about gender with them
- practise writing and reading little narratives with them
- share and debate visions for children with them
- regularly question with them the gender effects of the truths that guide early childhood education
- explore with them what restricts the desire and ability to experiment with teaching practices
- expose non-democratic practices
- recover hidden histories and knowledges
- place issues of difference at the top of the agenda
- discuss the political ramifications of their everyday teaching with them
- advocate a supportive policy context for their work.

To help in this process teachers can draw on the work of other early childhood educators who are contesting DAP truths (Walkerdine 1981, 1990; Davies 1989a; Cannella 1997; Jipson 1998; Smith & Campbell 1998).

Reconceptualising the self-gaze: self-styling as a teacher committed to gender equity

Gender equity in early childhood requires teachers who will self-style as teachers committed to gender equity. The teachers in the research group did this by seeing sexism, practising gender reflexivity, exercising power with feminist intent, advocating gender equity, challenging the normalisation of early childhood teaching and networking with others. These processes enabled them to:

- challenge colleagues about how to offer materials and equipment
- hold pedagogic knowledge up to critical reflection with others
- draw support from like-minded colleagues
- challenge colleagues' and parents' sexist understandings and practices
- desire improved understandings of gender
- link a clear social vision with their pedagogical imperatives.

There are considerable institutional and discursive challenges to managing such a self-styling in early childhood education. These have been discussed previously and include:

- the discursive dominance of DAP
- the professional isolation of early childhood teachers
- the policy silence on gender equity in preschool education
- the politics of truth concerning the developing child that need to be struggled over in developing a feminist pedagogy in early childhood education.

Taking on these challenges requires determination, a passion for a better world and a belief that it is possible through what is done in the name of teaching young children.

Finally

Feminist discourses, especially feminist poststructuralism, can be demonstrably and practically useful to teachers because they offer alternative ways to understand their own and other teachers' teaching praxis. Feminist discourses enable the gendering implications of DAP pedagogies to be reviewed and they provide alternative ways to understand children's learning. They also provided understandings of why and how children's curriculum choices are constructed. (The gendering praxis implications of how specific feminist discourses did this were detailed in Chapters 3 and 6.)

Feminist poststructuralist concepts can help teachers to:

- shift the object of their pedagogic gaze
- expand their readings of the construction of gender
- rethink the implications of how pedagogic space and materials are organised
- use their expanded understandings of how gender is being constructed to expand the teaching strategies they use to intervene in traditional gendering
- challenge the regulatory gaze of parents, colleagues and the academy and reconstruct these relationships
- challenge the will to truth.

Feminist poststructuralist ideas explored in this book suggest that we may create a stronger will to know gender in early childhood if we strive to:

- reject simplistic understandings of gender and gendering in early childhood (Chapter 2)
- reflect on and debate notions of good practice and their moral systems with others (Chapter 3)
- practise various feminist constructions of the gaze and reflect on their implications for people from diverse backgrounds (Chapter 4)
- reject discourses of childhood innocence and recognise the patterns of desire that constitute children's gender knowings (Chapter 5)
- explore different ways of remaking gender discourses with young children (Chapter 6)
- reject liberal humanism and explore how other feminisms might take gender equity policies and practices forward (Chapter 7)
- move from an ethics of individualism to an ethics of critical collectivism (Chapter 8)

- practise writing and reading little narratives in partnership with colleagues, children and parents (Chapter 9)
- fuse gender analysis with that of race, culture, class and sexuality (Chapter 10).

Finally, for feminists

The institutional and discursive challenges to being feminist early childhood pedagogues are considerable. The dominant knowledge-power regime constituting the developing child produces uncertain and shifting discursive dynamics. It requires fighting against marginalisation by many colleagues and parents, building supportive collegiate networks with those who share your vision, advocating a policy presence for gender equity, learning to critique the gendering implications of DAP traditions and practices, circulating and articulating feminist visions, and developing a gender reflexivity in and through teaching praxis. It was, therefore, not surprising that the feminist pathways research group members followed often shifted direction, took odd and unpredictable turns and constantly made each of us wonder where they might lead. It is also not surprising that our pathways represent only a few of those that might be possible.

Our pathways in the research group were varied, complex and intimately connected to the gendering and pedagogical discourses in which we made sense of ourselves, the children, other adults, teaching and our institutional and policy contexts. Consequently, there was no simple, coherent, obvious pathway to feminist pedagogies. Some pathways made it more possible to challenge patriarchal gendering in early childhood education, some pathways made it more possible to construct feminist ways of being with children.

Sharing these pathways and possibilities I hope offers others, and other feminists, in early childhood the opportunity to learn from our contradictions, tensions, flaws, frustrations, hopes, goals, successes and reflections. If others can learn from our efforts then the everyday gender myths unsettled in this book may not settle back into comfortable early childhood truths.

References

Adams, B. 1986, 'Training of Unskilled Child Care Providers', Ed.D. Nova University.

Allen, R. (ed.), 1990, *The Concise Oxford Dictionary*, Clarendon Press, Oxford.

Alloway, N. 1995a, 'The wearing of the badge: discourses of early childhood education and the possibilities of gender reform', paper presented to staff of the deLissa Institute.

——1995b, *Foundation Stones: The Construction of Gender in Early Childhood*, Curriculum Corporation, Melbourne.

Alloway, N. and Gilbert, P. (eds) 1997, *Boys and Literacy: Professional Development Units*, Curriculum Corporation, Melbourne.

Arndt, B. 1994, 'Gender Wars in Class', *The Weekend Australian Review*, Feb 19–20, pp. 1–2.

Arthur, L., Beecher, B., Dockett, S., Farmer, S. and Richards, E. 1996, *Programming and Planning in Early Childhood Settings*, 2nd edn, Harcourt Brace Jovanovich, Sydney.

Ashcroft, B., Griffiths, G. and Tiffin, H. 1998, *Key Concepts in Post-Colonial Studies*, Routledge, London.

Bakhtin, M.M. 1981, *The Dialogic Imagination: Four Essays*, ed. M. Holquist, trans. C. Emerson and M. Holquist, University of Texas Press, Austin.

Beaty, J. 1992, *Preschool Appropriate Practice*, Harcourt Brace Jovanovich, Florida.

Benish, J. 1978, 'Blocks: essential equipment for young children', *ED 165901*.

Benisom, E. 1992, 'Feminist thought as a source of critique and reconceptualization of multiculturalism in higher education', paper presented at the Annual National Conference on Racial and Ethnic Relations in American Higher Education, June 5–9, San Francisco.

Bentzen, W. 1985, *Seeing Young Children: A Guide to Observing and Recording Behaviour*, Delmar Publishers Inc., New York.

249

Bertens, H. 1995, *The Idea of the Postmodern: A History*, London, Routledge.

Blackmore, J. 1999, *Troubling Women: Feminism, Leadership and Educational Change*, Open University Press, Milton Keynes.

Blenkin, G. and Kelly, A. (eds) 1996, *Early Childhood Education: A Developmental Curriculum*, 2nd edn, Paul Chapman Publishing, London.

Bower, A. 1998, 'Boys and girls with disabilities: maternal expectations of gender behaviour and independence', in N. Yelland (ed.), *Gender in Early Childhood*, Routledge, London, pp. 36–54.

Brady, J. 1993, 'A feminist pedagogy of multiculturalism', *International Journal of Educational Reform*, vol. 2, no. 2, pp. 119–125.

Bredekamp, S. 1987, *Developmentally Appropriate Practices in Early Childhood Programs serving Children from Birth through Age 8*, National Association for the Education of Young Children, Washington, DC.

Bredekamp, S. and Copple, C. (eds) 1997, *Developmentally Appropriate Practice in Early Childhood Programs*, (rev. edn), National Association for the Education of Young Children, Washington DC.

Brenes, M., Eisenberg, N. and Helmstadter, G. 1985, 'Sex-role development of preschoolers from two-parent and one-parent families', *Merrill-Palmer Quarterly*, vol. 31, no. 1, pp. 33–46.

Brewer, R. 1997, 'Theorizing race, class and gender: the new scholarship of Black feminist intellectuals and Black women's labour, in R. Hennessy and C. Ingraham (eds), *Materialist Feminism: A Reading in Class, Difference, and Women's Lives*, Routledge, London, pp. 236–47.

Brooks, A. 1997, *Postfeminisms: Feminism, Cultural Theory and Cultural Forms*, Routledge, London.

Browne, N. and France, P. 1986, *Untying the Apron Strings: Anti-sexist Provision for the Under Fives*, Open University Press, Milton Keynes.

Buchbinder, D. 1994, *Masculinities and Identities*, Melbourne University Press, Melbourne.

Bulter, J. 1990, *Gender Trouble: Feminism and the Subversion of Identity*, Routledge, New York.

Cannella, G.S. 1997, *Deconstructing Early Childhood Education: Social Justice and Revolution*, Peter Lang Publishers, New York.

Caraway, N. 1991, 'The challenge and theory of feminist identity politics: working on racism', *Frontiers*, vol. 12, no. 2, pp. 109–29.

Cartwright, C. and Ward, C. 1982, 'Observation techniques', *Journal of Children in Contemporary Society*, vol. 14, no. 4, pp. 19–29.

Cartwright, S. 1998, 'Play can be the building blocks of learning', *Young Children*, July, pp. 44–7.

Chambers, I. 1996, 'Signs of silence, lines of listening', in I. Chambers and L. Curti (eds), *The Post-colonial Question: Common Skies, Divided Horizons*, Routledge, London, pp. 47–62.

Chattin-McNicols, J. and Howard Loeffler, M. 1989, 'Teachers as researchers: the first cycle of the teachers' research network', *Young Children*, vol. 44, no. 5, pp. 20–7.

Children's Services Office 1991, *Planning for Learning: a Framework for Planning Curriculum in Children's Services*, Education Department of South Australia, Adelaide.

Cleverley, J. and Phillips, D. 1987, *Visions of Childhood*, Allen & Unwin, Sydney.

Cohen, M. and Martin, L. 1976, *Growing Free: Ways to Help Children Overcome Sex-Role Stereotypes*, Association for the Education of Young Children International, Washington DC.

Collins, P. 1989, 'The social construction of black feminist thought', *Signs: Journal of Women in Culture and Society*, vol. 14, no. 4, pp. 745–73.

Commonwealth Schools Commission (1987) *The National Policy on the Education of Children in Australian Schools*, Commonwealth Schools Commission, Woden, ACT.

Connell, R. 1987, *Gender and Power*, Allen & Unwin, Sydney.

Cuffaro, H. 1975, 'Reevaluating basic premises: curricula free of sexism', *Young Children*, Sept., pp. 469–78.

Danby, S. 1998, 'The serious and playful work of gender: talk and social order in a preschool classroom', in N. Yelland (ed.), *Gender in Early Childhood*, Routledge, London, pp. 175—205.

Davies, B. 1988, *Gender Equity and Early Childhood*, Commonwealth Schools Commission, Canberra.

——1989a, *Frogs and Snails and Feminist Tales*, Allen & Unwin, Sydney.

——1989b, 'The discursive production of the male/female dualism in school settings', *Oxford Review of Education*, vol. 5, no. 3, pp. 229–41.

——1990, 'Agency as a form of discursive practice', *British Journal of Sociology of Education*, vol. 11, no. 3, pp. 341–61.

——1991, 'The concept of agency: a feminist poststructuralist analysis', *Social Analysis. Special Issue on Postmodern Critical Theorising*, vol. 30, pp. 42–53.

——1993, *Shards of Glass*, Allen & Unwin, Sydney.

Davies, B. and Harre, R. 1991/2, 'Contradiction in lived and told narratives', *Research on Language and Social Interaction*, vol. 25, pp. 1–36.

Department of Health and Family Services, 1996, *Equity Issues in Child Care: Child Care Matters*, Department of Health and Family Services, Canberra.

Department of Education and the Arts, 1996, *Kindergarten Development Check and Support Material*, Tasmanian Government, Hobart.

Dermon-Sparks, L. and the Anti Bias Task Force, 1989, *The Anti-Bias Curriculum*, National Association for the Education of Young Children, Washington DC.

Dirik, A. 1992, 'The postcolonial aura: third world criticism in the age of global capital', *Critical Inquiry*, Winter.

Dreyfus, H. and Rabinow, P. (eds) 1982, *Michel Foucault: Beyond Structuralism and Hermeneutics*, The University of Chicago Press, Chicago.

Dunn, S. and Morgan, V. 1987, 'Nursery and infant school play patterns: sex-related differences', *British Educational Research Journal*, vol. 13, no. 3, pp. 271–81.

Elkind, D. 1986, 'Formal education and early childhood education: an essential difference', *Phi Delta Kappan*, vol. 67, no. 9, pp. 631–6.

Endsley, R., Minish, P. and Shou, Q. 1993, 'Parent involvement and quality day care in proprietary centres', *Journal of Research in Childhood Education*, vol, 7, no. 2, pp. 53–61.

Faludi, S. 1991, *Backlash: The Undeclared War Against Women*, Vintage, London.

Faragher, J. and Mac Naughton, G. 1998, *Working with Young Children*, 2nd edn, RMIT Press, Melbourne.

Farquhar, S. 1990, 'Defining quality in the evaluation of early childhood programs', *Australian Journal of Early Childhood*, vol. 15, no. 4, pp. 16–23.

Fenby, B. 1991, 'Feminist theory, critical theory and management's romance with the technical', *Affilia*, vol. 6, no. 1, pp. 20–37.

Flax, J. 1990, 'Postmodernism and gender relations', in L. Nicholson (ed.) *Feminism/Postmodernism*, Routledge, New York, pp. 39–62.

Fleer, M. 1992, 'From Piaget to Vygotsky: moving into a new era of early childhood education', in B. Lambert (ed.), *Changing Faces: The Early Childhood Profession in Australia*, Australian Early Childhood Association, Canberra, pp. 134–49.

——1994, 'Does cognition lead development or does development lead cognition?', paper presented to the Pre-Conference Symposium at the 2nd Annual conference of Australian Research in Early Childhood Education, 28–30 January, Canberra.

Fleer, M. (ed.). 1996, *Play Through the Profiles: Profiles through Play*, Australian Early Childhood Association, Canberra.

Foucault, M. 1977a, 'Truth and power', in C. Gordon (ed.) *Power/Knowledge: Selected Interviews and Other Writings 1972–1977. Michel Foucault*, The Harvester Press, Sussex, pp. 109–33.

——1977b, 'Two lectures', ibid, pp. 78–108.

——1978, *The History of Sexuality. Volume 1: An Introduction*, Vintage Books, New York.

——1982, 'The subject and power', in H. Dreyfus and P. Rabinow, (eds) *Michel Foucault: Beyond Structuralism and Hermeneutics*, University of Chicago Press, Chicago, pp. 208–26.

Friere, P. 1980, *Pedagogy of the Oppressed*, Penguin, New York.

Fry, I. 1992, *Rediscovering Unit Blocks*, Australian Early Childhood Association, Canberra.

Ganguly-Scrase, R. and Julian, R. 1997, 'The gendering of identity: minority women in comparative perspective', *Asian and Pacific Migration Journal*, vol. 6, no. 3–4, pp. 415–38.

Ghandi, L. 1998, *Postcolonial Theory: A Critical Introduction*, Allen & Unwin, Sydney.

Gherardi, S. 1996, 'Gendered organisational cultures: narratives of women travellers in a male world', *Gender, Work and Organisation*, vol. 3, no. 4, pp. 187–201.

Giddens, A. 1991, *Sociology*, Polity Press, London.

Gilbert, P. and Taylor, S. 1991, *Fashioning the Feminine*, Allen & Unwin, Sydney.

Gilbert, R. and Gilbert, P. 1998, *Masculinity Goes to School*, Allen & Unwin, Sydney.

Gilligan, C. 1988, 'Remapping the moral domain: new images of self in relationship', in C. Gilligan, J. Ward, & J. M. Taylor (eds), *Mapping the Moral Domain*, Harvard University Press, Cambridge, pp. 3–19.

Ginsberg, H. and Opper, S. 1967, *Piaget's Theory of Intellectual Development: An Introduction*, Prentice-Hall Inc., New Jersey.

Gordon, A. and Williams Browne, K. 1993, *Beginnings and Beyond: Foundations in Early Childhood Education*, Delmar Publishers, New York.

Gore, J. 1993, *The Struggle for Pedagogies: Critical and Feminist Discourses as Regimes of Truth*, Routledge, London.

——1995, 'Foucault's poststructuralism and observational education research: a study of power relations', in R. Smith and P. Wexler (eds), *After Postmodernism: Education, Politics and Identity*, Falmer Press, London, pp. 98–111.

Gorelick, S. 1991, 'Contradictions of feminist methodology', *Gender and Society*, vol. 5, no. 4, pp. 459–77.

Greishaber, S. 1998, 'The State re-inventing the child', paper presented in the symposium The 'Scientific' Construction of the Education and Lives of Younger Human Beings at the Annual Meeting of the American Educational Research Association, San Diego, 13–17 April.

——1998, 'Constructing the gendered infant', in N. Yelland (ed.), *Gender in Early Childhood*, Routledge, London, pp. 15–35.

Grosz, E. 1990, 'Contemporary theories of power and subjectivity', in S. Gunew (ed.) *Feminist Knowledge: Critique and Construct*, Routledge, London, pp. 59–120.

Haas Dyson, A. 1994, 'The Ninjas, the X-Men, and the ladies: playing with power and identity in an urban primary school', *Teachers College Record*, vol. 96, no. 2, pp. 219–39.

Hall, S. 1996, 'When was "the post-colonial"? Thinking at the limit', in I. Chambers and L. Curti (eds), *The Post-colonial Question: Common Skies, Divided Horizons*, Routledge, London, pp. 242–59.

Heaney, C. 1994, 'Taskforce to Focus on Boys' Woes', *The Herald Sun*, Apr. 30, p. 5.

Hekman, S. 1991, 'Reconstituting the subject: feminism, modernism, and postmodernism', *Hypatia*, vol. 6, no. 2, pp. 44–63.

Hendrick, J. 1990, *Total Learning: Developmental Curriculum for the Young Child*, 3rd edn, Merrill Publishing Company, Ohio.

Hirsch, E. (ed.) 1987, *The Block Book*, National Association for the Education of Young Children, Washington DC.

hooks, b. 1989, *Talking Back: Thinking Feminist—Thinking Black*, Sheba Press, New York.

——1995, *Killing Rage: Ending Racism*, Owl Books, New York.

Hoy Crawford, S. 1996, *Beyond Dolls and Guns: 101 Ways to Help Children Avoid Gender Bias*, Heinneman, Portsmouth.

Hughes, P. and MacNaughton, G. 1998, 'Fractured or manufactured? Gendered identities and culture in the early years', paper presented to the Reconceptualising Early Childhood Education: Research, Theory and Practice 7th Interdisciplinary Conference, Hawaii, 6–10 Jan.

——1999, *Communication in Early Childhood Services: A Practical Guide*, RMIT Press, Melbourne.

Hughes, P. 1994, 'Modernist histories of communication: some problems with "grand narratives"', *Australian Journal of Communication*, vol. 21, no. 1, pp. 76–86.

Jayasuriya, L. 1991, 'The Australian response to diversity', *FOCUS: Newsletter of the Asian Australian Resource Centre*, July, pp. 2–6.

Jayawardena, K. 1986, *Feminism and Nationalism in the Third World*, Zed Books Ltd, London.

Jipson, J. 1998, 'Developmentally appropriate practice: culture, curriculum, connections', in M. Hauser and J. Jipson, (eds) *Intersections: Feminisms/Early Childhoods*, Peter Lang Publishing, New York, pp. 221–40.

Jones, A. 1993, 'Becoming a "girl": poststructuralist suggestions for educational research', *Gender and Education*, vol. 5, no. 2, pp. 157–66.

Jordon, E. 1995, 'Fighting boys and fantasy play: the construction of masculinity in the early years', *Gender and Education*, vol. 7, no. 1, pp. 69–86.

Jordon, G. and Weedon, C. 1995, *Cultural Politics: Class, Gender, Race and the Postmodern World*, Blackwell, Oxford.

Kamboureli, S. 1998, 'The technology of ethnicity: Canadian multiculturalism and the law', in. D. Bennet (ed.), *Multicultural States*, Routledge, London, pp. 208–22.

Kenway, J. 1990, 'Education and the Right's discursive politics: private versus state schooling', in S. Ball (ed.). *Foucault and Education: Disciplines and Knowledge*, Routledge, London, pp. 167–206.

Kenway, J. and Modra, H. 1992, 'Feminist pedagogy and emancipatory possibilities', in C. Luke and J. Gore (eds), *Feminisms and Critical Pedagogy*, Routledge, London, pp. 138–66.

Kenway, J. and Willis, S. 1997, *Answering Back: Girls, Boys and Feminism in Schools*, Allen & Unwin, Sydney.

Kenway, J., Blackmore, J. and Willis, S. 1996, 'Beyond feminist authoritarianism and therapy in the curriculum?', *Curriculum Perspectives*, vol. 16, no. 1, pp. 1–12.

Kenway, J., Willis, S., Blackmore, J. and Rennie, L. 1994, 'Making "hope practical" rather than "despair convincing": feminist poststructuralism, gender reform and educational change', *British Journal of Sociology of Education*, vol. 15, no. 2, pp. 187–210.

Kessler, S. 1991, 'Alternative perspectives on early childhood education', *Early Childhood Research Quarterly*, vol. 6, pp. 183–97.

Kilman, D. 1978, 'Avoiding sexism in early childhood education', *Day Care and Early Education*, Fall, pp. 19–21.

King, E. 1994, *Educating Young Children in a Diverse Society*, Allyn and Bacon Inc., Needham Heights, MA.

Kristeva, J. 1981, 'Women's time', *Signs*, vol. 7, no. 1, pp. 13–35.

Lambert, B., Clyde, M. and Reeves, K. 1986, *Planning for Individual Needs in Early Childhood Services. Part II*, Australian Early Childhood Association, Canberra.

Leeper, S. 1984, *Good Schools for Young Children*, Macmillan Publishing Company, New York.

Lewis, M. 1992, 'Interrupting patriarchy: politics, resistance and transformation in the feminist classroom', in C. Luke and J. Gore (eds), *Feminisms and Critical Pedagogy*, Routledge, New York, pp. 167–92.

Lewis, M. 1993, *Without a Word: Teaching Beyond Women's Silence*, Routledge, New York.

Lingard, B. and Douglas, P. 1999, *Men Engaging Feminisms: Pro-feminism, Backlashes and Schooling*, Open University Press, Milton Keynes.

Lloyd, B. and Duveen, G. 1992, *Gender Identities and Education: The Impact of Starting School*, Harvester Wheatsheaf, Hertfordshire.

Logan, L. 1988, 'Gender, family composition and sex role stereotyping by young children', *ED 290564*.

Lubeck, S. 1998, 'Is developmentally appropriate practice for everyone?', *Childhood Education*, vol. 74, no. 5, pp. 293–8.

——1994, 'The politics of developmentally appropriate practice: exploring issues of culture, class and curriculum', in B. Mallory and R. New (eds), *Diversity and Developmentally Appropriate Practices: Challenges for Early Childhood Education*, Teachers College Press, New York, pp. 17–43.

Lyotard, J. 1989, *The Postmodern Condition: Report on Knowledge*, University of Minneapolis Press, Minneapolis.

MacNaughton, G. 1993a, 'Gender, power and racism: a case study of domestic play in early childhood', *Multicultural Teaching*, vol. 11, no. 3, pp. 12–15.

——1993b, *Equal Play, Equal Work*, Office of Preschool and Child Care, Melbourne.

——1996, 'Collaborating for curriculum change in postmodern times: some ethical considerations', keynote address presented to the Weaving Webs Conference, Melbourne, 11–13 July.

——1997, 'Feminist praxis and the gaze in the early childhood curriculum', *Gender and Education*, vol. 9, no. 3, pp. 317–26.

——1998a, 'Beyond tokenism: a research agenda for gender equity in multicultural early childhood contexts', paper presented to the Australian Early Childhood Research Conference, Canberra, 16–18 Jan.

——1998b, 'Directions for early childhood education: do we need a compass?' Keynote address presented to Early Childhood Educators of Tasmania and the Kindergarten Teachers Association Annual Conference, Hobart, 25 July.

——1998c, 'Improving our gender equity "tools": a case for discourse analysis', in N. Yelland (ed.), *Gender in Early Childhood*, Routledge, London, pp. 149–74.

Maher, F. and Tetreault, M. 1993, 'Frames of positionality: constructing meaningful dialogues about gender and race', *Anthropological Quarterly*, vol. 66, pp. 118–26.

Mallory, B. and New, R. 1994, *Diversity and Developmentally Appropriate Practices*, Teachers College Press, New York.

Martinez, L. 1998, 'Gender equity policies and early childhood education', in N. Yelland (ed.), *Gender in Early Childhood*, Routledge, London, pp. 115–30.

Martino, W. 1995, 'Deconstructing masculinity in the English classroom: a site for reconstituting gendered subjectivity', *Gender and Education*, vol. 7, no. 2, pp. 205–20.

Mawson, B. 1993, 'The Construction of Gender in the Kindergarten', minor masters thesis, University of Tasmania.

McConnochie, I., Hollingsworth, K. and Pettman, R. 1988, *Race and Racism in Australia*, Social Science Press, Sydney.

McIntyre, A. 1994, 'Why the Women Rule', *The Herald Sun*, Apr. 14, p. 15.

McKay, V. 1989, 'Re-exploring feminist methodology', *South African Journal of Sociology*, vol. 20, no. 4, pp. 249–56.

McRobbie, A. 1996, 'Different, youthful, subjectivities', in I. Chambers and L. Curti (eds), *The Post-colonial Question: Common Skies, Divided Horizons*, Routledge, London, pp. 30–45.

McTaggart, R. 1991, 'Principles for participatory action research', *Adult Education Quarterly*, vol. 41, no. 3, pp. 168–87.

Millam, R. 1996, *Anti-discriminatory Practice: A Guide for Workers in Child Care and Education*, Cassell, London.

Minh-ha, T. (in conversation with A. Morelli) 1996, 'The undone interval', in I. Chambers and L. Curti (eds), *The Post-colonial Question. Common Skies: Divided Horizons*, Routledge, London, pp. 3–16.

Monacadu, C. 1984, 'Early childhood education in Minnesota: a position paper', *ED 259286.*

Moyer, J., Egerston, H. and Isenberg, J. 1987, 'The child-centred kindergarten', *Childhood Education*, vol. 63, pp. 243–7.

National Child Care Accreditation Council 1993, *Quality Assurance and Improvement Handbook*, Australian Government Publishing Service, Canberra.

O'Sullivan, T., Hartley, J., Saunders, D. and Fiske, J. 1983, *Key Concepts in Communication*, Sage Publications, London.

Orner, M. 1992, 'Interrupting the calls for student voice in "liberatory" education: a feminist poststructuralism perspective', in C. Luke and J. Gore (eds), *Feminisms and Critical Pedagogy*, Routledge, New York, pp. 74–89.

Pateman, C. 1988, *The Sexual Contract*, Harvard University Press, Cambridge, Massachusetts.

Perritt, R. 1988, *Girls and Boys: An Australian Early Childhood Association Resource Booklet*, Australian Early Childhood Association, Canberra.

Perry, L. and Morgan, A. 1993, 'Sex-role development in young children: relationships to behavioural and attitudinal measures of parental gender schemas,' paper presented at the Biennial Meeting of the Society for Research in Child Development, New Orleans, 25–28 March.

Pettman, J. 1988, 'Whose country is it anyway? Cultural politics, racism and the construction of being Australian', *Journal of Intercultural Studies*, vol. 9, no. 1, pp. 1–24.

——1992, *Living in the Margins: Racism, Sexism and Feminism in Australia*, Allen & Unwin, Sydney.

Pinar, W., Reynolds, W., Slattery, P. and Taubman, P. 1996, *Understanding Curriculum*, Peter Lang Publishers, New York.

Rabinow, P. (ed.) 1997, *Michel Foucault: Ethics, Subjectivity and Truth. Essential Works of Foucault 1954–1984. Volume I*, The New Press, New York.

Read, K. 1971, *The Nursery School: A Human Relationships Laboratory*, W.B. Saunders Company, Philadelphia.

Read, K., Gardner, P., & Mahler, B. 1993, *Early Childhood Programs: Human Relationships and Learning*, 9th edn, Harcourt Brace Jovanovich, Fort Worth.

Robinson, K. 1992, 'Class-room discipline: power, resistance and gender. A look at teacher perspectives', *Gender and Education*, vol. 4, no. 3, pp. 273–87.

Rogers, L. J. 1993, 'Sex differences in cognition: the new rise of biologism', *Australian Educational and Developmental Psychologist*, vol. 10, no. 1, pp. 2–5.

Said Khan, N. (ed.) 1992, *Voices Within: Dialogues with Women on Islam*, ASR Publications, Lahore.

Seefeldt, L. 1987, 'Today's kindergarten: pleasure or pressure', *The Principal*, vol. 64, no. 5, pp. 12–16.

Seidler, V.J. 1997, *Man Enough: Embodying Masculinities*, Sage Publications, London.

Silin, J. 1995, *Sex, Death and the Education of Children: Our Passion for Ignorance in the Age of AIDS*, Teachers College Press, New York.

Siraj-Blatchford, I. 1994a, *Laying the Foundations for Racial Equality in the Early Years*, Trentham Books, London.

——1994b, *Praxis Makes Perfect: Critical Educational Research for Social Justice*, Education Now Books, Ticknall, Derbyshire.

Skelton, C. (ed.) 1989, *Whatever Happens to Little Women? Gender and Primary Schooling*, Open University Press, Milton Keynes.

Smith, K. and Campbell, S. 1998, 'Images of the child: constructing the lived meaning of fairness', paper presented at the Representing the Child Conference, 2–3 October, Monash University, Melbourne.

Spivak, G.S. 1990, 'Strategy, writing, identity', in S. Harasym (ed.), *The Post-colonial Critic: Interviews, Strategies, Dialogues*, Routledge, London, pp. 50–8.

Spodek, B. 1988, 'Conceptualising today's kindergarten curriculum', *The Elementary School Journal*, vol. 89, no. 2, pp. 203–11.

Stone, L. 1984, 'A staff development program to improve the quality of infant and toddler caregiving'. Practicum Report, Nova South Eastern University, Fort Lauridale, CA.

Stratton, J. and Ang, I. 1998, 'Multicultural imagined communities: cultural difference and national identity in the USA and Australia', in D. Bennett (ed.), *Multicultural States: Rethinking Difference and Identity*, Routledge, London.

Tang Nain, G. 1991, 'Black women, sexism and racism: Black or antiracist feminism?' *Feminist Review*, vol. 37, Spring, pp. 1–24.

Taylor, C. 1992, 'Issues in preservice early childhood teacher education in Australia', *Australian Journal of Early Childhood*, 17(2), pp. 35–41.

The Children's Services Centres Regulations 1988. Statutory Rule No. 467/1988. Reprint No. 1.

Tong, R. 1989, *Feminist Thought: A Comprehensive Introduction*, Allen & Unwin, Sydney.

Tsolidis, G. 1993, 'Re-envisioning multiculturalism within a feminist frame-work', *Journal of Intercultural Studies*, vol. 14, no. 2, pp. 1–12.

Usher, R. and Edwards, R. 1994, *Postmodernism and Education*, Routledge, London.

Walby, S. 1992, 'Woman and nation', *International Journal of Comparative Sociology*, vol. XXXIII, no. 1–2, pp. 81–100.

Walkerdine, V. 1981, 'Sex, power and pedagogy', *Screen*, vol. 38, pp. 14–24.

258

——1982, *Girls and Mathematics*, Virago, London.

——1984, 'Developmental psychology and the child-centred pedagogy', in J. Henriques, W. Holloway, C. Urwin, C. Venn, V. Walkerdine, *Changing the Subject*, Methuen, London, pp. 153–202.

——1988, *The Mastery of Reason: Cognitive Development and the Production of Rationality*, Routledge, London.

——1989, *Counting Girls Out*, Virago Press, London.

——1990, *Schoolgirl Fictions*, Verso Books, London.

——1992, 'Progressive pedagogy and political struggle', in C. Luke and J. Gore (eds), *Feminisms and Critical Pedagogy*, Routledge, London, pp. 15–24.

Walkerdine, V. and Lucey, H. 1989, *Democracy in the Kitchen: Regulating Mothers and Socialising Daughters*, Virago Press, London.

Weedon, C. 1987, *Feminist Practice and Poststructualist Theory*, Basil Blackwell, Oxford.

——1997, *Feminist Practice and Poststructualist Theory*, 2nd edn, Basil Blackwell, Oxford.

Weiler, K. 1988, *Women Teaching for Change: Gender, Class and Power*, Bergin and Garvey Publishers, Inc., Massachusetts.

Williams, J. 1997, 'The romance of the intellectual and the question of profession', in H. Giroux with P. Shannon (eds) *Education and Cultural Studies: Towards a Performative Practice*, Routledge, London, pp. 50–64.

Wright Sexton, A. 1996, 'Sowing and reaping: the seeds of parent involvement in a pre-K co-op', *Focus on Early Childhood*, vol. 9, no. 2, pp. 1–4.

Yelland, N. and Grieshaber, S. 1998, 'Blurring the edges', in N. Yelland (ed.), *Gender in Early Childhood*, Routledge, London, pp. 1—14.

Zack, N., Shrage, L. and Sartwell, C. 1998, *Race, Class, Gender and Sexuality: The Big Questions*, Blackwell Publishers, London.

Zinn, M. B. and Dill, B. T. 1996, 'Theorizing difference from multiracial feminism', *Feminist Studies*, vol. 22, no. 2, pp. 321–31.

Index

abstract thought, 93, 95
accountability, educational, 190
action research study
    background, 4–7
    overwriting, 6
action research team, 8, 235, 241,
    242, 244–5
    Anna, 8, 10
    Anne, 8, 9, 65–73, 75–6, 85,
        135, 136, 172
    Carlie, 8, 9, 134, 136, 140,
        144–5, 184–6, 196–7
    Edna, 8–10, 12–24, 29–30, 71,
        91–2, 94–6, 116, 133, 135–6,
        138, 163
    Emma, 8–10, 71, 136, 209–10
    Fay, 8, 71, 135, 136, 139
    Matti, 8, 10, 163
    Nellie, 8, 9–10, 36–41, 44–6,
        48, 50–1, 54–7, 70–1, 93–6,
        137, 140, 172, 210, 211
    Nette, 8, 9, 136, 139, 161–9,
        172, 175
    Sally, 8, 36–7, 41–6, 54–6, 92–6,
        123, 136, 137, 140, 144–6,
        153, 172, 184, 186–9, 192,
        196–7, 210–11
    Sue, 8, 10, 133–6, 138, 192
    Tina, 8, 10, 71

advocacy, for children's rights,
    194
affirmative action, for girls, 134
Alloway, N., 45, 150, 151, 168, 239
alterity, 212, 214–15, 216–17, 221,
    222
androgyny, 139, 140
    androgynous personalities,
        139–40
Ashcroft, B., 214
Association for Childhood
    Education International
    (ACEI), 14
Australian Early Childhood
    Association, 191

Benisom, E., 216, 221, 222, 225
best practice, 51
binary oppositions, 148
    contesting those of gender, 150
    deconstructing, 149
biological determinism, 18, 24,
    25, 29
Blackmore, J., 77, 201–2
block play
    boys as the problem, 118
    equal access, 12–19
        badge system, 15, 17
        gender rules, 15, 17

intervention strategies,
14–17
fragile girl/boy interaction, 116
gendered power dynamics, 68–9
girls need to change, 117
girls-only days, 133–4
minimum teacher
involvement, 66–7
negative consequences for
girls, 68–9
patriarchal area, 119–20
play dynamics, 113
power relations, 120, 121–2
sexist behaviour, 12, 24
shunned by girls, discovering
why, 94–5
strategies to increase girls'
involvement, 116–18
feminisation, 113, 117
fusion, 113, 114–15, 117
policing, 113, 116, 118
separatism, 113–14, 117
boys, 202
aggressive, 11, 41, 112
challenge to girls' presence, 69
disruptive, 67
dominating, 68, 70
expansive, 69, 70, 112
extension of experiences, 135
focus on, 136–7
intimidating, 69
learning a non-patriarchal
masculinity, 144–6
macho discourse, 121
noisy, 11, 112, 185
power over girls, 76
remaking the meanings of
masculinity, 149, 150–4
remaking their subjectivities,
147–8
reverse discrimination, 134, 139
revolting behaviour, 65, 66
strategies for owning play
spaces, 37–8
under-achievement, 132–3
undermined by peers, 135

boys' needs, alternative
understandings, 142–54
Buchbinder, D., 146–7

Cannella, G.S., 53, 95, 97, 168–9,
194
case studies
Barbie's baby wants a daddy, 80
Barbie's boobies, 126–8
Boys are mean, 204–6
My traffic lights, 228–30
Painting the playhouse, 58–60
Paul and Amber at mud-play,
83–4
Pippa prefers home corner,
105–8
Reece, Bradley and the
bouncing dolls, 154–8
Snack time at Nellie's, 86–7
The daffodil curriculum,
178–81
Tom and the after-shave
bottle, 30–3
change see social change
child development
feminine qualities/skills in
boys and girls, 138
room organisation, 192–3
child-centred education, 141, 142
child-choice, 17, 45, 48, 55, 56
childhood innocence, 95
children
constructed as 'Other', 168–9
gender-fairness, 240
as gendered beings, 82–5
rights, 194
working hard to be normal,
118–19
class, 220
and multiracial feminism, 78–80
Cohen, M., 14
collectivism, 172–3, 174–6
critical, 176, 177–8, 242
importance of dialogue, 176–8,
242
communication, with young
children, 38

confrontation, avoided by girls, 112, 120
connectedness, 177
Connell, R., 143
consciousness raising, 41
countersexism, 54–5
Crawford, Hoy, 226–7
critical reflection, 243–4
Cuffaro, H., 114, 118
cultural diversity *see* multiculturalism and gender equity
cultural excuses, 222–3
culture
  common, 216
  dynamic, 217
curriculum, 66
  class-based goals, 53
  countersexist, 40
  developmentally appropriate practice (DAP), 45, 66
  equal access to sites, 12–13
curriculum planning, 66, 74

Davies, Bronwyn
  children learning gender, 104
  gender discourses, 194–5
  identity construction, 22–3, 24, 144
  need to reform early childhood truths, 2–3
  subjectivity, 100–2, 142–3
  subverting assumptions about gender, 151
decolonisation, 219
deconstruction, 149
  postcolonial, 219–20
Dermon-Sparks, L., 227
Derrida, Jacques, 148, 150, 165
  hinge words, 150
desire, patterns of, 101–2, 103–4, 118
developmental psychology, 2, 45, 74, 141
  child in need of protection, 95–6

effect on learning and gendering, 54
  truths of the developing child, 96
developmentalism, 73, 74–5, 200, 201
developmentally appropriate practice (DAP), 51, 65, 66, 96–7, 142, 241
  DAP gaze, 73, 241
  dominant discourse, 2, 3, 52–3, 191–2
  onespeak, 45–6
  principles, 45–6, 96, 117–18
  reconceptualists' critique, 48–9
  truths of the child, 192
Developmentally Appropriate Practice in Early Childhood Programs Serving Children from Birth Through Age 8, 46, 48, 49
difference, 184–6, 202
  gender-based, 11, 67–8, 238
  moving from margin to centre, 221, 225–6
Dill, B.T., 78, 79
discourses, 53, 237–8
  dissensus, 203
  influence on teaching, 57–8
  meanings, 49–50, 51
  multiple, 54
  unequal social power, 55
dissensus, 198–9, 201, 203
Douglas, P., 202
Dyson, Haas, 124–5, 126

early childhood education, 203
  good practice, 44, 45, 56, 58, 191
    alternatives, 48–58
    Piaget as guide, 47
    reconstruction of, 171
  lack of gender equity policy, 3, 140
  lack of gender reflexivity, 6–7
  mapping the ethics, 170
  political and ethical, 171–2, 175
  reconceptualising, 48–9, 235

traditions and truths, 2–3, 6–7,
169–70
Edwards, R., 190
Elkind, D., 45
encouragement, 14, 20
Enlightenment
free will, 22
ideals of progress, 22
equality, 13, 139, 150
equipment reorganisation, source
of tension, 161–4
equity, 85
essentialism, 202, 238
ethic of the self, 172, 174
ethics
of collectivism, 172–3
Foucault's sense of, 170, 242
of individualism, 170–1, 172,
178
exclusion, 124–5, 129

fairness, 123, 124–5, 225, 227, 240
Faludi, S., 146
femininity, 50, 84, 119, 129
changed understanding of, 126
emphasised, 143, 148
multiple femininities, 101
feminism, 199, 201–2
alternative ethic of the self, 172
gendered child, 76
ideal of commonality, 216
liberal, 77, 139, 140, 141–2
men's reactions to, 153
and multiculturalism, common
concerns, 221, 225–6
multiracial, 77–80
political implications of
teaching discourse, 56, 57
postcolonial, 219–21
radical, 138, 140, 163, 167
reconstruction of pedagogic
gaze, 77, 247–8
feminist poststructuralist
possibilities
exploring children's gender
knowings, 108–9

gender equity and cultural
diversity, 231
good practice to counter
sexism, 61
innovation and the ethics of
individualism, 181
observing daily gendered
politics, 87–8
remaking gender discourses, 129
strategies for talking about
gender, 33–4
ways of being masculine, 158–9
see also poststructuralism,
feminist
Fenby, B., 238
Foucault, Michel, 7, 194
disciplinary gaze, 173
gendering of power, 203
regimes of truth, 164–6, 167–8,
170
Foucault's care of the self
applied to children, 82
ethical substance of
relationship with self, 82
mode of subjection, 82
self-forming activities, 82, 83
telos, 82, 83, 176
Foundation Areas of Learning, 75
free play, 37, 39, 48, 55, 56
no moral agenda, 39–40, 41
and sexism, 43–4
Freud, Sigmund, 51

Ganguly-Scrase, R., 217
Gardner, Howard, 46
gaze, of teacher, 74, 76, 77, 79,
84, 241
reconceptualising, 236–7
see also lenses
gender, 64, 129, 220
children's attitudes, 40
delineating categories, 50
differences based on, 67–8, 238
hidden by DAP gaze, 73–4,
75–6
importance in understanding
behaviour, 71, 72

influence on play, 65–6, 91
and multiracial feminism,
    78–80
new category to observe, 71
silenced, 238
third gender of girl/boy, 149
western cultures' ideas of, 143
gender boundaries
crossed, 43, 136
interruption of, 238–9
gender discourses, 104, 129, 194–5
bringing about change, 104–5
gender dynamics, 65, 68–9
in Jewish kindergarten, 209–10
gender equity, 36, 141, 201
alternative understandings,
    121–6
attempts to increase,
    marginalised, 169, 170–1
commitment of teacher, 244–5
in early childhood, myths, 1,
    4, 6, 234–5
innovation, 111–12, 122
interrupting gender
    boundaries, 238–9
interventionist teaching, 39,
    41, 48
policy, 140
promoted in curriculum, 189
revitalising, 235
teachers' role in children's
    play, reimagined, 125–6
teaching strategies,
    reconceptualised, 238–41
gender goals, 213
gender knowledge, of young
children, 90–4, 96, 101, 102,
105
alternative understandings,
    97–105
exploring, 93–4, 103–4
hearing children's voices, 96–7
gender order
challenges bring uncertainty,
    145, 146
patriarchal, 143–4
gender pleasure, 104–5

gender politics, deconstructing,
    151
gender reflexivity, 6–7, 244
gender relations, 70
exercise of power, 71
patriarchal, 76
remaking, 126
see also power; power relations
gender security, 104–5
Gherardi, S., 27
Gilbert, P., 143, 151
Gilligan, C., 26
girls, 112, 201, 202
controlled, 69
desirable qualities, 13
ostracised, 210
rights, 40, 43, 57
subordinate, 122
timid and passive, 18
traditional feminine discourse,
    121–2
good practice see early childhood
education
Gorelick, S., 218
Greishaber, S., 75
Growing Free, 14

Harre, R., 142
Head Start programs (US), 53
Hekman, S., 20–1
hinge words, 150
homogeneity, gender, 212,
    213–14, 215–16, 217
hooks, b., 218
human rights, 41, 52

identity formation, 11–12, 13–14,
    78, 225
alternatives, 23–8
as a dialogue, 26–7, 29
genetic, 12, 17–18
individual in the social, 24–6
many different messages, 21
modernist accounts, 22–3
as a narrative, 27–8, 29
poststructuralist themes, 28–9,
    33–4

social duping, 20–2, 23, 25
sponge model, 19–20, 21–2, 23, 25
imprisonment, 154
inclusion, 124–5, 129
individual-in-the-social-world, 24–6, 81, 82
individualism, 45, 73, 74, 200, 201
  displacing of, 175, 176
  ethics of, 170–1, 172, 178
  and liberal feminism, 141–2
inequality, 143–4
innocence, 95
innovation, 169, 171
institutions
  provision of frameworks, 51
  support for ways of being, 166–7
intervention, in children's play, 18, 38–9, 41–2, 43–4, 54–5, 61

Jordon, E., 149, 152
Julian, R., 217

Kenway, J., 6, 77, 178, 222
Kessler, S., 55
Kilman, D., 114
Kindergarten Development Check, 75
knowledge
  control of access to, 95–6
  validation through dialogue, 176–7
Kristeva, J., 150

language
  and accounts of the world, 197–8
  and power, 101
  and subjectivity, 97–8, 100
learning, 47
  adult intervention, 47
learning environment, 47
lenses
  developmental, 65
  ethics of the self, 84, 87–8, 236
  gender, 65
  masculinities, 236–7

multiracial feminist, 79–80, 87–8, 236
observational, 65
radical feminist, 65, 77, 236
storyline, 84, 87–8, 236
Lewis, M., 239, 240
liberal feminism, 77, 139, 140, 141–2
  view of gender/identity, 142
liberal humanism, 140–1
liberalism, 199, 200, 202
Lingard, B., 140, 202
little narratives, 197–8, 199, 201, 203, 204, 244
Lyotard, J., 165, 201
  little narratives, 197–8, 200

marginalisation
  of attempts to increase gender equity, 169, 170–1
  of feminist discourses, 191–2, 193
  of women, 202
Martin, L., 14
Martinez, L., 3
Marxism, 199
masculinity, 50, 84, 119, 129
  backlash literature, 146–7
  changing boys' understanding of, 125–6, 146–7, 149, 150–4
  hegemonic, 143, 148
  men's movement, 146
  multiple masculinities, 101, 148
  connections with femininities, 148
  non-traditional, 126, 146–7, 184–5
  non-violent, 152–3
  problematising it, 151–2
  traditional, 195
  violent, 150, 154
meaning-making, 102
men's movement, 146
metanarratives, 199–201
modelling, 14, 18, 20
modernism, 22–4, 148
moral systems, 104, 166

morality, 52, 53–4
multiculturalism and gender
  equity
  alterity, 212, 214–15, 216–17,
    221, 222
  alternative understandings,
    212–21
  common projects, 221–2, 224
  feminist postcolonial theory,
    219–21
  gender conflict in many
    cultures, 217
  gender/culture dualism
    cultural excuses, 222–3
    deconstructing, 222–6
  homogeneity, 212, 213–14,
    215–16, 217
  intersections between
    gender/race/culture,
    reconceptualising, 220
  silences, 208–12
  simultaneity of
    gender/race/culture,
    227–8
  tokenism, 212–13, 215
multiracial feminism, 77–80
  complexity of women's lives,
    78
  connectivity of women, 78
  identity formation, 78
myths, of gender equity in early
  childhood, 1, 4, 6, 234–5

narratives
  local/little, 197–8, 199, 201,
    203, 204, 244
  metanarratives, 199–201
National Association for the
  Education of Young Children
  (US), 46, 48, 75, 191
National Child Care
  Accreditation Council
  (NCAC), 75
National Policy on the Education
  of Girls, 140
New Right, rise of, 190
normality, 166

the 'Other', 167, 169

observations, 66, 71
  alternative understandings,
    76–80
  basis for knowing child, 96
  DAP-based, 73–4
  gender-specific, 76
  power-related concepts, 72–3
  prioritising gender, 71, 72
oppression, exposing, 221, 227–8
Orner, M., 173
osmosis socialisation, 20, 25
ourselves-in-the-world, 101–2
  categorisation, 102
  positioning, 103
  social practices, 102

parents
  discussion of gender, 196–7
  encouraging parental support,
    186–7, 196–7
  and gender equity
    alternative understandings,
      193–204
    concerns about, 185–8, 195–6
  involvement in early
    childhood education,
    189–90, 191, 197
  as 'Other' to teacher, 191
  partnerships with, 183, 194
  remake of knowledge/power
    relations, 244
  supportive of difference,
    184–5, 195
  surveillance of teachers, 190–1,
    193, 193–4
patriarchy, 119, 124, 143, 177
  binary opposition of
    men/women, 148
  gender relations, 76, 238
  interrupting patriarchy, 240
peer groups, 101, 135
Pettman, Ralph, 216, 217
philosophy, 200
Piaget, Jean, 44–5, 46–8, 51
  self-directed learning, 47

play
and gender relations, 122–3
girls' silences, 239–40
initiation of, 103
intervention, 38–9, 41–2, 43–4,
54–5, 61
power and resistance, 121
sexist, 39
teachers reimagining their
role, 125–6
play patterns
among NESB girls, 210–11
challenging patriarchy, 117
choice of area, 112, 163
control of space, 37, 69, 112
demand for teacher time, 112
use of auditory space, 69, 112
use of time, 113
poststructuralism, 24, 25–6, 203
feminist, 1–4, 7, 22–3, 194, 195
alternative understandings
for teachers, 245–7
conceptual tools, 81–2, 237–8
discourses and power, 52,
54, 55–6, 237
disruption of patriarchal
gender order, 143–4
good practice, 49–50, 61
identity formation, 33–4
learning discourses, 57–8
redefining the self, 142–3
relationships between
discourses, 52
subjectivity, 237–8
teacher's gaze, 84–5
theories of change, 196
meaning of discourse, 50, 51
themes of identity formation,
28–9
power, 70, 129, 237–8
of discourses, 52, 54
physical, 122
sexist, 41
of teacher, 16–17
through storylines, 84, 122
power relations, 54, 57, 237
intercultural, 224

masculinist (macho), 119, 122,
202
in play, 15–16, 69–70, 120, 121–2
psychology, 199, 200

Quality Assurance and
Improvement System (QAIS),
74–5
questioning, 95, 96, 240
asking 'why', 91–3, 94, 95, 105
ways of avoiding 'why', 92

race, 78, 220
and multiracial feminism,
78–80
racism, 39, 78, 216, 217, 218, 227
radical feminism, 138, 140, 163,
167
Read, K., 38
readings of the child, 241
reconceptualising, 237–8
reconceptualisation
of early childhood education,
48–9
of intersections between
gender/race/culture, 220
of pedagogic gaze, 236–7
of readings of the child,
237–8
of relations with
colleagues/parents/academy,
241–4
of self-gaze, 244–5
of teaching strategies, 238–41
reconceptualists, 48–9, 52, 53
DAP contributes to social
inequality, 49
DAP denies role of social
contexts, 49
DAP offers little guidance on
values/goals, 49
reinforcement, 38
rights, for girls, 40, 43, 57
role models, 13–14, 18
role-play, 29
room organisation, 168, 192–3
attempts to change, 161–4

safety, 192–3
science, 199, 200, 202
Seefeldt, L., 45
self-directed learning, 45, 47, 48
self-discipline, 17
self-gaze, reconceptualising, 244–5
self-motivation, 45, 48
sex-role socialisation, 14
sexism, 39, 52, 56–7, 227
   changing the storyline, 41–3
   cultural, 221–2
   effects on play, 37–8, 76, 123
sexuality, 220
   and multiracial feminism, 78–80
silenced histories/lives, recovering, 221, 226–7
Silin, J., 96–7
Siraj-Blatchford, I., 218–19
Skinner, B.F., 51
social behaviour, 40
social change, 176, 178, 198, 200, 201
social justice, 85
social practices, 50–1, 53
socialisation theory, 24
storylines
   aggressive, 37
   analysis of, 81–2
   boys', 114
   children making sense of their world, 81–2
   domestic, 41–2
   exercise of power through, 84, 122
   girls', 115
   importance, 101
   key to change, 123
   noisy, 37
   recreating through discussion, 123–4
   remaking, 126, 129
   teacher help with, 42
   use of books, 123
subjectivity, 97, 105, 219, 237–8
   and language, 97–8

process of formation, 100–1, 102–3
reimagined, 142–3
remaking boys', 147–8

Taylor, S., 143
'The Author's Theatre', 124–5
tokenism, gender, 212–13, 215
Tong, R., 139–40
truth, 241
   competing interpretations, 165–6, 167–8
   Foucault's view, 175, 241
   institutional and personal support, 166–7, 171
   parochial professionalism, 169–70

understandings, 124
   hybridisation, 124–5, 177
Usher, R., 190

Vygotsky, Lev, 46, 49, 51

Walkerdine, Valerie, 2, 22, 121, 170, 200–1, 211
Weedon, C., 54, 103, 178, 203
Willis, S., 6, 77, 222
women, 201
   backlash against feminist gains, 193
   equity for, 141, 150, 201
   in history, 226, 227
   marginalised, 202
   positive bias in radical feminism, 138
   and sexism, 13–14, 138, 221–2
   silenced, 202

Young, Iris, 216
youth suicide, 154

Zinn, M.B., 78, 79